Leadership for Sustainable Futures

Leadership for Sustainable Futures

Achieving Success in a Competitive World

Gayle C. Avery

Professor of Management, Macquarie Graduate School of Management, Macquarie University, Sydney, Australia

Edward Elgar
Cheltenham, UK • Northampton, MA, USA

Published by
Edward Elgar Publishing Limited
Glensanda House
Montpellier Parade
Cheltenham
Glos GL50 1UA
UK

Edward Elgar Publishing, Inc.
136 West Street
Suite 202
Northampton
Massachusetts 01060
USA

A catalogue record for this book
is available from the British Library

Library of Congress Cataloguing in Publication Data
Avery, Gayle, 1947–
    Leadership for sustainable futures : achieving success in a competitive world /
Gayle C. Avery.
        p. cm.
    Includes bibliographical references and index.
    1. Leadership—United States. 2. Industrial management—United States. 3. Success in business—United States. 4. Leadership—European Union countries. 5. Industrial management—European Union countries. 6. Success in business— European Union countries. 7. Competition, International. 8. Leadership—Case studies. I. Title.

HD57.7.A938 2005
658.4'092—dc22

2004058448

ISBN 1 84542 173 6 (cased)

Typeset by Manton Typesetters, Louth, Lincolnshire, UK
Printed and bound in Great Britain by MPG Books Ltd, Bodmin, Cornwall

Contents

Tables

Boxes

Preface

I would like to start this book with a riddle. How is it that a company that, according to conventional wisdom, gets almost everything 'wrong' yet is a stellar performer in the allegedly toughest capitalist market in the world, the USA? The company I am referring to is Nordstrom, a nationwide fashion specialty chain of retail stores. Nordstrom breaks all the traditional rules that aspiring managers are taught at the best MBA schools across the USA. Instead of focusing on shareholder value, it invests money in its employees, customers, the environment and the rest of society. Instead of worrying about quarterly returns, it challenges the financial markets by insisting on taking a long-term view. Instead of training its sales staff in standard procedures, it just tells them to do their best. Instead of watching the bottom line, it pays people more than it is obliged to. It focuses on customer service and looking after its employees. In other words, instead of running a tight ship, Nordstrom embraces concepts like fun, family and virtue.

If this sounds like a recipe for disaster to you, then how do you explain the fact that, in over 100 years of operation, the company became one of the most successful and admired in the USA? For example, in 2004, *Fortune Magazine* cited Nordstrom for the sixth consecutive year as one of the 100 Best Companies to Work For in the USA. All this may seem hard to explain. Perhaps this is why an outside CEO appointed to the company in 1997 got it wrong by doing things right. He shifted the primary focus to shareholder value. The result was a decline in the company's performance. This time the 'right' answers produced the wrong results.

Predictably, the analysts were not impressed when the family took charge again. This also went against conventional wisdom. Instead of downsizing and re-engineering, the family went back to the values that had made the company great in the first place. Three years later the company was given a clean bill of health again.

This raises the question of how a company that seemingly gets it so wrong on its approach, gets it so right on results? Is it just a freakish one-off case or are there lessons to be learned? This book is about the kinds of leadership processes that made Nordstrom a success. However, our starting point is Europe, where a group of companies follows the 'Rhineland model'.

Since 1999, I have researched over 30 European organizations headquartered in Germany and Switzerland, usually meeting senior management and other employees on several occasions. During the visits, employees kept mentioning that these organizations are 'special' places. This made me curious. A growing concern for how organizations in the Anglo/US world of Australia, the UK and the USA are faring made me look at these European enterprises more closely.

I found that these European businesses generally operate quite differently from typical public companies in Australia and the USA. In fact, they often operate in exactly opposite ways to the companies I was used to. Although each organization is unique, there was an underlying pattern. These enterprises are 'special' because of their leadership practices and philosophies. *Leadership for Sustainable Futures* reveals this pattern, giving the practicing manager concrete examples of how to lead organizations in a more sustainable way.

What does sustainability mean? To many it suggests being environmentally friendly and certainly this is part of sustainability. But the concept goes way beyond being 'green'. It refers to the very survival of a business, and this includes the survival of the community in which it operates.

In reflecting on the differences between Anglo/US and European patterns of leadership, I was led back to the fundamentally different assumptions of the European model of capitalism compared with those of Anglo/US capitalism. This focus affects how organizations are led. Developments in Anglo/US capitalism since the 1980s have focused managers' attention essentially on the short-term maximization of shareholder value and the self-interest of each firm.

By contrast, I found a strong emphasis on the interdependence of a business and the society in which it operates in the Rhineland approach. These managers believe that the long-term sustainability of the organization depends on fostering positive relationships inside, as well as with the outside world and environment. In achieving this, leadership involves long-term thinking and employment; valuing people; developing managers from within; loyalty; team-based top management; innovation in products, services and processes; concern for the interests of multiple stakeholders; social responsibility; and environmental friendliness.

In this book I want to share my first-hand lessons from successful European enterprises, using concrete examples to bring the ideas within reach of both practicing managers and researchers. In investigating the organizations I visited in Germany and Switzerland further, I identified 19 elements that distinguish European and Anglo/US leadership.

To my initial surprise, I found that, on the whole, family-run businesses seem to follow European leadership principles. The principles also operate elsewhere, as examples from Scandinavia and South Africa show. The biggest surprise of all is that some leading US corporations, such as Colgate Palmolive, Continental Airlines, IBM, Marriott and Nordstrom, also closely follow Rhineland leadership principles. The good news in this is that location and the prevailing business culture do not prevent managers from adopting sustainable leadership practices – it is a matter of choosing to do so.

I also consulted the management literature. There I found many calls and ideas for leading sustainable organizations along the principles that I had uncovered in the European companies. Eminent management thinkers are urging business leaders to become more people-focused, innovative, ethical, long-term in their thinking and planning, and to provide for the interests of a broad range of stakeholders, including the environment and future generations.

This book develops and expands on some of these ideas. It challenges current ways of doing business under the Anglo/US approach. This is not new, but people who already recognize the problem are often left searching for answers. What can be done differently? How can a business be led in more sustainable ways? *Leadership for Sustainable Futures* addresses these questions by showing what 28 successful organizations from a variety of industries and based in different countries are doing. Many of them are turning conventional wisdom on its head.

The real challenge in writing a book like this is to have it read by the skeptics. Not much is gained by preaching to the converted. In trying to engage the skeptics, it is tempting to water down the message to make it more palatable. Early drafts of the manuscript were far more equivocal about the relative merits of different leadership approaches than the final book is. However, this is not the result of early attempts at ingratiation giving way to honesty. No, the more research I did, the more convincing the merits of the European approach to leading organizations became.

Having worked with managers on sustainable leadership over several years, there is probably not a 'yes ... but' objection that I have not been confronted with. I try to address those concerns throughout this book. Skeptics who are willing to challenge their dearly held prejudices with an open mind are encouraged to read on. At the very least, readers will see an alternative to the prevailing Anglo/US approach and understand how, in practice, it can lead to sustainable organizations.

I realize that many managers are under pressure from various sources, including the financial markets, investors and shareholders, to follow the Anglo/US shareholder value approach to leading an organization. However, this approach is flawed and contains the seeds of its own destruction, as I show later. This is not the leadership for creating sustainable enterprises.

Some managers will say that they are just doing what business schools taught them to do. While this may be true, it is no excuse for keeping on doing the wrong thing. Even academics are criticizing their colleagues. Thus Professor Dexter Dunphy from the University of Technology, Sydney supports the search for alternatives because 'business as we practice it and teach it is unsustainable. We cannot continue to conduct business as usual'.[1] Professor Henry Mintzberg from Canada's McGill University strongly criticizes how managers are educated in typical MBA programs, and the dehumanizing consequences of their actions on organizations and society.[2] Mintzberg and his colleagues are also very concerned about the sustainability of Anglo/US business leadership.[3]

Even those managers without an altruistic bone in their body can surely be motivated by considerations of self-interest. Immediate self-interest lies in making what many argue is an imperiled system survive. This might be for no other reason than to maximize their own stock options (especially now that option plans are focusing more on the long-term performance of an enterprise), or because, to maintain their value in the job market, managers need to demonstrate success. Increasingly this will refer to long-term success. This alone should make people interested in leadership for the long term.

Another objection often raised is that European companies do not perform well for shareholders. However, this is dispelled by both research findings and many of the case studies in this book that are about public companies that follow sustainable leadership principles *and* produce a generous return for shareholders. As for maximizing shareholder value, even the wealthiest shareholders are affected by environmental catastrophe. Even the most profitable companies suffer from skyrocketing fuel prices. Even CEOs are susceptible to cancer from air pollution. At the basest level, firms cannot sell as many of their products and services to people devastated by climatic and social disasters, or to poorly paid and unemployed workers.

Many voices are echoing calls for Anglo/US corporations to act more in the interests of the broader society.[4] Those who dismiss these voices are dismissing not only the Rhineland model's example, but also evidence of growing numbers of residents in the USA (41 per cent), Canada (50 per cent) and the UK (51 per cent) favoring laws requiring corporate social responsibility – even at the perceived risk of higher prices and fewer jobs.[5] In the UK and the USA, corporate social responsibility is now strongly on the governments' agenda, as it has been for some time in South Africa. This increases the pressure on leadership to move in the direction of fairness for all stakeholders, as the Europeans espouse.

Misconceptions abound about the relative success of the European and Anglo/US economies. A detailed analysis by Will Hutton[6] concludes that the Europeans are in fact, outperforming the USA when all factors are taken into account. Related to this misconception is the idea that European labor laws prevent companies from adjusting their workforce. The companies I studied certainly prefer to avoid downsizing their highly skilled workforce, but, if it needs to be done, it can be done. It is just a matter of how well the affected employees are supported during the process. This is the right way to treat human beings in any case. Some people object to taking a collaborative approach in working with unions. However, in Europe, once unions accept the need for change, they can assist in getting acceptance from the rest of the workforce.

Then there are objections that environmental initiatives cost money and take away from shareholders. A number of the companies featured in this book show that this is a myth, and that they actually save money and avoid future damage claims by being proactive in protecting the environment. A major objection often raised is that Europeans only engage in sustainable leadership practices because they have to, through legal or other regulations. European managers tell me that not only is protecting the environment the right thing to do, but their employees would get upset if their employer were not environment-friendly and did not care for the community. Similarly, European employers have good business reasons for other practices.

As a final example, many Anglo/US managers assure me that it is impossible for a modern firm to be innovative and employ people for a long time, particularly retaining the CEO for a long time, as European enterprises generally do. Yet innovation is at the core of the European companies I studied. They place great store on getting ideas and contributions from all over the organization. These enterprises do not wait for innovation to be driven from the top down. They develop systems for capturing, evaluating and, where appropriate, rewarding stakeholder suggestions. This generates large amounts of money for the firm and the person behind the idea.

Clearly, no one leadership model is a universal panacea. Globalization and other forces are challenging the European and Anglo/US models. Initially it looked as if adjustment in both directions was going to occur, with the possibility of the Anglo/US model prevailing. This no longer looks likely. Not only have corporate failures tarnished the shareholder value model, but an increasing demand for sustainable leadership is driving business – willingly or unwillingly – towards leadership principles reflected in the European model. Perhaps it is better to be a willing leader than an unwilling follower.

Being asked to accept that alternative business models may perform as well as, if not better than, the one we are familiar with is admittedly challenging. For many, the first hurdle lies in even becoming aware that other management practices and philosophies exist, and accepting that they can be effective and sustainable. Second, people tend to interpret new experiences and ideas through their existing frameworks. I have led many groups of managers on visits to companies practicing the Rhineland model. Initially the visitors often respond with denial. People are unable or unwilling to 'see' the difference. For example, one manager lamented how much of a handicap it must be to have to take account of the local community in conducting business: he could not envisage that this also brings advantages to the enterprise. Others were amazed to see their belief in the need for continual growth challenged, or the idea embraced that shareholders could be patient and take a long-term view.

Therefore, even if you have heard it all before, even if you feel that your way is the best and needs no modification, I suggest you take a close look at the case studies, and the principles I have extracted from them. The results will surprise you.

Readers who keep an open mind will be rewarded with practical examples showing how managers lead their organizations towards greater sustainability. This might inspire some to move closer to sustainable leadership practices by adapting some of these examples to their own circumstances. Please come with me on this journey. Your shareholders could thank you for it.

Gayle C. Avery

Acknowledgments

A book like this does not suddenly appear, but is the result of the influence and support of many people and organizations. In thanking key individual supporters, loving thanks go first to my husband and partner, Dr Harry Bergsteiner. He is my harshest critic and greatest supporter. I am also very grateful to Dr Grant Jones from Macquarie Graduate School of Management for his detailed comments and suggestions on an earlier draft of the manuscript. Thank you to Gillian Lucas, who was unstinting in her research assistance and support on many fronts throughout the entire writing process. Dr Robert Rich provided insights into my writing style and ideas for improving the manuscript, which are greatly appreciated. Professor Martin Hilb from the University of St Gallen was also highly supportive and provided ideas from his area of expertise in corporate governance. Finally, thanks are due to my many students who provided feedback on early drafts of the manuscript or otherwise contributed to its development. I would like to single out the following in particular: Chris Fitzpatrick, Dr Sooksan Kantabutra, Gerry McDonald, Dev Mookerjee, Heidi Oldman, Win Rangan, Michael Still, Alison Strange and Fred Trost. To all the other unidentified individuals who have helped in this project, a big thank you as well.

The generosity of a number of organizations has been exceptional. First, I would like to express my gratitude to the many European companies who hosted my visits to meet their senior managers, and to staff of the JW Marriott Hotel in Hong Kong. In addition, I appreciated the support from many of the enterprises around the world featured in this book, whose communication departments supplied missing information and corrected my errors. I hope I have successfully removed the latter in the final manuscript and, if not, I take responsibility for them. Thanks are also due to Macquarie Graduate School of Management and Macquarie University for funding. The Macquarie University library and its staff have been outstandingly supportive as always. I am also very grateful for the generous support and trust of Catherine Elgar and the team at Edward Elgar Publishing Limited, without whom this project would never have come to fruition.

Finally, I want to say a loving thank you to all my patient family and friends who have not deserted me, despite the fact that this book demanded so much of my time over 18 months.

PART I

Setting the scene

In the Rhine view, the company is a true community which offers a lasting place for each of its members. This is sharply different from the Anglo-Saxon model, in which the company is no more than the sum of a series of contractual arrangements between temporarily convergent interests: in short, a cash-flow machine, a collection of assets. The Rhine company is a living institution to be guarded and nurtured through work. In return, the company pledges to protect its own members through numerous social benefits (M. Albert, President, Assurances Générales de France[7])

1. Towards sustainable leadership

This book starts with the two forms of capitalism described in the above quotation and looks at their profound influence on the leadership and sustainability of organizations. One form of capitalism, referred to as Anglo/US capitalism, stems from the USA and focuses on short-term maximization of shareholder value. It is often called 'neoliberalism' or 'liberal market economics'. Variations are typically found in other parts of the English-speaking world, including Australia, Canada, Ireland, New Zealand and the UK.[8] Anglo/US capitalism is widely celebrated as the ideal form of capitalism.

The second form of capitalism is less widely publicized. It is based on concepts of social justice, and recognizes the interdependence of businesses and their local community. It is known as 'Rhineland capitalism', 'stakeholder capitalism' or 'coordinated market economics'. This approach is concerned about the long-term sustainability of an enterprise and its relationships with many interest groups, not just with shareholders. It is typically found in countries like Austria, Denmark, Finland, Germany, The Netherlands, Norway, Sweden and Switzerland, and in more widely varying forms in Italy and Japan.[9]

Capitalism has not always been popular. After the Second World War, capitalism was considered morally objectionable because it appealed to individual greed instead of idealism, promoted inequality and, through industry's collusion with Hitler, was partially blamed for the war itself.[10] European countries like France, Italy and the UK chose somewhat different economic systems, some with considerable state involvement. Most other 'isms', including various attempts at socialism and communism, have since failed.[11] Former communist Russia and Poland turned to capitalism to revive their emerging economies through 'the free determination of prices in the market place and the private ownership of the means of production'.[12] Capitalism has once again gained in popularity, particularly the Anglo/US variety.

The predominance of Anglo/US capitalism stems in large part from US financial and cultural dominance since the end of the Second World War. Although US financial power now dominates world stock markets, Joseph Stiglitz shows how US financial beliefs spread beyond the business world. For example, so-called 'Washington policies' reflect a faith in the general effectiveness of the financial capital markets that influences major international institutions like the International Monetary Fund and World Trade Organization.[13] Originally these organizations were set up to assist countries in crisis and to promote economic stability in the world. Instead, Stiglitz demonstrates how they operate on the premise that what is good for the Anglo/US financial community will be good for everyone else. Obviously this is not always the case. Another strong US global influence stems from America's military power, which increased even further after the collapse of the eastern bloc and the end of the cold war.

Spreading US values worldwide also favors Anglo/US capitalism, and this occurs in many ways.[14] One way is by exporting US culture. This is helped by English becoming almost a universal language thanks largely to mass communications and the Internet. The mass media transmit US culture via films, television and music around the world. US elite universities attract bright minds from abroad, thereby enriching intellectual capital in the USA, and imparting US culture and business practices in many students returning home. US academic journals have an impact on universities almost everywhere.[15]

Pressure to adopt the Anglo/US model also comes from American corporate law, which even influences companies headquartered in other countries. Furthermore, the US dollar has long been the preferred currency for international trade. This has allowed the USA to trade in its own currency, print more money when required and thus gain access to large amounts of additional liquidity.[16] Through these and other mechanisms, the USA influences business around the world. But does the USA export the ideal form of capitalism from the point of view of a business organization?

Economists often debate the impact of different forms of capitalism on national economies. They rarely investigate the effects of different forms of capitalism on leadership inside individual firms. Closing this gap, *Leadership for Sustainable Futures* explores the implications of Anglo/US and Rhineland capitalism for organizational leadership and sustainability. This is particularly timely as the Anglo/US form of capitalism is coming under strong criticism and managers are looking for alternatives. The Rhineland model offers one alternative that has operated for decades in some parts of Europe. However, not all European countries operate on the Rhineland model. France, for instance, has adopted a centralized business model. Managers there are educated in particular elite schools that were originally established to produce public servants rather than business leaders.[17]

Comparative and political economists have long known that different models of capitalism can underpin successful businesses. The employee-oriented Japanese approach and the hierarchical family-oriented model traditionally found in many parts of Asia provide examples. Ozaki's[18] view is that Japan's human capitalism, with its strong employee focus, places Japan at the most advanced stage of capitalism. Although recently in a long recession, Japan achieved sustained economic success while maintaining an egalitarian society in terms of income and low crime rates. The price of this is that the company becomes the employee's 'extended family' and the meaning of his life. South-East Asian businesses often work under a model of capitalism that relies on governments taking an active role in creating, shaping and guiding markets, requiring firms to take considerable responsibility for the social welfare of their employees.[19] Singapore is one highly successful example. Other Asian governments are also actively moving towards sustainability. Box 1.1 illustrates an example from Thailand.

BOX 1.1   THAILAND'S APPROACH TO SUSTAINABILITY[20]

In Thailand, steps are being taken towards more sustainable development through the 'Sufficiency Economy' philosophy stemming from His Majesty, King Bhumibol Adulyadej.[21] The philosophy stresses the middle path as the overriding principle for Thai people's conduct and way of life at the individual, family and community levels. It allows choice of balanced development strategies for the nation in line with the forces of globalization, while affording protection from internal and external shocks. To achieve this, the prudent application of knowledge is essential, particularly the application of theories, technical know-how and methodologies for planning and implementation. At the same time, the moral fiber of the nation must be strengthened, so that everyone – particularly public officials, academics, business people and financiers – adheres first and foremost to the principles of honesty and integrity. In Thailand, a balanced approach combining patience, perseverance, diligence, wisdom and prudence is considered indispensable to cope appropriately with critical challenges arising from extensive and rapid socioeconomic, environmental and cultural changes occurring as a result of globalization.

This book focuses on leadership within Anglo/US and Rhineland contexts. As we will see, the philosophy and pressures from the prevailing model of capitalism influence executives in the way they lead organizations. Depending on their beliefs and priorities, managers will lead their organizations in fundamentally different ways. This influence arises partly because the social, political and economic contexts in which organizations operate provide particular opportunities and constraints. These influence an organization's strategy.

Strategy in turn influences decisions about how resources are invested and valued, external impacts are dealt with, people are treated and innovation is fostered. Strategy and leadership are closely related, and part of the role of leadership has long been recognized as developing and implementing strategy.[22] In this way, the broader social context influences leadership decisions.

Others have examined the Anglo/US and Rhineland varieties of capitalism. Albert, in his book *Capitalism vs Capitalism*, systematically compared these capitalist models, highlighting some major differences.[23] Surprising many, he concluded that the Rhineland model was superior. Hall and Soskice have shown how the basic market philosophy underlying a country's economy provides specific advantages and disadvantages for the firms operating in that country compared with firms based elsewhere.[24] They argue that both Rhineland and Anglo/US forms of capitalism provide satisfactory economic performance in the long run, judging by major indicators like gross domestic product (GDP) and unemployment. However, Will Hutton disputes that the two models are comparable. He argues, like Albert, that the Rhineland approach produces superior outcomes.[25] Irrespective of which is superior in measures of GDP, these writers all agree that the two forms of capitalism have major implications for a nation's innovation, how income is distributed, the nature of employment and people's quality of life.

Despite research showing the advantages of the Rhineland model, managers, academics, business analysts and the media have tended to promote the Anglo/US model as the only worthwhile business model. Managers everywhere have come under enormous pressure to lead their businesses according to the Anglo/US model, particularly since the early 1990s. The growth of the global economy has been fuelled partly by the new exportable capital from a number of nations, particularly from the USA, and partly by growth in information and communications technology and transport. Global markets have become highly unregulated, volatile and unpredictable. Financial transactions can, and do, take place almost instantly, enabling cash to flow in practically uncontrollable ways. This places pressures on organizations to react quickly, perhaps to stop investors selling their shares. This makes it difficult to counter the influences of Anglo/US capitalism with its short-term focus.

Nonetheless, now, even US writers have started to question this myopic view. 'Have we become slaves to our own financial and corporate creations?' Shearer[26] asks. Henry Mintzberg and his associates[27] are concerned that Americans are getting poorer as a society. This is occurring despite massive increases in wealth for a fortunate minority since the early 1990s. Mintzberg asks what the relationship of the Anglo/US economic system is to the rest of the community and how sustainable it is. Is it right for economic entities to be concerned merely with their own welfare, largely ignoring the social, political and other contexts in which they operate? Are people caught in a global economic system that they feel powerless to deal with, let alone change?

The message from a wide range of management and economics writers is that it is time for leaders operating under the Anglo/US model to face the unsustainability of many of their prevailing beliefs and practices.[28] It is time to consider the moral and social dimensions of modern economic life. This is an important perspective for corporate leaders because organizations can only prosper in sustainable societies. Some CEOs (Chief Executive Officers) are in denial that there is anything wrong. This can even lead to the temptation to resort to fraudulent practices like falsifying figures during poor financial quarters.[29] Others recognize the limitations of what they are doing, but do not know how to act differently.

In the coming chapters, we will see that much of what eminent management thinkers such as Peter Drucker, Henry Mintzberg, Tom Peters, Warren Bennis, Margaret Wheatley, Stephen Covey, Charles Handy and others are calling for has already been practiced under the Rhineland model for many decades. They are urging business enterprises to become better corporate citizens, look after their stakeholders and the environment, and take a long-term perspective. Since the Rhineland model incorporates these practices, it makes sense to see how the Rhineland model actually works in practice in creating successful and enduring enterprises using these and related principles.

Leadership for Sustainable Futures challenges the assumed supremacy of the Anglo/US model by contrasting its implications for leadership in individual firms with those of the Rhineland model. These differences in philosophy and behavior have major implications for the sustainability of an enterprise. The Rhineland model provides a serious alternative to the Anglo/US model, bringing a focus on stakeholders in addition to shareholders, on the long term, and on social and environmental responsibility. Surprisingly, Rhineland leadership can be found in Anglo/US regions. In all, 28 organizations provide living examples of how they follow Rhineland practices, including examples from Australia, the UK and the USA.

The rest of this chapter describes the context that has allowed leadership philosophies based on Anglo/US capitalism to dominate, examining their strengths and weaknesses. The Rhineland model is introduced, starting with a focus on the Germanic variant because it provides a dramatic contrast to Anglo/US approaches.[30] The 'Sustainable Leadership Grid' frames this analysis, using 19 criteria to compare leadership under the two models.

In Part II, a series of case studies from 15 leading Rhineland organizations in Germany and Switzerland brings the criteria forming the Sustainable Leadership Grid to life. These European case studies provide practical examples of the Rhineland approach, using diverse publicly listed and privately owned organizations that have weathered hard times. We look at concrete examples of the way these enterprises approach management and decision making, focus on their people, and develop their systems and processes to address issues like social and environmental responsibility, people loyalty and development, innovation and promoting organizational longevity. The examples reveal that there are many individual routes to sustainability under the Rhineland model, including routes for publicly listed companies.

Part III shows that Rhineland leadership is not confined to Europe; it also occurs in successful enterprises elsewhere. This includes some public companies based in Finland, Sweden and South Africa. It is not surprising that Rhineland principles occur in family businesses that are free of the strong pressures from the financial markets to conform to the Anglo/US model. In the Anglo/US world, some major corporations also display Rhineland leadership consistent with the Sustainable Leadership Grid criteria. Two US cases highlight successful public corporations where the founding family is still involved in the business. Rhineland practices are easily seen in these organizations.

An even greater challenge confronts Anglo/US public companies no longer associated with the founders or their descendants. They operate in a capitalist context that does not favor the Rhineland model. Nonetheless, some publicly listed companies from Australia, the UK and the USA show how they conform to the Sustainable Leadership Grid criteria, or are striving to do so. This leads to the conclusion that it is possible to implement Rhineland practices in Anglo/US countries, even though the economic and cultural context and infrastructure support a quite different approach to leadership. Thus, the terms 'Anglo/US' and 'Rhineland' leadership are not restricted to specific geographic regions, but refer to two philosophies and sets of actions underpinning leadership.

Part IV concludes with some future scenarios and questions that managers seeking to adopt more sustainable leadership practices should be asking.

The next sections describe each model in turn, starting with Anglo/US capitalism.

ANGLO/US CAPITALISM

A comment is needed on the term 'Anglo/US capitalism'. It could also be called the 'neo-American' model, except that its influence reaches way beyond US shores. Some observers find the pairing of the UK and US approaches uncomfortable because of the fundamental difference in social welfare and values in the two countries.[31] The UK has a long tradition of social welfare, contrasting with what Albert[32] terms 'the absence of any system of protection at all' in the USA. Further, through its membership of the European Union

(EU), the UK is destined to draw closer to the extensive social welfare typically found on the Continent. Even though moves are afoot to reduce the extent of the social safety net in various European countries, it is unlikely to disappear.

Despite sharing many values with the EU, the UK appears willing to adopt US views on defence, finance and corporate leadership. Margaret Thatcher's American-style changes to the UK economy, extensive listing on the stock exchange, and similar systems of corporate governance in the UK and USA, provide reasons for referring to the Anglo/US model.[33] The emphasis is less on a particular geographic region than on the US neoliberal form of capitalism, particularly the approach based on short-term shareholder value. Box 1.2 summarizes broad demographic, geographic and political characteristics in the USA for the non-American reader.

Essentially, the idea behind Anglo/US capitalism is that the purpose of business is to maximize shareholder value. According to Kennedy,[34] the idea of maximizing shareholder value began to be popularized by academic accountants who noted that they could better predict stock market price levels 'by discounting future cash-flow streams associated with a business rather than analyzing accounting measures of performance like earnings per share'. In the late 1970s and early 1980s, US investment bankers used the academics' ideas to raid companies whose stocks appeared to be undervalued. The raiders then restructured the firms to release their hidden reserves of value and sold them. This not only enriched the raiders, but also started to focus managers' attention on the idea of maximizing shareholder value.

Boards began to align managers' compensation to their success in raising the company's stock prices, using stock options as incentives. Soon many managers were focused on their own self-interest, and restructured their businesses to maximize the share price as the corporate raiders had done. This turned into a widespread short-term corporate culture with managers getting as much as they could within as short a time as possible, underpinned by what Mitchell[35] terms 'the ethic of personal advantage'.

Anglo/US executives now experience considerable pressure to conform to the shareholder value idea. First, managers risk losing the equity holders to whom they report if they fail to maximize shareholder returns. Continual growth is a must for these managers. Second, failure to act in shareholder interests puts the firm at risk of being acquired by a stronger company or losing access to capital markets. Third, this reflects on the managers' own pocket and his or her value in the employment market. Thus, 'in theory at least, self-interest and self-preservation ensure that no rational executive will engage in activities that clearly erode shareholder value'.[36] Yet this self-interest might be illusionary unless the enterprise is also sustainable as well as able to grow.

BOX 1.2   DEMOGRAPHIC, GEOGRAPHIC AND POLITICAL CHARACTERISTICS OF THE USA[37]

The USA occupies the North American continent with its northern neighbor, Canada, and borders in the south on Mexico. According to the Economist Intelligence Unit,[38] a population of about 287 million generated the largest GDP in the world, valued at US$10.4 trillion, in 2002. The economy entered recession in 2001, and a sluggish recovery began in 2002. Tax cuts boosted GDP in 2003, with GDP forecasts for growth of 4 per cent in 2004, and 3 per cent between 2005 and 2008. In 2003, the expansion in the economy reduced the chance of a macroeconomic crisis in the short term, but the economic imbalances built up during the late 1990s boom continue to threaten long-term economic stability. These imbalances in the economy include a low propensity to save, and a large current account deficit that has increased since 11 September 2001 owing to the cost of the war in Iraq and funding tax cuts. Tax cuts are expected to boost private consumer spending but not to stimulate investment growth because of firms' excess capacity.

The executive head of the US federal republic is a president elected by popular vote via a complex system of 538 electoral colleges. An administration is appointed and reports to the president following senate approval of senior officials. The Supreme Court is the ultimate court of appeal on questions of federal law, and the president appoints judges with approval of the senate. The USA, which operates on a two-party system fostering rivalry between the Democratic and Republican parties, is regarded as politically stable. The income gap between rich and poor grew in the 1990s but has apparently not led to extensive class resentment. However, tensions can arise between the races because of large gaps in income, education and employment between whites and African–Americans, and African–American feelings of discrimination and prejudice from the white population. Hispanic and Asian populations are becoming increasingly important political forces.

How is it that shareholders, and even then only the lucky ones, have been able to appropriate so many of the benefits in a shareholder value-focused organization? One theory is that shareholders have done this by coopting the CEOs, and rewarding them disproportionately for increasing quarterly profits, through personal options and bonuses.[39]

What happens to other stakeholders? Proponents of shareholder value maintain that the interests of other groups are adequately protected through explicit or implicit contractual arrangements.[40] For instance, Shearer reports an amazing economic argument as to why firms are not responsible for their pollution beyond that of maximizing their own profits: the disutility of breathing smoke coming from a factory chimney will be reflected in the wages paid by the factory owners or prices of their goods.[41] The factory's responsibility for fouling the air in the community in which it operates is thus discharged by the wages and employment it brings. How far from reality can economic theory take us!

Obviously, pursuit of shareholder interests does not necessarily serve the collective good of the local community, as the above example reflects. Under this view, people's lives and well-being, and that of non-human life and ecosystems, are made subservient to the pursuit of shareholder profit. These external effects are presumed to be taken care of via the 'benefits' flowing from the corporation.[42] This example also shows that some stakeholders, like employees and investors, can choose to be part of a firm, becoming *voluntary stakeholders*. Other members of a community who may be unknowingly harmed or advantaged by a corporation's activities are *involuntary stakeholders*. Governments, communities and the environment itself are typical examples of involuntary stakeholders.

In a nutshell, the major principles underlying the Anglo/US approach are as follows:[43]

1. the main organizational goal is maximizing the stock price;
2. top management shall strictly adhere to the interests of the shareholders. To ensure this, a large part of managerial compensation will depend on the stock prices, including compensation via stock options;
3. organizations should have transparent standards for accounting such as the US GAAP (Generally Accepted Accounting Principles);
4. the validity of financial reports is controlled by experienced auditors. The stock exchanges shall prosecute misinformation harshly; and
5. organizations should only invest in projects that bring a return significantly higher than the cost of capital.

Clearly, finance stands at the very heart of the way Anglo/US capitalism operates: Wall Street demands that managers focus on short-term profitability. Achieving quarterly profits encourages short-term thinking and action. It can result in quick actions like cuts to research and training budgets, or reducing the workforce to meet analysts' expectations. As we will see, these short-term actions can undermine the very foundation on which a future should be built by reducing the firm's innovation, knowledge base and capacity for learning. Another way to create profits quickly can be to break up and sell parts of companies or take over others. Albert harshly condemns these methods as a high price to pay for capital.[44] To paraphrase Kennedy:[45] despite undoubted gains in productivity and performance during the 1990s, US corporations have mortgaged their long-term futures after less than two decades of obsession with maximizing shareholder value.

How could this happen? In switching to a market-driven economy in the 1980s, President Reagan abolished punitive rules and regulations (such as airline safety regulations, oil prices and protection in areas like telecommunications) in an effort to stimulate US markets and promote open competition. Although this deregulation led to price decreases in affected industries and a much-needed restructuring of the oil industry, it produced two unfavorable consequences.[46] The first is greater vulnerability of deregulated industries to the customer's disadvantage, as with the savings and loan bank collapses, ironically bailed out with massive federal government funds in this market economy. The second is a lowering of quality and service standards; for example, United Airlines admitted falsifying some safety checks to cut costs and maximize profits; and many depositors with the savings and loans banks lost their money.

Given the bail-out of the banks, for example, the claim that competition and self-regulation are the principles of US business is clearly a myth.[47] The market is in fact highly controlled and doing business in the USA is tightly regulated.[48] Is the acclaimed success of the Anglo/US model sustainable?

Major corporate collapses in 2002 led media and business people alike to loudly question the business model based on short-term shareholder value. They suggested that the Anglo/US model is fundamentally flawed.[49] Professor Fredmund Malik[50] from the University of St Gallen attributes the disaster on the stock markets and the sad condition of many enterprises – particularly those in the finance and telecommunications sectors – to the shareholder value approach. Various writers assert that shareholder value theory is behind the moral corruption in many parts of the financial sector.[51] Another view is that the financial scandals in the USA are more than moral errors.[52] They have revealed the structural weaknesses of the shareholder value concept. In any case, the destruction of about €15 billion in investor capital, of which €7 billion were lost in the USA alone,[53] makes people wonder how this is benefiting shareholders.

The promises of the Anglo/US model have often not come true; instead of organizations becoming strong and their shareholders rich, enterprises have been weakened and their owners made poorer. Malik[54] counters those who propose that the shareholder value approach was merely misinterpreted by emphasizing that the theory is fundamentally flawed. The destructive flaw lies in the focus on financial perspectives and the interests represented by the stock markets, fund managers and analysts who have no interest in enterprises themselves, just in relatively short-term paper dealings. Everything is measured except the organization itself, such as its leadership, although this is changing. When the leadership is scrutinized it is often limited to the top person, or at best to the top team, as if leadership at lower levels in the organization was an incidental factor. The departure or arrival of a CEO can move the share price either up or down quite dramatically.

Clearly, the pursuit of profit brings benefits: it is necessary for corporate survival and, when balanced, can bring social benefits like salaries for employees and taxes to government.[55] The issue is how profits are pursued and how the needs of stakeholders are addressed. 'Taken to its logical extreme, the pursuit of profit is, paradoxically, a threat to capitalism,' Albert wrote.[56] This is largely because the focus on short-term profits discourages long-term thinking, investing and planning.

A stakeholder backlash has already started. Marginalized stakeholders like employees, suppliers and customers have started to strike back at shareholder-value driven corporations. One irony is that US citizens enjoy extensive rights and liberties – except as employees of organizations, where their existence is not even included in corporation law.[57] Anglo/US corporations have downsized, outsourced, merged, globalized and automated to the extent that employees have ceased to identify with their employer. Employees have started realigning themselves from 'my corporation' to looking out for themselves under a 'me-incorporated' view. Instead of loyal, motivated employees, corporations are dealing with self-interested, self-motivated freelancers, who seek the best short-term deal for themselves. Some involve their lawyers in job negotiations to protect their interests.

For many years, suppliers were squeezed mercilessly on price and other conditions in corporate attempts to lower costs while increasing supplier service. Those who survived tended to band together to stand up to their major customers. Today the power relationship is reversing, with the remaining suppliers often in the driver's seat.[58] Customer power is also rising, particularly in the USA. Through various tactics designed to maximize shareholder value, customers have been disadvantaged: for example, by reduced choice of brands and outlets. US customers are now fighting back by withdrawing their loyalty as they search for the lowest priced items instead. This contrasts with Rhineland regions where there is less pressure from consumer groups for deregulation and liberalization than in the USA and UK. By contrast, Rhineland consumer groups often sympathize with producer groups such as farmers or retailers, because consumers value social stability, product safety and/or environmental protection over economic efficiency.[59]

Even the capital markets are changing, with some investors also influencing corporate behavior by investing in environmentally and socially responsible stocks. The fact that these stocks in aggregate outperform traditional stocks is not lost on these investors.[60] Thus the environment and other neglected stakeholders are starting to compete for corporate attention, supported by government regulation.

In short, the widespread and globally well promoted shareholder value model has come under considerable criticism for being theoretically, practically and socially flawed. It is accused of containing the seeds of its own destruction and being unsustainable. Some warn that the US economy may eventually fall into ruin if the Anglo/US model does not change.[61] What is the alternative?

RHINELAND CAPITALISM

Rhineland capitalism derives its name from the 1959 conference held on the banks of the Rhine in Bad Godesberg, Germany. Here the German Social Democratic Party committed itself to capitalism. For these Democrats, capitalism involved the need to protect and promote private ownership of the means of production within a free and competitive market.[62] The Rhineland aspect refers to the clear social component in economic policies and practices. A Germanic company is expected to serve anyone who holds a stake in its operation, including clients, suppliers, employees, stockholders and the local community. The Rhineland's stakeholder approach is associated with long-term investments that support innovation and foster stakeholder loyalty. Employees are seen as assets who need to be looked after like any other asset. The community is regarded as essential in protecting the individual and stabilizing society, but, beyond that, the free market dominates.

Although details of the model differ from country to country, Rhineland countries tend to share a particular set of values.[63] First, they are egalitarian, with disparities between the highest and lowest wages more moderate than in the USA; they levy tax on assets; and direct taxation is favored over indirect taxation. The vast majority of citizens are comfortably well-off. Even small towns have swimming pools, pedestrian malls and other communal infrastructure. Second, the interests of the group are put ahead of narrow individual interests.

Social benefits are typically widespread in Rhineland countries, and include universal health access for virtually the entire population. Social insurance covers all the major hazards for Rhineland workers: illness, work-related accidents and unemployment, as well as providing a basic retirement pension. Although the costs of Rhineland countries' social welfare systems are straining national resources, especially in times of poor economic performance, people generally have a socially responsible attitude to the welfare system, relatively few cheats aside.[64]

The focus in this book is on German and Swiss versions of the Rhineland model, although examples from Finland, South Africa and Sweden, covered later, show that the model applies outside the Germanic regions. Germany operates on a form of capitalism known as a 'social market economy'; Switzerland has a similar emphasis. A social market economy is no less capitalist than Anglo/US capitalism, but bears a pronounced social dimension. The commitment to this social dimension is often falsely equated with socialism by those who do not fully understand the subtleties of this version of capitalism. Economic elements are the core, alongside concepts of freedom and social justice. The social market economy was intended to provide goods and services efficiently, eliminate poverty and distribute income and resources more fairly.[65] It is based on consensus, corporatism and collective achievement over the long term.[66] Broad demographic and political characteristics of Germany and Switzerland, summarized in Box 1.3, provide some context for the following discussion.

BOX 1.3   DEMOGRAPHIC, GEOGRAPHIC AND POLITICAL CHARACTERISTICS OF SWITZERLAND AND GERMANY[67]

Switzerland is dominated topographically by the Alps, while Germany's terrain ranges from the Alps in the south to the Baltic and North Sea in the north. Germany is a member of the European Union (EU). For Switzerland, EU membership is only a remote possibility although it has extensive trade and other bilateral ties to the EU. About 98 per cent of the German population speaks German; about 65 per cent of the Swiss people are German-speaking, with French the second language.

According to data from the Economist Intelligence Unit, in 2003, Germany's population was about 82.5 million people and Switzerland's 7.3 million.[68] Germany has the third-largest economy in the world. Its GDP in both 2002 and 2003 was estimated at about €1990 billion, expected to grow by about 1.8 per cent in 2004 and 2005. Partly as a result of reunification with eastern Germany, Germany is no longer one of the wealthiest economies in the region. Its breaching of the EU budgetary ceiling of 3 per cent deficit is predicted to continue until 2005, although major social and economic reform initiatives were introduced in 2003. A serious problem facing Germany is the aging of its population, which is predicted to strain its social services and lead to a labor shortage in 2010–20. Swiss GDP fell by 0.4 per cent from 2002 to US$314 billion in 2003, but GDP growth is predicted to rise between 1.3 per cent and 1.5 per cent in 2004 and 2005, respectively. Substantial deficits are predicted in 2004 and 2005, but economic sentiment is improving.

Politically both countries are federal republics, and are considered stable democracies. Germany comprises states that have a high degree of discretion, particularly in cultural affairs like education, politics and industrial relations. A federal president elected by parliament heads the country, with the chancellor heading the government of the day.

The Swiss confederation is based on the principle of subsidiarity. This means that, what the individual family cannot do, the community does; what the community cannot do, the canton does; and similarly the state does what the canton cannot do. Switzerland retains elements of direct democracy, with individuals voting directly in referenda on many important issues. The head of state, a ceremonial office that rotates among members of the Federal Council, is elected for one year as council speaker, a *primus inter pares* (first among equals). Swiss concerns about neutrality and sovereignty remain strong.

Germany and Switzerland have few natural resources and depend on trade. Germany is the world's second largest exporter after the USA,[69] and is Europe's dominant industrial power, specializing in automobiles, heavy engineering, chemicals and electronics. For the Swiss economy, services, particularly tourism, contribute most heavily to GDP, and many Swiss hotels and restaurants are traditional family-owned establishments. Products include machines, electronics, chemicals and pharmaceuticals, watches and jewellery.

A major priority of social market economies is to establish and maintain social consensus. This requires balancing individual rights within a context of social justice and solidarity.[70] Three clearly articulated moral principles underlie this approach:

1. *principle of individuality*: this incorporates the liberal ideal of individual freedom;
2. *principle of solidarity*: humans are embedded in a society which makes them mutually dependent and obliges them to overcome injustice;
3. *principle of subsidiarity*: an institutional rule that shapes the relationship between individuality and solidarity. The intention is to give highest priority to individual rights. Whatever the individual can do, he or she should do, rather than the state. The German constitution states that

government cannot substitute for the market, and its role is restricted to providing direction and encouragement.

An extensive regulatory framework, referred to as *Ordnungspolitik*, allows market forces to operate within prescribed rules. The regulatory nature of the social market economy in Germany has changed over time within its basic framework, adapting to circumstances. Further changes are likely. The rule-based *Ordnungspolitik* may well prevail at the EU level, even if in a somewhat modified form.[71] This would mean a big change for governments used to greater discretionary powers, particularly France and Italy.

One way of looking at Rhineland capitalism is as a system of long-term cooperative relationships between different parties. The parties include firms and labor, firms and banks, and different firms. Best known are Rhineland partnerships with banks and labor unions.[72] Other parties include a range of stakeholders with interests in the firm and its well-being, from shareholders to employees, from the local region (through taxes generated by the firm and its employees) to clients and suppliers.[73] Future generations are also regarded as stakeholders. All stakeholders expect good relations with the company, and this generates pressure for the organization to behave in an environmentally and socially responsible way.

In turn, stakeholders have certain obligations, because these ethical and social achievements can only be sustained if the company can survive financially. For example, customers are expected to repay the company's social investments through increased demand and loyalty to the firm's products and services. With reciprocity expected from various groups of stakeholders, it is in the company's interests to behave responsibly and ethically.

Stock markets play a lesser role in Germany than in the USA. Few large German corporations allow the majority of their shares to be floated publicly. Given the traditional strength of the banks, public floats have not been necessary to raise capital, and banks have traditionally been patient and loyal shareholders. They make loans and, because of their connections to other firms and throughout the economy, provide a network of economic, financial, business and industrial information for the benefit of client companies. Their special relationship to businesses makes banks strong and their services valuable to their clients. Banks appear to have the long-term interests of the businesses at heart. However, the contribution of the banks as shareholder and financier in Germany, although perceived as very strong from abroad, is overestimated: the contribution is only 13 per cent in West Germany compared with the UK (21 per cent), France (25 per cent) and Switzerland (46 per cent).[74]

Power sharing is common, starting at the top, even in large firms. The board of management, the *Vorstand*, is responsible for the day-to-day running of the enterprise. A separate board, the supervisory board or *Aufsichtsrat,* is elected by shareholders to make strategic decisions. It appoints and oversees the *Vorstand.* Both boards are required by law to assist one another to ensure the smooth running of the organization and may have no members in common at any one time. This structure symbolizes the role of propriety over efficiency by having the two boards chaired by different people. It provides checks and balances between the two boards.

Workers share power with management via works councils, to which social issues such as training, redundancies, schedules, payroll matters and working patterns are brought. Consensus is important, and both management and works council need to come to agreement about these issues. Employees also sit on the supervisory board, thereby influencing broad policy.

Employer organizations, industrial trade associations and trade unions play a powerful, strategic role in the German economy. For example, in helping develop Baden-Württemberg, one of the most prosperous German states today, a coalition of local companies and industry associations decided to attract manufacturers in specialized niches to their region. Today Baden-Württemberg is the center of Germany's machine-tool and machine-making business. This in turn has attracted automobile and other manufacturers to the region, using the smaller companies as suppliers. Another town, Tuttlingen, has become the center of medical manufacturing, home to about 400 businesses related to medicine. Other regions specialize in different fields, including glass production, insurance, banking and publishing.

The Rhineland approach centers on achieving consensus among the many stakeholders involved, but it is not a substitute for conflict and disagreement. It provides a process in which conflicts can generate a solution acceptable to the community as a whole.[75] The Rhineland view is that dialogue and consensus are the oil keeping the wheels of business turning smoothly.

This consensual approach might seem time wasting, but, in the final analysis, consensus management enhances competitiveness.[76] An example from the industrial relations area arose during the 1981–2 recession. German trade unions agreed to take 3–4 per cent salary cuts. Similar salary sacrifices still occur within given firms in tough times. This cooperation is made possible by having a small number of industry-specific trade unions in Rhineland areas. Other benefits also occur under this form of industrial relations. Predictable wage demands have enabled employers to combine paying high wages with constant rises in productivity, while pursuing long-term goals. Furthermore, the strength of vocational training stems from the close collaboration between unions and management, and this in turn provides real wealth in terms of technical expertise and human resource (HR) potential. It would clearly damage the economy if Germany's acclaimed vocational training were not sustained. Relatively high levels of employment security, and hence low staff turnover, provide management with the incentive to invest in high levels of skills training and research and development (R&D). These practices are central to the Rhineland model.

Some see the greatest windfall in Rhineland economies as the system's support for seeking and achieving excellence, particularly in the face of a strong currency that makes it hard for countries like Germany to be more productive and compete abroad.[77] Rhineland systems support production techniques, training and investment in R&D.

Critics argue that the Rhineland model is not as consistent as many think.[78] Regional differences (such as in the former East German states), company-specific organizational forms (such as large transnationals) and industry differences influence the form of the model. Thus, even within Germany, variations on the Rhineland model exist.[79]

This variability can also be interpreted as evidence of the Rhineland model's adaptability. Adaptability is needed because several factors are straining this model.[80] First, governments are under pressure because money and entire businesses can rapidly leave the country. This would decrease tax revenue and increase local unemployment, both undesirable outcomes. Second, powerful forces like the US government, and international organizations such as the World Trade Organization and the EU, are promoting more liberal markets and common regulations. If successful, this would require modifications to the Rhineland model. Similarly, some people believe that the Rhineland model discourages new developments in the information technology (IT) and biotechnology areas, and are pressing for change. Finally, Germany and Switzerland have been experiencing slow economic growth and government budget constraints in recent years. This generates political pressure to cut government spending and focus on deregulation and other changes that promise to improve economic growth without increasing spending.

Other observers point out strengths in the Rhineland approach.[81] First, it involves the intentional blurring of boundaries between business and society, the public and private spheres, and between markets and politics, encouraging collaboration between these sectors. Second, the strengths of the model are part of the system and are not easily imitated. This feature provides additional competitive advantage to the model. Third, the system has continually adapted itself to change since its inception. This adaptability is fortunate because of the enormous changes called for in tough economic times, including those that lie ahead in the EU. Fourth, the Rhineland labor market is less prone to strikes, more predictable and more accountable than in many other countries.

To outsiders, the social market economy sometimes appears to constrain managers but, paradoxically, these constraints probably increase the flexibility and responsiveness of the entire economic system.[82] This happens as the many players in the Rhineland system adapt to change, build consensus and ready all parts of the economic system for change. Powerful trade associations, unions and corporations are involved, including the banks.

Continuous innovation is central to Rhineland organizations, in services and products, as well as the way they do business. Although Rhineland economies have been criticized for being slow in the area of radical innovation, particularly high-technology innovation, German enterprises outperform US and Japanese firms globally in R&D for intensive high-value goods markets and in patent notifications.[83] Furthermore, there is evidence that Germany is adapting its institutions and organizational processes to make radical innovation possible.[84] For example, considerable German government support has created technology parks and made venture capital available to stimulate this sector. The industry association research model has been adapted to support more innovative industries like biotechnology, while still remaining within the Rhineland business model. We will see later that German technology firms have adapted their business strategies to take advantage of the context in which they operate, rather than being constrained by it.[85]

Some ask whether Rhineland capitalism can remain a cohesive economic and social system as it adapts continuously to changing requirements. Will it survive today's huge challenges as well as it has mastered others in the past? The same questions could be asked of the Anglo/US model. In the following section, the models are compared.

COMPARING APPROACHES

Many differences between the two models of capitalism are evident from the above discussion. However, the fundamental difference is that the link between business and society is clearly stated in the Rhineland approach but is generally not made explicit in Anglo/US businesses.[86] Mintzberg and other US management experts emphasize that corporations are indeed social entities that must justify their existence by their overall contribution to society.[87]

Things are slowly changing. Mainstream Anglo/US economists are starting to include non-economic variables in explaining market behavior. These variables include viewing human resources as capital, judging productivity by social and environmental, as well as economic, criteria and making corporations responsible to multiple stakeholders rather than just to their shareholders. The basic idea behind the Anglo/US corporation is gradually shifting from shareholder value to answering questions such as 'For whose benefit and at whose expense should the firm be managed?'[88] The vision of US pharmaceutical giant Pfizer illustrates this change in emphasis. In the 1990s, Pfizer's vision referred to dominating the market. It has since shifted to a vision of being highly valued by a range of stakeholders.

Given evidence that the Rhineland model is both economically and socially more efficient than its US counterpart,[89] it is ironic that the Anglo/US model exerts a psychological and political superiority over the European model. Even European leaders have started questioning their own model, seeking deep reform.[90] The Europeans were reinforced in this questioning by many US policy makers. Enthused by the apparent successes of the Anglo/US business model, these policy makers refused to believe that what they saw as overregulated, tradition-bound Europe could function efficiently in a globalized economy.[91] Then the collapse of Enron, Worldcom and other US corporations tarnished the Anglo/US model. This encouraged Europeans not to abandon their own model, but to seek modifications to it and find new courage to follow their own ways. Many European business leaders refuse to buckle to Wall Street's new 'reform' demands on the grounds that they take a well functioning – but different – approach to business.

The Rhineland model is far from perfect, and has its critics. One weakness is attributed to the long-term personal relationships that make the model relatively rigid.[92] However, these relationships also bring support in times of need. Other major criticisms regarding publicly listed companies in particular include inadequate focus on shareholder interests, the two-tier system of executive board and supervisory board, poor financial transparency, inadequate independence of supervisory boards, limited independence of financial statement auditors and inadequate disclosure of top executives' pay.[93] Poor transparency is not an inevitable component of the Rhineland approach, nor is it an inevitable component of the Anglo/US approach. Rather, it is an issue that needs to be addressed by both models.

The German Corporate Governance Code that took effect in 2003 addresses all five major criticisms made of the German model. The code's aim has been to make corporate governance rules for German public companies transparent, but it recommends that non-listed companies also adhere to its principles. The code has blended international best practice within the prevailing German legal context. Codes of corporate governance have also been instigated in the Anglo/US world, including the USA and South Africa, through the US Sarbanes–Oxley Act of 2002 and the King Reports, respectively.

The Anglo/US model has its critics too. One problem relates to innovation. Undoubtedly, many significant innovations have emerged from the USA, but Albert[94] points out that overall R&D has suffered in the USA because most of it is directed towards military purposes. The Pentagon's research budget is greater than the total R&D expenditure of Japan or Germany. Most of Germany's 2.5 per cent of GDP spent on R&D goes to non-military programs, whereas in the USA about 2.7 per cent of GDP is spent on R&D, with 1 per cent devoted to weapons research alone. On the plus side, military research led to the development of the Internet and the whole world is benefiting from this. However, emphasizing high-level research specialized for the military presents a problem for the broader US economy. This is because military research is often narrowly focused and its results classified, making its benefits slow or even impossible to spread to industry. This compares with basic R&D that can be used in different industries, typical of Germany and Japan.[95]

Another concern is that the Anglo/US approach promotes competition between employees because, among other things, individual employee salaries are negotiated at market rates.[96] If people are competing, it can make collaboration a challenge. The Rhineland model has a different set of priorities. It does not treat employees as so many productive units or raw materials to be bought and sold on the market. The Rhineland enterprise, as part of the community, has an obligation to provide a certain level of job security, earn staff loyalty, and offer educational and training opportunities to employees. These obligations cost money, and so the firm may not be able to pay each worker his or her market value in the American sense. Instead, it lays the basis for a long-term career. Thus, under the Rhineland model, there is nothing to be gained by cut-throat in-house competition between employees. This in turn favors collaboration and teamwork.

The Anglo/US shareholder value model is often accused of overpaying managers, who receive vastly more than Rhineland managers.[97] Traditionally, the difference between wages paid to the lowest and highest Rhineland salary earners is significantly lower than in the USA, where the average CEO's salary is 475 times that of the average worker's wages.[98] According to *Business Week*, the ratio of CEO pay to factory worker pay in Germany was about 21 to 1 in 1995. Only Norway, Sweden, Denmark, Finland and Belgium have a lower level of wage differences than Germany, according to the OECD.[99] However, these figures may be somewhat inaccurate. They tend to disguise the fact that the differences have probably increased in the years since that research, and that wages paid above union-agreed levels and additional payments extend these differences somewhat. Despite the emphasis on equality, the centralized bargaining system has not been able to prevent a working poor class from developing in Germany, showing that the Rhineland model does not achieve its social goals perfectly.[100] However, relatively egalitarian wage levels promote social peace.[101]

Perhaps the two models might each suit different circumstances. Bischof[102] points out that British managers are under pressure to deliver profits, have an inferior infrastructure to contend with and have a less skilled workforce by German standards because they invest less in staff development and training. It is no wonder, then, that British managers have to manage differently from their German counterparts. The result is that the Germans are better at managing complex processes like car manufacturing, whereas the British are faster off the mark, more creative and adaptable, and outsource as much as they can to make it simple. In other words, the Anglo/US model suits short-term relationships with workers and economies that compete on cost rather than quality[103] and require short-term flexibility.[104] But is this approach sustainable over the long term and for the whole economy?

BROADER ECONOMIC CONTEXT

It is tempting to assume a relationship between how well a country is performing on various broad economic indicators and how its business models operate. Various writers have pointed out the difficulty of linking apparently global economic developments and trends to specific impacts within different countries.[105] There are many reasons for this difficulty.

First, the definition and choice of different economic statistics and measures complicate international comparisons. For example, the way the USA calculates productivity gains (using 'hedonic' price indexing) leads to the USA appearing more productive than Germany purely through statistical manipulation.[106] If Germany used hedonic fixing, its GDP would look considerably better than it currently does. Following a detailed analysis that compensates for measurement differences, Hutton[107] argues that GDP in Europe actually exceeds that of the USA, contrary to prevailing wisdom.

Second, an economy works within a set of assumptions and values that differ from country to country. Whose set of values should one adopt in comparing economies, and do these values provide a meaningful basis for comparison? Low unemployment, for example, may seem like a key value. However OECD evidence suggests that the level of unemployment within a European nation has little to do with how much the country's fiscal policies copy the American model. Three countries that feature a strong Rhineland focus achieved low unemployment levels in the period 2000–2002: The Netherlands, Norway and Switzerland.[108] Clearly one feature of an economy, unemployment, results from many political and economic factors and the values on which they rest.

Third, the impact of models of capitalism and a country's economic performance depend on the positive or negative effects of individual components in the models. This is also difficult to evaluate. Throughout the 1990s, people were predicting trouble for the German economy. For example, experts predicted that, in bursting out of the post-unification recession, Germany's social commitment would drive up labor costs, and the cradle-to-grave social welfare system would stifle energy and innovation.[109] This does not appear to have happened.[110] Instead Germany's business model has provided the nation with considerable social stability.[111] So what is the effect of the social commitment: is it positive in creating stability (that benefits firms) or negative because of costs to firms?

How wide a net should economists cast in evaluating an economy? Looking at society broadly, the US economy is embedded within a strained and vulnerable society that appears to be becoming increasingly polarized into two groups.[112] One group is affluent and enjoys access to the best services and advantages; the other is chronically poor, undereducated and excluded from the benefits and privileges available as a matter of course to the other group. Rhineland countries are more egalitarian. Is distribution of wealth and access to services not important in evaluating the success of an economy?

Similar arguments can be made about global disparities in wealth and living conditions.[113] Some forms of capitalism strive to reduce these disparities more than others, and it becomes a question of values as to whether this is an appropriate goal. The Anglo/US model would tend to say no, the Rhineland model would say yes.

Thus it is very difficult to link models of capitalism to broader macroeconomic indices of 'success'. In fact, because they use different criteria for success, it is almost impossible to compare outcomes, except using Anglo/US criteria of financial success. In financial terms, successful corporate outcomes occur under both Rhineland and Anglo/US paradigms, and each contains acknowledged weaknesses.[114] Nonetheless, it is useful to explore the broader economic context in which each model is embedded, before concluding this chapter by introducing the Sustainable Leadership Grid.

German Context

Many people were concerned about Germany's overall economic performance in the early 2000s. Switzerland's economy was also performing poorly at that time, while another Rhineland country, Finland, was considered to have the most competitive economy after the USA.[115] Let us look at Germany's economy in order to better understand the context within which Rhineland enterprises operate. Box 1.4 describes an important element in that economy, the role of SMEs (small and medium-sized enterprises), known as the *Mittelstand*.

Certainly Germany's postwar economy grew well into the early 1990s, creating what many refer to as an economic miracle. Skeptics attributed this postwar growth to a reconstruction boom, but closer analysis suggests that it was indeed a growth 'miracle' in its own right.[116]

As the *Economist*[117] pointed out in a review of the German economy, commentators have been predicting the demise of the German economy for decades, and it has not yet arrived. Growth has slowed significantly and governments at all levels are running out of cash, but life is still comfortable for the majority of Germany's residents. The question is, how long will the good life continue?

The German economy contains various apparent weaknesses, including slow responsiveness to changing environments.[118] High labor and social costs like six weeks' annual vacation, and annual bonuses of one month's extra pay (known as the 13th salary) are often touted as weaknesses because they add to the cost of labor, but they also contribute to employee quality of life and well-being. Well-paid employees consume products and services both at home and abroad.

Being a resource-poor nation, Germany is dependent on its people's knowledge, its intellectual capital. This requires a focus on innovation, technology and education. Alarm bells should start ringing now that Germany's expenditure on R&D has fallen from 2.9 per cent of GDP to under 2.5 per cent in only a few years.[119] Furthermore, the ambivalent relationship between Germans and technology needs re-examining. Although Germans use advanced technology in their cars and households, many are wary of large-scale technologies such as genetic engineering and biotechnology, where almost all key patents are held by the USA.[120]

Further cause for alarm came from a recent international comparison of educational systems. Germany's once envied education system fell almost to the bottom of the ratings. German universities need urgent reform, and so do secondary schools and the once acclaimed apprentice system.[121] Education needs to be lifelong if people are to keep pace with the rapid changes facing the world. This will require a shift in thinking away from one-off diplomas or certificate qualifications to continuing learning.

Some economists argue that employers are suffering under the high costs of providing pensions and health cover for their staff, which inhibits taking on new employees, in turn flooding the labor markets with unemployed citizens.[122] Consensus building is also blamed for adding to labor costs and hence to unemployment. Close analysis refutes all these claims. For example, Hutton provides considerable evidence that shows how unemployment is the short-term by-product of major economic shocks that the German and broader European economies have suffered.[123] Some of these shocks are discussed below. Even if German managers agreed with commentators who blame rigid labor markets for high labor costs, decreasing competitiveness and high unemployment in Germany, they often remain ambivalent about deregulating labor markets because doing so might destabilize society.[124]

Despite structural weaknesses in need of reform, the German economy is still a major force and, to some extent, a miracle. Since the 1990s, Germany has faced four major financial and economic hurdles that have severely affected the economy, and might well have brought a weaker economy to its knees. Let us look at each of these hurdles.

First, Germany has been the largest net contributor to EU finances since its inception, consistently contributing more money than it takes out of the EU treasury. In 2000, Germany contributed a net €11 billion,[125] money that did not go directly into stimulating its own internal economy. To put this contribution into perspective, all but three other EU countries are net beneficiaries.

A second economic shock arrived in the 1990s, during the reunification of the two Germanys. The state stepped in to provide heavy assistance to this exceptional process. First, it provided massive fund transfers from west to east. Second, it intervened in market forces by establishing a trustee to handle the sale of former communist enterprises. Despite the 1991–2 boom, reunification is estimated to have involved roughly €108 billion in net transfers in 1995 alone, and large transfers have continued ever since.[126] Furthermore, the unexpected and unplanned incorporation of a large proportion of the east German population into the social welfare system strained the economy, as did heavy spending on environmental protection necessitated by severe pollution in the eastern states. Nonetheless this kind of investment is expected to pay off in the medium-to-long term, even if it is painful in the short term.[127]

Third, a deep economic crisis occurred in 1992–3. At this time, the impact of the weak global economy reached Germany, which is heavily dependent on exports. A highly valued currency coupled with expensive production costs made the economic crisis worse. Moving production abroad and instigating major restructuring at home eliminated 900 000 jobs between 1992 and 1994. A heated debate as to whether Germany was a viable production location centered primarily on the high production costs and business failing to move into new industries.[128] High wages could be tolerated when Germany exported into quality, niche markets. However other nations (such as Japan) had risen to challenge Germany's uniqueness in quality, dependability and service. This made price more of a competitive factor than in the past. In innovation, German companies tended to focus on sectors where they had traditionally been strong: aviation and space, mechanical engineering, vehicle construction and parts of the chemical industry.

Fourth, adoption of the euro brought another economic shock. This was partly because Germany joined the monetary union at a disadvantageous exchange rate. Its currency was exchanged at a rate estimated to be up to 20 per cent too high.[129] Being part of the monetary union also means that Germany can no longer manipulate the exchange rate of its currency. This intervention had assisted its export economy in the past.

Thus at least four major forces reduced the German economic miracle over about a decade. Rather than condemning Germany's current economic performance, perhaps we should marvel that the country has been able to weather all these economic shocks over such a short time and still retain social harmony and world-class organizations. How have they done it?

BOX 1.4   THE *MITTELSTAND* (GERMAN SMEs)

The German economy is dominated by about 3.3 million small- and middle-sized enterprises (SMEs), known as the *Mittelstand*, a significant part of the economy. Mittelstand firms employ fewer than 500 people, although over 65 per cent of them have fewer than 250 employees,[130] and about 40 per cent are privately owned.[131] The Mittelstand represents about 99.3 per cent of all enterprises subject to turnover tax, 44.8 per cent of all taxable turnover, 57 per cent of GDP of all enterprises and 46 per cent of the gross investment, creates 70 per cent of jobs and offers 80 per cent of trainee positions in Germany.[132] Thus the Mittelstand represents the backbone of the German economy and is the motor behind job generation. The Mittelstand has traditionally dominated small global niches, particularly in the important machinery and chemical sectors, and provided a powerful engine for the recent economy.

Institutional arrangements for assisting small firms are traditionally well established in Germany, with special SME policy being part of regional policy. German policy makers try to improve economic efficiency by compensating SMEs for recognized disadvantages of being small. Part of this support for the Mittelstand is directed at human resources, particularly via Germany's strong technical education. This contrasts with interventions in Britain that generally would only be used to remove or compensate for market imperfections.[133]

All is not well with the Mittelstand, however. According to the president of the Bavarian Business Association, Randolf Rodenstock, the future of the Mittelstand lies in innovation and major change. By destroying old structures, new opportunities emerge: coal and steel become bio- and high-tech industries as the old economy gives way to the new economy.[134] However, SMEs tend to be conservative, do not generally enter risk gladly, and thus do not easily embrace new and different enterprises and industries.[135] Some positive action is being taken to help the Mittelstand. In Bavaria, for example, SMEs form industry-based associations that in turn have banded together as part of a broader, united Mittelstand association. This association has been able to lobby the state to direct more funds to assisting the Mittelstand. Financing for the Mittelstand is also in a state of transition in moving towards more financial transparency, controlling and strategic optimization.

Despite these constraints and challenges, some members of the Mittelstand are flourishing, as the case studies in Part II show.

US Context

The USA is the largest economic power in the world at the beginning of the 21st century. Since its decline in the 1980s, when it became the largest debtor nation, the USA has made a major comeback. Using the country's economic, financial and technological advantages, the Reagan government generated an economic boom that brought America back, larger than ever. This appeared to continue under Clinton, until George W. Bush's era and heavy borrowings to fund the so-called 'war on terror'. The US economy and its achievements tend to be widely reported and lauded, being greatly admired in many parts of the world. There is therefore no need to go into too much detail about its successes here.

However, according to the OECD's 2003 *Economic Outlook* and other analyses, the US economy is not in as good shape as its reputation suggests.[136] The 1990s US productivity 'miracle' was somewhat illusory. It was based on a consumer boom built on record domestic borrowings and foreign capital. A massive rise in share prices made citizens feel rich and enticed foreigners to want to buy a share of the action. According to Hutton's analysis,[137] this approach is not sustainable because essential relationships between the market, society, patient investors and government have been weakened.

Going beyond economic factors, observers are increasingly arguing that the USA is in social decline. This is indicated partly by the growing drugs economy, crime and the associated two million people in prison, of whom about 15–20 per cent are said to be mentally ill.[138] Barricades are being put up throughout society, with a split into two societies that sharply contrasts the advantaged and disadvantaged.[139] It is polarizing not only rich and poor, but also institutions such as hospitals, schools and universities, which are either elite or in 'tatters'.[140] Poverty statistics make the social divide clear. According to OECD figures between 1985 and 1995, 17 per cent of the US population was defined as poor.[141] This was the highest poverty rate in the industrialized world, and compared with 5 per cent in Denmark and Finland, and 9 per cent in Canada, Germany and the Netherlands. In 2004, the OECD[142] reported continuing social challenges in the USA, with poverty rates edging up. Continuing this theme, Mintzberg[143] and his colleagues ask whether a society should feel comfortable when 'more than 30 per cent of households have a net worth, including homes and investments, of less than $10,000'. They point out that poverty in the USA increased during the boom years of the 1990s. Furthermore, the inflation-adjusted minimum wage was 21 per cent lower in 2002 than in 1979.

On the business and political fronts, American observers note that the USA has experienced major problems stemming from the values and behaviors of legitimized leaders who have not been held accountable for their actions.[144]

This started to change in the early 2000s, when US law prescribed and imposed forceful sanctions on managers who failed to comply with new antitrust, securities and environmental regulations.[145]

Various writers point out that Reagan supported the trend away from business concerning itself with social issues and explicitly supported greed as an acceptable value.[146] Early founders of the American constitution predicted that, without 'civic virtue' exercised by private citizens, American society would descend into factional chaos and could end in authoritarian rule. The founding fathers of the American Republic would be amazed at the accuracy of their predictions in today's US society. Since the Reagan presidency, concern for the economy seems to be the main binding force keeping US society together: the citizen has been transformed into 'economic man'.[147] Is this the kind of world we want to work towards? Can we operate in a better way?

SUSTAINABLE LEADERSHIP GRID

We have seen that at least two forms of capitalism have coexisted for many decades. The Anglo/US version has threatened to dominate the other, primarily through the influence of the capital markets and US world dominance. Many writers have contrasted the short-term, shareholder value focus of the Anglo/US model with the long-term, stakeholder-driven European approach, questioning the apparent pre-eminence of the Anglo/US approach.[148] The differences between the assumptions underlying the two forms of capitalism affect the way organizations are led and their sustainability in significant ways, as we will see.

Major differences between the two models are highlighted in the 'Sustainable Leadership Grid' shown in Table 1.1. Here the Rhineland and Anglo/US models form two ends of a series of dimensions. The dimensions are described using short phrases, but their fuller meaning is discussed in Chapters 3, 4 and 5. The dimensions cover the role of the CEO and top team; where decisions are made; the value placed on ethical behavior; dependence and independence from the financial capital markets; innovation in products/ services and processes; how knowledge is managed; taking a long-term or short-term perspective on CEO tenure, strategy, planning, investment, growth, stock options and work processes; developing managers from within versus bringing in new people from outside; exhibiting a strong or weak organizational culture; making people a high or low priority; ensuring high quality in products and services or being laissez-faire about quality; retaining or downsizing staff; promoting a skilled workforce or not; displaying social and environmental responsibility or not; considering a broad range of stakeholders

Table 1.1 Sustainable Leadership Grid comparing Rhineland and Anglo/US models

Grid elements	Rhineland	Anglo/US
CEO concept	top team speaker	decision maker, hero
Decision making	consensual	manager-centered
Ethical behavior	an explicit value	ambivalent
Financial markets	challenge them	follow them
Innovation	strong	a challenge
Knowledge management	shared	a challenge
Long-term perspective	yes	no
Management development	grow their own	import managers
Organizational culture	strong	a challenge
People priority	strong	lip-service
Quality	high is a given	difficult to deliver
Retaining staff	strong	weak
Skilled workforce	strong	challenged
Social responsibility	strong	underdeveloped
Environmental responsibility	strong	underdeveloped
Stakeholders	broad focus	shareholders
Teams	self-governing	manager-centered
Uncertainty and change	considered process	fast adjustment
Union–management relations	cooperation	conflict

versus giving priority to shareholders; working through self-governing or manager-directed teams; managing uncertainty and change; and the extent of cooperation or conflict between management and unions.

While reducing a complex system to the 19 elements in the Sustainable Leadership Grid oversimplifies the real world, the grid is intended as a device for understanding essential differences between the models. It facilitates the comparison of leadership philosophies and behaviors in the case studies presented later. Table 1.2 summarizes the elements in the Sustainable Leadership Grid from Rhineland and Anglo/US perspectives, as many of their proponents would see them, showing subcategories for some elements.

Corporate governance is not a separate element in the Sustainable Leadership Grid because both Rhineland and Anglo/US models are converging in this area. Clearly, effective corporate governance is critical to sustainable leadership to ensure that companies are run in transparent, ethical ways that retain investor confidence. Corporate governance guidelines and codes of conduct for boards are being introduced in both Anglo/US and Rhineland regions. The 2003 German code has already been discussed. The Swiss equivalent is the 2002 corporate governance code of best practice issued by the Swiss Business Federation. In the USA, the Sarbanes–Oxley Act 2002 introduced government regulation of the capital markets sector by specifying corporate responsibilities, regulating auditors and financial reporting, and providing penalties for fraud. The 2002 South African King 2 Report (discussed further in Chapter 6) detailed the responsibilities directors have in financial, social and environmental areas. However, adherence to King 2 is largely voluntary except for companies listed on the Johannesburg stock exchange. These codes represent contrasting approaches to ensuring that companies are well managed – compare punitive US legislation with voluntary South African guidelines – but the end goal is to ensure that the public can have confidence in the way businesses are run.[149] The tendency is for principles of corporate governance to be aimed at similar objectives throughout the world, while respecting local values and laws. Therefore, these mechanisms no longer provide a major point of difference between Anglo/US and Rhineland leadership. For this reason, corporate governance has not been made an explicit element in Table 1.2, although related practices like ethical behavior and a stakeholder focus are included.

Note how the various elements at each end of the Sustainable Leadership Grid tend to *align* and be self-reinforcing in many ways. The elements combine to create a system whose overall effectiveness is greater than the sum of its individual parts. An example of alignment can be seen in the Rhineland's long-term employment policies ('retaining staff'). Policies like this are driven by the fact that a 'skilled workforce' that is imbued with a 'strong organizational culture' is capable of working in 'self-governing teams' to deliver 'high quality'. This is a valuable asset that managers would not readily dispose of and it would be costly to replace.

Another example of alignment is where power is concentrated in the hands of top management, as in Anglo/US CEOs. A single decision maker only needs to pay lip-service to 'people are our priority', and finds it easier to downsize a less 'skilled workforce' to cut costs when faced with pressure from 'financial markets'. For Rhineland companies, power is shared with employees, making such decisions more difficult. Furthermore, access to finance and other benefits often depends on a Rhineland firm's reputation, and so Rhineland companies value enduring 'stakeholder relationships'.

Of course, in practice, the alignment will not be perfect in all firms. For example, Rhineland organizations may have a CEO who wants to be the ultimate decision maker rather than the speaker of a top team that has to come to consensus. However, a broad conformity to one or other of the two ends of the Sustainable Leadership Grid is likely to occur because of the self-reinforcing pressures for alignment that come from the other elements. Box 1.5 explains the derivation of these elements from a combination of observations and theory.

Table 1.2   Sustainable Leadership Grid criteria from Rhineland and Anglo/US perspectives

Element	Rhineland perspective	Anglo/US perspective
CEO concept	*Primus inter pares*, personality cults are rare; team speaker	CEO often enjoys hero status, decides and leads from the front
Decision making	Consensual and participative decisions	Managers often decide or make final decisions
Ethical behavior	Usually a core value	Under pressure because of short-term considerations
Financial markets	Strong resistance to capital market pressures, or balancing stakeholders	Typically driven by the capital markets
Innovation	Pervasive, continuous in process, service and product	Limited, emphasis is on radical innovation
Knowledge management	Often a managed process; supported by staff retention	Difficult to achieve with low staff retention and low skills
Long-term perspective	Yes	No, short-term; driven by capital market demands
CEO and top team tenure	CEOs and top teams have lengthy tenures	CEOs have to perform to remain, with increasing turnover
Strategic thinking	Allows long-term planning, investment, managing growth and reinventing work processes	Planning, investment, growth and re-engineering tend to be limited by short-term factors
Stock options	Tend to reward achieving long-term objectives	Reward short-term results
Stakeholder relationships	Supplier, customer, employee and other stakeholder relationships tend to be valued over the long term	Supplier, customer, employee and other stakeholder relationships tend to be short-term, changing to lowest-cost supplier
Management development	Promotion from within reinforces the culture and values, minimizes knowledge loss; requires extensive management development	Importing managers from outside transfers cost of training to others, can result in knowledge transfer but also loss within the firm; can challenge the culture and staff morale and commitment

32

Organizational culture	Being strongly rooted in history, vision, values and philosophy seems core; reliance on high trust	Developing a strong culture takes time; this is difficult when a firm is short-term, growth-driven, merger-dominated; reliance on control
People priority	Staff development and retention are valued as investments in people	Development is often the employee's responsibility
Quality	High quality is a given	Limited where the emphasis is on speed and cost cutting
Retaining staff	Low turnover rates, strong staff development focus	Downsizing and outsourcing common
Skilled workforce	Continuing technical and behavioral training for most employees, who develop firm-specific skills	Unstable workforce acts as a disincentive for 'upskilling' employees, except for managers; employees bring generic skills to a firm
Social responsibility	Permeates these organizations' thinking and actions	Often seen as reducing shareholder value and profits
Environmental responsibility	A given, brings competitive advantage and savings	Not widely considered, often seen as reducing profits
Stakeholders	Broad stakeholder focus includes employees, customers, suppliers, government, communities, industry associations, society and future generations	Shareholders win over other stakeholders, although customers and employees are rising in importance
Teams	Teamwork is a core process, often via self-governing teams	Effective teamwork is a challenge, requires management intervention
Uncertainty and change	Change is a considered and managed process	Constant change may not allow initiatives to really take hold
Union–management relations	Employees, unions, management share power; employees represented on boards of large companies	Normally adversarial relationship as unions battle for better work conditions; boards and management typically hold the power

BOX 1.5   METHODOLOGY FOR GENERATING THE SUSTAINABLE LEADERSHIP GRID

In generating the elements in the Sustainable Leadership Grid, I employed two main conceptual approaches: middle-range thinking and grounded theory. These approaches contrast sharply with traditional research methodologies such as formal surveys, using instead case studies, informal observations and archival documents (for example, annual reports, analyst commentaries and the academic literature).

Laughlin[150] envisages middle-range thinking as lying midway between empirical research approaches (for example, surveys and statistical testing) and non-empirical research (for example, qualitative and subjective approaches not driven by hypothesis testing). At the empirical end of this dimension, the researcher is assumed to be irrelevant to finding the 'facts', whereas, at the other end, the investigator is recognized as part of the discovery process. Middle-range thinking provides a balance between these two extreme approaches to research. This book adopts middle-range thinking by employing case study data that I collected and interpreted, supplemented by observations made during visits to enterprises in Germany and Switzerland, and referring to documentation and information supplied by, or published about, the case study organizations. Often issues were also discussed with senior management of these enterprises. In this sense, practicing managers have contributed to the elements in the Sustainable Leadership Grid.

In developing the Grid's dimensions, I also employed grounded theory, an iterative process that calls for comparison, contrasting, cataloguing and classifying to develop variables with significant explanatory power.[151] Thus, the elements in the grid were derived through a combination of published literature relating to the Rhineland and Anglo/US models and information acquired during visits to the organizations. (Note that the element, 'long-term perspective', has been divided into smaller elements since it covers a range of activities.)

This inductive process has allowed me to hypothesize about key characteristics distinguishing the two models in practice, based on available information and other people's published research. The value in doing this is that the context in which the Rhineland model operates is preserved. In addition the complex ways in which the elements in the two models align become apparent. Organizations are not static, and the Sustainable Leadership Grid is intended to reflect continuing processes, not specific events.

In the following chapters, case studies of successful organizations show how the Rhineland model works in practice using each dimension in the Sustainable Leadership Grid. The grid serves as a framework for discussing the current leadership philosophy and practices within a particular enterprise.

PART II

Rhineland leadership practices

The practices of successful US organizations are often described in books like *Built to Last* and *In Search of Excellence*, and in magazines like *Fortune* and *Forbes*. European managers tend to be familiar with these kinds of publications and are relatively well-informed on the Anglo/US business model. However, Anglo/US executives rarely learn much about leadership in successful organizations in other parts of the world. The next four chapters reveal some of the thinking and practices of successful European enterprises that follow Rhineland principles. The intention is to show how sustainable leadership is put into operation by taking an inside look at selected enterprises.

Chapter 2 introduces the case study firms. The following three chapters illustrate how the elements in the Sustainable Leadership Grid operate in practice in these firms. The grid elements are grouped for convenience into three areas: management and decision making practices, focus on people, and broader systems and processes. Within each of these areas, the elements of the grid are discussed in alphabetical order. We will see at the end that the various practices combine to form a self-reinforcing system. However, the three criteria that most differentiate Rhineland organizations from their Anglo/US counterparts are the *long-term perspective* taken by Rhineland companies, how they manage the influence of the *financial capital markets*, and their focus on employees and other *stakeholder groups*.

All grid elements are also recognized as important by well-known management thinkers. To show the link between the elements and the views of eminent Anglo/US scholars and practitioners, each section in Chapters 3, 4 and 5 is introduced by a quotation from a leading US management thinker in the field. To demonstrate that these introductory quotations have not been culled from many obscure sources, all have been taken from articles published in the *one* issue of a US professional magazine aimed at management practitioners: the 20th Anniversary Issue of *Executive Excellence*. Covering so many characteristics of the Sustainable Leadership Grid in this single issue reinforces the growing demand for Rhineland elements to be incorporated into Anglo/US leadership.

It is important to understand the thinking and philosophy behind the elements in the Sustainable Leadership Grid. Therefore, in Chapters 3, 4 and 5, current discussion from the published literature on each element is summarized before the element is illustrated with examples from the European organizations. Furthermore, if an organization is not chosen to illustrate a particular element in the grid, this does not mean that it does not follow that principle. Examples have been selected to provide diversity rather than for completeness.

2.   Rhineland case study enterprises

This chapter introduces 15 case studies from enterprises based in Germany and Switzerland. Many others could have been used to illustrate the Rhineland model in operation. The organizations included here were selected because they are consistent leaders in their fields, have been in business for at least two decades, exhibited growth in sales in 2002 and have weathered difficult times. All have two things in common: success and leadership following Rhineland practices in the Sustainable Leadership Grid.

Some are household names, while others tend to be known only to specialists requiring their services or products. Aesculap is a leading supplier of surgical equipment and services; Allianz and Munich Re dominate in their respective global niches in the financial sector; Rohde & Schwarz leads in test measurement for radio and IT communications; BMW, Porsche and ZF star in the automobile industry; Migros dominates Swiss retailing; Loden-Frey is a trend setter in fashion and textiles; Fraunhofer is acclaimed in contract research; Holcim and Seele excel in the global construction sector; Kärcher shines in cleaning products and solutions; Novartis specializes in pharmaceuticals and health care; and WACKER leads in organic and inorganic chemistry.

Well-known BMW and Porsche were also the top scorers in a German industry ranking of firms on image and profile. In 2004, they were both rated 'excellent' by *Manager Magazin*.[152] In the same survey, ZF and Allianz ranked forty-fourth and fifty-first, respectively. The performance of privately held and smaller companies is rarely published, excluding them from formal rankings, but the companies covered in this chapter are all recognized leaders in their markets. Some of the privately held firms would qualify as Simon's[153] 'hidden champions', including Aesculap, Kärcher, Loden-Frey, Rohde & Schwarz, Seele and WACKER. These are the quiet achievers, privately owned and rarely seeking publicity, but recognized for excellence in their products and services.

A brief description of the featured organizations, their history and markets follows. Table 2.1 provides a summary. The organizations come from diverse industries. They range in age between 20 and over 160 years, and employ between 250 and 174 000 people. Loden-Frey and Migros have a mostly local focus, but the rest are international. Eleven are clearly global in scope.

Table 2.1 *Overview of German and Swiss case study organizations*

Organization	HQ	Industry	Date	Staff (approx.)
Aesculap	Germany	medical supplies	1867	6 400
Allianz	Germany	insurance/finance	1890	174 000
BMW	Germany	automobiles	1916	104 000
Fraunhofer	Germany	R&D	1949	12 700
Holcim	Switzerland	cement	1912	45 000
Kärcher	Germany	cleaning systems	1935	5 400
Loden-Frey	Germany	textiles and fashion	1842	385
Migros	Switzerland	retail, hotels, banks	1925	81 000
Munich Re	Germany	reinsurance, primary insurance, asset management	1880	41 400
Novartis	Switzerland	pharmaceuticals	1996	78 500
Porsche	Germany	automobiles	1900	10 699
Rohde & Schwarz	Germany	test and measurement, radio communications, IT security broadcasting, radiomonitoring and location, mobile radio	1933	5 900
Seele	Germany	glass and metal structures	1984	350
WACKER	Germany	mixed chemicals	1914	15 622
ZF Friedrichshafen	Germany	automobile parts	1915	53 000

Note: N/a = information not available.

Scope	Ownership	Turnover* (millions)	Financial Year*	2002 One year sales growth (%)	Sustainability Index
global	B. Braun (family)	€780.8	2003	7.2	
global	public	€85 000	2003	9.8	Dow Jones; FTSE4Good
global	public + family	€41 525	2003	17.6	Dow Jones; FTSE4Good
international	non-profit	€1 038	2003	N/a	
global	public	CHF12 600	2003	15	Dow Jones
global	family	€1 000	2003	N/a	
Munich region	family	N/a		N/a	
Switzerland, Austria, Poland, Turkey	customers	US$14 548	2003	0.1**	
global	public	€45 959	2003	19	Dow Jones; FTSE4Good
global	public	US$24 864	2003	7.4	Dow Jones
global	public + family	€6 359	2003	32.6	
global	family	US$992	2003	20.8	
international	family	€70	2003	N/a	
global	family + corporate	€2 467	2003	N/a	
global	Friedrichshafen city	€8 928	2003	60.5	Dow Jones

Source: Company annual reports and/or Hoover's financial data. **Low because of calculations changed in 2002.

The enterprises differ in ownership, ranging from being family and founder-owned, to customer and community ownership, public shareholder ownership and combinations of these. Revenues in 2003 (the latest available) range from about €70 million to €85 billion. A financial criterion for selection was that all those firms for which published figures were available exhibited positive sales revenue growth in 2002 over the previous year. Membership of the Dow Jones Sustainability Index and/or FTSE4Good Index is indicated in Table 2.1.

A brief description of the case study companies follows. One of the challenges in preparing these descriptions is that changes occur rapidly in these enterprises. The information is believed to be current as of May 2004.

AESCULAP: 'ALL IT TAKES TO OPERATE'

The Aesculap brand name, created in 1895, evolved from Gottfried Jetter's international ventures. A qualified cutler, in 1867 he began manufacturing surgical instruments in Tuttlingen, Germany. Today, Tuttlingen (population 35 000) is the world center for medical manufacturing, being the regional hub for around 400 surgical instrument manufacturers, of which Aesculap, with about 2400 employees, is the largest. Aesculap's global production facilities employ 6000–7000 people to generate 18 per cent of market share worldwide.

During its history, Aesculap established landmarks in medical technology with the invention of the first surgical electric motor in 1935 and the first pneumatic motor in 1967, and later with its entry into implants and container systems. Aesculap's global reputation is as a manufacturer of high-quality medical products under the motto 'all it takes to operate'. Offering innovative products and services for the core processes of surgery, its showroom displays 50 000 products, in addition to the company's comprehensive instrument management systems, services and procedure kits.

In 1976, Aesculap began to cooperate with the family-owned B. Braun Group of companies, eventually integrating into the Braun Group in 1997 to form the Group's second-largest division. This division operates largely independently of the B. Braun Group because of major differences in R&D, production and customers. For example, the doctor is the major decision maker for Aesculap, the hospital management for the B. Braun Group's other divisions. 'We will continue to demonstrate our responsibility and reliability to both our customers and our staff,' said Ludwig Georg Braun, Chairman of the B. Braun Group.[154]

In 2002, the Braun Group turned over €2.75 billion, representing organic growth of 4.1 per cent over the previous year. Profit on ordinary activities was

€111.5 million (an increase on the fiscal year 2001's €70.5 million), an impressive performance given the overall depressed economic conditions in its European and the US markets. Over 75 per cent of turnover was achieved internationally. Aesculap contributed €780.8 million to the Braun Group, that is 29.5 per cent of total group sales in 2003, and over one-third of the Group's profit. Since its inception, Aesculap claims to have written black figures in all but one year.

The five-year strategy is to double sales and triple products from the current 500 plus new products/processes generated annually, accepting some financial losses in the process. A strategic shift is occurring to partnering with doctors and hospitals beyond selling instruments. Aesculap now provides solutions for managing instruments, such as leasing instruments to hospitals.

Aesculap states, as company policy, that environmental protection forms part of its corporate identity, as does responsibility to the Tuttlingen region, town and future generations.

ALLIANZ: GLOBAL FINANCE

The origins of the Allianz Group, a huge publicly listed, integrated finance company, date from 1890. Based in Munich, Allianz has developed into one of the world's fastest growing insurance and financial service organizations, operating through around 700 subsidiaries in over 70 countries, and employing about 174 000 people worldwide in 2003. Allianz provides its 60 million clients with a broad range of services via international subsidiaries that typically command a strong position in their home markets. In 2001, Allianz acquired Germany's fourth-largest bank, Dresdner Bank.

The Group offers first class security (AAA Moody's, AA+ Standard and Poor's, A++ A.M. Best), and the *Financial Times* placed the Group at twelfth among the world's most respected financial institutions. In 2001, *Business Week* rated Allianz as Germany's largest global company and among the world's 50 largest in terms of market value.

Worldwide pretax revenue was €85 billion from five business segments in 2003. Revenue derived from Allianz's original core business of property and casualty insurance was over €5.5 billion, generating more than half the Group's worldwide premium income. About 25 per cent of this revenue is derived in Germany, making Allianz the country's market leader in property and casualty insurance. The second core business area, an area that is predicted to grow, is life and health insurance, with 2003 sales of €757 million. Asset management is the third core business activity at Allianz, where assets-under-management make it one of the five largest investors in the world, equivalent to the GDP of countries like Canada. Fourth, Allianz reinsures most companies within its group, and is among the top worldwide reinsurance companies by virtue of its size, shareholders' funds and strong reserves. In selected segments, Allianz also reinsures companies outside its own group. The overall 2003 result was reduced by a €2.2 billion loss in the fifth area, the banking segment. The Dresdner takeover, 9/11 and falling global share markets continued to affect the group's financial performance adversely in 2002. However 2003 saw a dramatic turnaround, with net income of €1.6 billion.

Allianz and its subsidiaries held 21.5 per cent of the holding company's shares at the end of 2001, providing considerable flexibility. Munich Re, a company bound with Allianz through a 'principles of cooperation' agreement, held a further 23 per cent, although this form of cross-shareholding is reducing. The publicly listed Group thus has long ensured strong control over its own operations and future by controlling large parcels of its own stock.

Allianz's commitment to sustainability is widely recognized. Its 2004 sustainability status report underscores that sustainability is a key driver of its strategy, providing an opportunity for innovation and developing a future-oriented corporate culture. A sustainability strategy team advises management on the integration of corporate and social responsibility factors into the firm's business decisions. An international team reports directly to the CEO of the Group and to the CEOs of the largest subsidiaries worldwide. The input of a network of internal environmental and other specialists is drawn upon in this process.

BMW: 'PREMIUM BRAND STRATEGY'

Gustav Otto founded BMW (Bayerische Motoren Werke) in 1916. Starting with aeroplane engines, the company shifted to automobile production in the late 1920s. Today the Munich-based Quandt family owns over 48 per cent of this publicly listed company that enjoys a worldwide reputation for highly engineered vehicles. One of the world's 12 largest car manufacturers, BMW remains an independent automobile manufacturer in an industry that the *Economist* describes as being in a 'fever of consolidation', and that faces a worldwide oversupply of cars as a whole. The company has so far resisted takeover and hostile consolidation attempts.

Headquartered in Munich, BMW employed over 104 000 people in 2003, operating at sales and distribution locations in over 26 countries, 15 production sites and eight plants. Under a strategy of 'survive by growth', BMW acquired British Rover in 1994. This was unsuccessful and Rover was sold in 2001, creating heavy losses for BMW, and leading to the dramatic departure of its previous CEO to Volkswagen. Joachim Milberg, responsible for production on the management board since 1993, took over as CEO, becoming a member of the supervisory board after his retirement in 2002. According to the current chairman of the supervisory board, Volker Doppelfeld, 'under Milberg, the enterprise experienced the most successful period in its history'. The firm continues to achieve record results in a stagnant world market. It increased retail sales by over 10 per cent in 2001 and achieved a record result in 2002 that was almost repeated in 2003, with the €1.947 billion profit falling only just below the 2002 record on a turnover exceeding €41.5 billion.

The company claims that its brand profile has become synonymous with energy, performance and sheer driving pleasure, as well as determination, high standards and professionalism. BMW protects its valuable brand, building its growth strategy of a 'premium' brand in every market sector. This creates an obvious distinction from most of the competition.

A major challenge for BMW as a large, distributed manufacturing organization is how to be innovative and agile in responding to the fierce pressures of a fast-changing, competitive global environment. BMW continuously reinvents its production and people processes, doing things the 'BMW way'. The company is almost entirely structured around teams from the board of management to the factory floor. People and their development are a major focus, including extensive team-based training. As part of this process, every two years management and others rotate jobs within their areas, applying formally for particular roles. The human resource (HR) policy at BMW is an integral feature of overall corporate policy in both strategic and operational decisions, although the shape of the HR policy has changed over time.

Innovation, quality, partnership, social responsibility and environmental protection are key values at BMW, which is a member of various sustainability indexes. BMW was rated second to VW in the automobile sector on the 2003 Dow Jones Sustainability Index.

FRAUNHOFER-GESELLSCHAFT: PROFESSIONAL INTELLECT

The non-profit Fraunhofer-Gesellschaft (FhG) is dedicated to the conduct, management and coordination of application-oriented research. From inauspicious beginnings, FhG grew into a renowned applied research organization based on contracts with clients from industry and government. It wins about 3 per cent of the total contract research business in Germany. In terms of being an employer of choice, number of patent registrations, repeat customers and many other criteria, FhG is a leader in its field. By 2000, FhG research covered most areas in engineering and the natural sciences, including microelectronics, microsystem technologies, factory organization, production and manufacturing technologies, data processing and communications technology, company management, new materials development, environmental protection, preventative health care, traffic logistics, biotechnology and processing technologies (especially those relating to biological processes). In 2002, Fraunhofer applied for 449 patents, ranking 27th among applicants in Germany.

Headquartered in Munich, FhG comprises 58 geographically dispersed research institutes, most of which are instrumental in generating regional employment throughout Germany. Six others are located overseas. Turnover in 2003 was about €1038 million, of which 90 per cent stemmed from contract research and more than 60 per cent was covered by FhG's own contractual revenues. With 12 700 employees, FhG operates through flexible structures that enable it to respond quickly to changes as required by industry and the market. A primary focus is training university scientists to become commercially oriented, and an indication of FhG's success is that, in 2001, staff turnover was 12 per cent, with 87 per cent of the ex-staff going into industry. Highly innovative, FhG has generated about 350 spin-off businesses with its staff in recent years, and helps retain employees by allowing them also to run their own companies.

At FhG, continuous change and international expansion are on the horizon because Germany's contract research market is essentially saturated. FhG's internationalization strategy aims to transfer knowledge and enhance expertise, expanding FhG's business fields and opening up new markets. FhG strives to remain sufficiently agile to be able to adapt to changing market and research needs and, to achieve this, institutes are organized largely as 'fractal organizations', consisting of self-organizing project groups.

Close interlinking relationships occur between universities, FhG and industry. Universities educate young scientists who learn to conduct research and undertake consulting projects for FhG. University professors direct over half the FhG institutes while remaining active at their universities. The professor, whose primary job is heading the FhG institute, maintains offices and staff at the institute rather than at the university. This starts a virtuous cycle because, through their university links, these professors can identify the brightest students, many of whom use FhG projects as doctoral and undergraduate thesis topics. In this way, a strong research/teaching loop is established between FhG and universities.

Universities find this arrangement very attractive since they gain access to a research institute at no cost to the university. Private industry and government also benefit from the FhG–university link through the research projects that are carried out, and also because industry can later attract the FhG-trained researchers into innovation management.

HOLCIM: CEMENTING RELATIONSHIPS

Holcim was founded in 1912 in the small Swiss village of Holderbank, from where it has grown into one of the world's largest suppliers of cement, aggregates (gravel and sand) and concrete, with majority and minority interests in over 70 countries. Internationalization began early. By the 1920s, the company had already invested in cement businesses in other European countries, expanding into many other parts of the world. Today, based in Zurich, Holcim's international presence consists of a balanced mix of companies in industrialized and emerging markets, with about 45 000 employees. Former owner, chairman and CEO, Dr Thomas Schmidheiny, is still the major shareholder, with 23 per cent of the shares in publicly listed Holcim. However, the roles of chairman and CEO are now separate.

In 2001, world cement markets became significantly more difficult, but with market-oriented structures, new products, skilled employees and efficient environmental management systems, Holcim executives consider that the company is well positioned for the future. Consolidated operating profit in 2003 grew by 1.2 per cent to CHF1.925 billion (compared with 2002's CHF1.903), while consolidated net income jumped 35.6 per cent to CHF686 million (2002 was CHF506). Net turnover declined by about 3 per cent in 2003, partly owing to a weaker US dollar, following 2002's increase of 15 per cent over 2001.

Holcim has embarked on several strategies, as outlined in its annual report. These include growth through expanding capacity, and acquisitions providing access to new markets. Another strategy of geographical diversification allows business cycles to be smoothed out, and businesses to be integrated commercially on a regional basis. Although the Holcim Group has the widest and deepest portfolio of all the international cement groups, opportunities exist to cluster the different countries into a wider group still. Global standardization is a third strategy, aimed at evolving the business from its current structure of a 'group' of companies to one 'Group', achieving standardization step by step. This is most visible in the new Holcim logo, but sharing services such as IT in regional clusters is another step to align the business. Although Holcim is a global business as much as it is a local business, the big challenge continues to be transferring the values created within the Group's headquarters to new companies joining the global brand.

Corporate social responsibility is prominent at Holcim, which sees itself playing a role in the rural communities where it operates. Holcim strives to influence the health and education of the less developed regions it enters, and delivers surplus power from its own plant to the community. A corporate taskforce manages the Group's overarching social policy. The firm ranked second in the building materials sector on the 2003 Dow Jones Sustainability Index.

Cement production has a considerable impact on the environment, and Holcim recognizes its obligation to the environment, particularly as legislation and regulation become more demanding in the developed world. The company's close involvement in sustainable cement industry projects supplements its own efforts to continue improving performance in environmental responsibility. Holcim aims to align its corporate objectives around the globe with respect to environmental priorities. Operationally it seeks to meet new, stricter clean air standards likely to be implemented in different parts of the world.

KÄRCHER: 'SIMPLY CLEAN'

Alfred Kärcher founded this company in 1935, specializing in heating equipment for industry and submersible heating elements. Headquartered in Winnenden, Germany, the company was operating internationally by 1955 using Kärcher's patents, with formal subsidiaries established from 1962 onwards. In 1959, the 58-year-old founder suddenly died, and his wife, Irene, led the company's 250 employees for three decades. Kärcher's double digit growth up to the mid-1970s was achieved through diversification, at times financed by selling some of Alfred Kärcher's many patents. The strategy then changed, returning the company to its core competence in industrial cleaning based on high-pressure water. After 10 years, new products were introduced. It was during this time that the change to Kärcher's yellow trademark colour occurred. In 1984, Kärcher entered the domestic market, seeking to build on its reputation in the industrial sector. Today Alfred and Irene's son and daughter, Johannes Kärcher and Susanne Zimmermann von Siefart, are members of the supervisory board and continue the family business into the second generation.

Roland Kamm, former managing director significantly influenced the focus and direction of family-owned Kärcher. He implemented a bold strategy, taking the company from three countries to 30. In 2001, Hartmut Jenner became managing director after nine years' experience with the company in five or six positions. Today the company comprises 38 sales and service companies with a closely knit dealer network. With a global staff of about 5400, Kärcher holds a dominant market position in the provision of industrial and professional standard cleaning equipment through high-pressure washers, vacuum cleaners, steam cleaners, sweepers, scrubber-driers, cleaning agents, brush-type vehicle washers and water treatment plants. Total annual sales exceed €1 billion (being privately held, exact figures are not available). Organic growth is preferred to acquisition.

The company still follows the guiding principles established by Alfred Kärcher. It adopts very long-term thinking, tending to develop in 30-year steps. Innovation is a core principle and competency. The Kärcher Cleaning Academy allows the company to keep in touch with universities, train the sales force, and work with customers such as hotel housekeepers, as well as obtaining feedback and new ideas from customers and scientists.

To Kärcher, cleaning is no simple service that can be uniformly applied across various industries and applications, but a customized process that requires machinery for specific applications. Kärcher products are supported by a range of specialized accessories and cleaning agents, designed to facilitate cleaning using the applicable system. Furthermore, Kärcher sees itself as more than a manufacturer of cleaning equipment: as a provider of cleaning solutions. The company not only regards part of its corporate success as having environment-friendly products, but aims to be a responsible corporate citizen. Kärcher is widely recognized with awards for innovation, environmental responsibility and community contribution. Its voluntary adherence to ISO9001 and ISO14001 testifies to the desire to produce the finest quality equipment, while minimizing the impact on the environment and providing a safe, clean working environment for employees.

LODEN-FREY: 'BITTEN BY THE LODEN-FREY VIRUS'

Munich's famous Loden-Frey Modehaus was founded in 1842. The 22-year-old founder, Johann Georg Frey, started with a weaving business in Munich. In 1854, Johann Frey won a gold medal at the Paris World Exhibition for developing Loden cloth, and his son in turn developed this cloth further into the first really water-resistant Loden. Continuing this trend for innovation, as early as 1880 the company used mail order marketing for their water-resistant Loden coats. From a single company, Loden-Frey split into two separate business areas in 1957. One business manufactures clothing, the other retails a range of fashion goods. Today's businesses are owned by Frey's fifth-generation descendents, the Frey and Nagel families. Portraits of previous generations hanging in the store cafeteria reinforce the family connection.

Designing textiles and manufacturing garments are managed by CEO Dr Peter Frey and his sister. Products include fashion coats and other garments, and the design and manufacture of traditional costumes. Production takes place largely in eastern Europe, particularly in Hungary and Romania. The business has received the Bavarian Quality Prize for Leadership and Processes.

However, the focus of this case study is the retailing side. Selling fine fashion from some of the world's prominent fashion houses is operated by a different branch of the family. The Nagel brothers walk through their store each day, making direct contact with staff and customers. The CEO is an outside manager with experience in retailing and working in a family-owned business. These three senior managers work together with 15 department heads who are responsible for buying, selling and staffing their areas. The store employs about 385 people, equivalent to 275 full-time employees. The store attracts a large number of customers from all over Germany and abroad.

Loden-Frey's main feature is providing excellent service, and its reputation is so high that recruitment from unsolicited applications is relatively easy. The largest component of the business is people and service. In 2000, service standards were introduced to provide consistency, and the entire workforce is trained every three years. Most people who start with Loden-Frey at age 16 remain with the firm, creating low staff turnover and high loyalty. Innovators are rewarded, but many people volunteer ideas without seeking a reward.

As Loden-Frey is a private company, financial information is not publicly available. However, like many small family-owned companies, the owners are prepared to work for low profit if necessary, typically operating from their own rent-free premises. If the family itself does not have the capital to expand, the owners accept low growth in order to avoid the financial markets. For this reason, the Loden-Frey fashion store intends to remain in the one building in Munich, and not expand.

MIGROS: 'THE MORAL MARKET'

The giant Migros Group began with a single truck in 1925, from which Gottlieb Duttweiler (1888–1962) sold six staple products to housewives. His aim was to cut out the middleman between producer and consumer, which remains part of the Migros philosophy. The Migros Group, derived its name from the French word *mi-gros*, or semi-large. It is today's largest retailer in Switzerland, one of the top 10 companies in Switzerland and the nation's largest employer. Retailing in Switzerland is the core of Migros's business, although other activities like banking, travel and hotels contribute about one-third to turnover. Recent acquisitions have included operations abroad, for example from Britain, France and Germany. Some parts of the Group (such as Globus and Hotelplan) operate in foreign locations. In 2003, turnover exceeded CHF20 billion, largely from retailing activities in 528 stores, with about 81 000 staff (around 70 000 are women). Revenue increased by 2.6 per cent in 2001, but only grew 0.1 per cent in 2002 due to changes in calculating turnover in the hotel area.

This conglomerate is owned by its customers. Originally Duttweiler had incorporated his business, but in his will the childless entrepreneur left the company as a mutual association, or cooperative, to its customers. Interestingly, there are no dividends, discounts, capital growth or other tangible benefits from being a customer–owner of Migros, but the 1 953 531 cooperative members can have input into the organization via one of 10 regional cooperatives. Being outside the financial markets allows Migros to continue its traditions. Offering the consumer choice is central to Migros's marketing, and in many lines it offers three levels: budget, medium and premium. Characteristic of Migros's products are value for money, quality control (for example, through its own taste kitchens) and low prices. Prices are calculated from the bottom up as follows: price = costs for good material + operations + right salaries + low transport + modest profits.

History is central to understanding today's Migros, which is both strongly bound to its traditions and responsive to changing times. For example, in the 1920s, producers boycotted Duttweiler's young business, so he produced his own wares. This is still done at Migros today. Management is guided by a set of 15 principles and values left by the founder, and one consequence is that Migros has never sold tobacco or alcohol. Duttweiler believed in customer loyalty and stipulated that women must form the majority in the governing bodies of Migros, which they do. Remaining true to its principles, which includes being close to the customer as well as innovative and ethical, is fundamental at Migros. Environmental protection and socially responsible practices rank highly. The organization uses its surpluses for community social projects, public education and lowering the prices of its wares. Duttweiler's moral market lives on in Migros's highly ethical approach to the environment. An example is its seeking out suppliers of palm oil (the basis of many modern products) who do not sacrifice tropical rainforest animals or plants in producing the oil. All suppliers must meet stringent criteria and are monitored for compliance.

Migros is monitoring changes occurring in the EU, and further internationalization is a future consideration. Since Switzerland is not a member of the EU, pressure is felt as the borders of Europe are opened up, and Migros will need to adapt.

MUNICH RE: 'CREATING FUTURES'

Carl Thieme and some influential business partners established Munich Reinsurance in 1880. They started from two rented rooms with five employees and a share capital of three million marks. The company grew rapidly and, in 1888, Munich Re's shares were listed on the stock exchange. Operations expanded into other European countries, with London opening in 1890 and the USA following in 1892. Dr Nicolaus von Bomhard became CEO in 2003. Today, reinsurance is one of three main business areas of the Munich Re Group, along with primary insurance and asset management. Acquiring about 90 per cent of the ERGO insurance group placed Munich Re second only to Allianz in Germany's direct insurance market. Taking over American Re has provided Munich Re with strong access to US markets. Reinsurance customers include over 5000 primary insurers in 150 countries.

Profits fell dramatically in 2001, and continued to be low in 2002 and 2003 as this enterprise encountered difficult times. Key figures for the business year 2003 include increased gross premium income of €41.5 billion (previous year: €40.0 billion), stemming largely from underwriting in both reinsurance and primary insurance business segments. Sales revenues are increasing, up 19 per cent in 2002 and 35 per cent in 2003.[155] However, the firm reported an overall loss of about €434 million in 2003.

Declining profitability was due to major events, such as the €2.2 billion payment for losses in New York and Washington following September 11, the largest claim in the history of the company. The terrorist attacks in the USA have had a serious impact on the insurance industry, as has the decline in global share markets and the European economy, and uncertainty created by the Iraq war. However, the future looks bright, given that the demand for reinsurance cover from companies with top ratings like Munich Re rose disproportionately after September 11. Munich Re's strategy is to strengthen its role as market leader.

The Group, which includes the world's largest reinsurer, employed over 41 000 staff globally at the end of 2003. The company views staff as a primary competitive advantage in liaison and service delivery to clients, with employees a decisive resource for securing market leadership. An emphasis on training and human resource development reflects this position.

Munich Re is one of the leading companies in the insurance sector in the 2003 Dow Jones Sustainability World and FTSE4Good indexes, and in 2003 was ISO14001 certified. It also focuses on sustainable investment funds and strategies.

Professional risk management, a key to the Group's operations, is both centralized and decentralized, given the complexity of these operations. Munich Re undertakes research into a wide range of sectors including aviation, natural catastrophes, agriculture, social security, life sciences, environmental awareness and genetic engineering. The company makes the results available to its clients. Engineers and scientists from more than 80 different disciplines (including meteorologists, geologists, geographers and medical doctors) analyze insurance information to improve operations.

NOVARTIS: CHEMISTRY THROUGH PEOPLE

The story begins with three firms that generated this publicly listed pharmaceutical company in 1996: Geigy, dating back to the middle of the 18th century, Ciba, established around 1860 and Sandoz, founded in 1886. Headquartered in Basel, Switzerland, but with extensive facilities abroad, Novartis operates through 360 independent affiliates in 140 countries. The USA is the largest market (41 per cent of sales), followed by Europe (35 per cent). Novartis employed 78 500 people in 2003, when Group sales increased by 19 per cent, to US$24.9 billion, of which pharmaceuticals comprised $16 billion. Net 2003 income was US$5 billion and the Group invested approximately US$3.8 billion in R&D, an increase of 32 per cent over 2002. The CEO, Daniel Vasella, described 2003 results as a 'record'.

Novartis's pharmaceuticals division accounted for 64 per cent of sales in 2003. It comprises business units for primary care, oncology, transplantation, ophthalmology and 'mature' products. Prescription drugs include treatments for cardiovascular diseases, cancer and nervous system and ophthalmic disorders. The Consumer Health division generated 36 per cent of sales revenue in 2003, covering generics, over-the-counter drugs, animal health, medical nutrition, infant and baby products and CIBA vision (eye drops, contact lenses and contact lens solutions). Gerber baby foods is a major Novartis consumer brand.

The firm's aspirations are to be recognized for having a positive impact on people's lives; to create sustainable earnings growth, rank in the top quartile of the industry and secure long-term business success; to build a reputation as an exciting workplace in which people can realize their professional ambitions; to provide a motivating environment where creativity and effectiveness are encouraged and cutting-edge technologies applied; to benefit to society through its economic contribution, the positive environmental and social benefits of its products, and open dialogue with stakeholders.

Science magazine rated Novartis as one of only two European companies ranked among the 10 top places to work in the biotech and pharmaceutical industry, placing Novartis at number eight. Novartis also ranked among the 100 best employers for working mothers in the USA. By US standards, company benefits are generous. They include 23 vacation days, 10 paid holidays, a pension plan (partially funded by employees), two child-care centers, child allowance ($165 monthly), five days of paid paternity leave, up to eight weeks of paid leave for adoptive parents and 16 weeks of paid maternity leave.

At Novartis, sustainability translates into managing risks to ensure the health and safety of employees, neighbors, customers, and all others affected by the firm's business activities, as well as protecting the environment. Most sites are certified according to ISO14001 and/or OHSAS18001. Financial analysts consistently rate Novartis among the leading companies for sustainability performance. However, one index on which Novartis is not included is the FTSE4Good, which currently penalizes producers of substitutes for breast milk for babies. FTSE4Good requires baby food producers to conform to the strict International Code on marketing of breast milk substitutes. In 2003, Novartis shared second position on the Dow Jones Sustainability Index in the pharmaceutical sector.

PORSCHE: 'DOING THINGS DIFFERENTLY'

Porsche's core competence is not just its excellent engineering, or its pride and passion for perfection. Rather Porsche sells driving enjoyment. The history of Porsche is the story of Ferdinand Porsche and his remarkable vision, energy and determination to follow his own rules and philosophies rather than the mainstream thinking of the times – an approach followed by Porsche to this day. The company was founded in 1931, following several other Porsche inventions, including the Volkswagen. The first factory was set up in 1950 in Zuffenhausen, a second in Leipzig in 2001. Porsche went partly public in 1972, when the family gave up its day-to-day control of the company. Shares outside family ownership (about 50 per cent) tend to be held primarily by investment funds, banks and insurers.

The worldwide group includes more than 60 subsidiaries in sales, consulting, finance and engineering services. That Porsche has thrived after experiencing extreme difficulties in 1993 and employed 10 699 people in 2003 has been attributed to a total reinvention of the company. Not a single movement in the production process is the same as in 1993. Porsche is performing very strongly today. Sales increased by 32.6 per cent to a record US$6.3 billion from 1 August 2002 to 31 July 2003, despite difficult times. Strong cash reserves can finance the company's future independently of the capital markets. Furthermore, Porsche has rejected the listing requirem ent to provide quarterly financial reports, which it regards as bureaucratic, short-term and unnecessary. It reserves the right to report to shareholders at intervals of its own choice. As a result, Porsche was dropped from the German MDAX stock index, but was invited to join another European index. It is not part of the Dow Jones Sustainability Index.

Porsche's latest success is not a sports car, but a luxury off-road/on-road four-wheel-drive vehicle, the Cayenne. This vehicle was developed jointly with VW, building on Porsche's considerable experience in four-wheel-drive technology, a dramatic strategic change for Porsche.

In 2002, his peers nominated the Porsche president, Dr Wendelin Wiedeking, as the executive who had increased the profitability of a company most convincingly over the past year by demonstrating leadership quality and innovation in the face of economic uncertainty. Porsche consistently shines, having the most positive image among German companies, and receives many awards for excellence. Peter W. Schultz, former CEO of Porsche, believes that a firm's only lasting competitive advantage lies in its ability to obtain extraordinary results from ordinary people. At Porsche, people can make the most of their skills and experience, reaching beyond their limitations and real or imagined boundaries. Porsche's current management and supervisory board echo this theme as they consistently promote staff and management development.

Passion and optimism abound at Porsche today. Staff express pride in their work, especially when a staff member sees a car on the road or in a movie, and can say, 'I built that car.'

ROHDE & SCHWARZ: INDEPENDENCE IS A CORE VALUE

Rohde & Schwarz is the largest manufacturer of electronic test and measurement equipment in Europe. It is the leading manufacturer of professional radio communication, broadcasting, monitoring and location, and IT security technology. The firm originated in 1931 from a Munich laboratory, where Dr Lothar Rohde and Dr Hermann Schwarz began experimenting and developing their first measuring instrument, a precision frequency meter. They registered a company five months later.

Rohde & Schwarz's triangle of service continues to emphasize price, quality and time in order to tailor services to suit customer needs. The company continuously looks for advancement and improvement by providing comprehensive global service; enhancing quality, efficiency and security in communication and information systems; and improving its capabilities, processes, partnership and customer relationships. Rohde & Schwarz is recognized as a high-quality firm in business procedures, behavior and attitudes, as well as in product and service. The company is accredited with well-known international certifications from ISO9001, ISO14001, AQAP, FAA and other military approvals. Its instruments and systems set standards worldwide in research, development, production and service.

Having subsidiaries and distribution representatives in over 70 countries underpins a worldwide presence with excellence in global technical support and services. Driven by the executive management board, the company is structured into profit centers and central service. Profit centers focus on leading-edge technology and product development, whereas central service provides the main back office support. Each strategic business unit reports directly to the executive management board.

Family-owned, Rohde & Schwarz avoids taking on debt, being willing to grow only from earned revenues. Whenever forecasts indicate that revenue will fall, the company acts proactively to ensure that it does not need to borrow money and can retain its independence. The prevailing ethos is that only an independent company can decide its own development future. The company was badly hit by falling orders following the dot.com collapse. Despite poor economic conditions in major markets, Rohde & Schwarz has shown continuous growth in sales since 1995, and turned over in excess of €992 million in 2003, with about 5900 employees. Current growth is around 12 per cent. Rohde & Schwarz invest about 12–13 per cent of revenue in R&D even in difficult times, preferring growth through innovation to mergers. In competing against asset-rich giants like Hewlett Packard, Hitachi and Agilant Technologies, Rohde & Schwarz relies on speed and flexibility.

People are regarded as the most important asset in the business, and Rohde & Schwarz was ranked number 37 on *Capital*'s 2004 best employers in Germany list. Staff commitment and motivation contribute to the firm's sustainable achievement. Management is by objectives. Regular communication enables people to spot potential areas of concern early on and take any necessary action to achieve transparent objectives. Various measures are used to develop an innovative culture, including providing an enjoyable workplace where people can freely express their ideas and develop their potential. Moreover the vision and values of the company are communicated to all levels of the organization to provide employees with clear direction.

SEELE: 'BEAUTY IS THE RADIANCE OF TRUTH'

Seele designs and constructs customized roofs, walls, steps and other building elements out of glass and steel. The company specializes in the creation of unique roofs and façades and does not touch standard glass and steel structures.

Founded in 1984 by the glazier Gerhard Seele and his steel design engineering partner Siegfried Gossner, Seele has created its reputation by building revolutionary designs that appear to defy the laws of physics. The less steel, the more expensive the construction, and Seele has managed to reduce the 30kg/sqm steel component of normal structures to 4–5kg/sqm in its own structures. To ensure the quality and supply of appropriate glass, Seele even considered manufacturing its own. Seele also offers cleaning and maintenance contracts for their projects on the principle that it is a challenge to create structures that are inexpensive to maintain.

The company conducts 80 per cent of its business outside Germany, but benefits from the 'made in Germany' image. Seele now has offices in various foreign locations, including the USA, UK, Dubai, the Czech Republic, Austria, Hong Kong and Singapore. Abroad Seele typically uses its own people alongside local installers, supervised by a 'hands-on' German foreman.

Highly profitable in an otherwise depressed sector, this privately held company has avoided entering the capital markets to retain its independence. Quality and profitability make this €70 million organization stand out, although figures are not publicly available. The last projects on which they made a loss were reportedly from the mid-1990s.

At Seele knowledge permeates the entire organization, and constant communication is essential to achieve the high level of quality and customer service the company strives for. The focus is on transparency of people, process and product, as well as on quality and creativity. This is reflected not only in the firm's transparent glass buildings and offices, but also in the way the business is run. Mistakes are openly discussed and posted on the website for all to learn from. Clearly, this culture is not for everyone. The 'Seele person' is characterized by openness, innovation and creativity, teamwork, a solution orientation, liking an open environment and being well-oriented to the customer.

To maintain its culture, which is highly relationship-focused and centered on meaningful, creative work for employees, Seele has capped the growth of the organization at about 350 people world-wide. Beyond this size, executives found that they had no thinking time or weekends, and concluded that further staff growth is unsustainable. Seele pays relatively high wages by industry standards, so its staff remain non-unionized. In-house equity is a goal, with compensation openly seen to be comparable between people doing the same work.

The top management team has remained stable since its inception, except for the addition of a third managing director, Thomas Geissler, in 1999.

WACKER: 'THERE IS STILL SO MUCH MORE TO INVENT'

WACKER is a highly innovative limited liability company, held 51 per cent by the WACKER family holding company and 49 per cent by Hoechst. Its activities focus on semiconductor technology, silicone chemistry, specialty chemicals and ceramic materials. Founded in 1914 by Alexander Wacker, the company is a global player in the top league of organic and inorganic chemistry, with four divisions: WACKER Siltronic, WACKER Silicones, WACKER Specialities and WACKER Ceramics.

One of the two largest divisions, WACKER Siltronic, is among the top three manufacturers of hyperpure silicon wafers for the semiconductor industry. The other major division, WACKER Silicones, is among the world's four leading silane and silicone producers, with products used in many daily customer applications such as airbag coatings and masonry protection agents. WACKER Specialities is the global technology leader in high-quality binders and polymer additives, and a customized solutions expert in special chemicals and biotechnology. Biotechnology, genetic modification of microorganisms and metabolic engineering are seen as highly promising avenues of research. WACKER Ceramics[156] is a leading global producer of high-performance materials. These include exceptionally hard and damage-resistant ceramic components for the mechanical and automotive sectors.

Sales turnover was €2.5 billion in 2003, down from €2.7 billion in 2002, due to a strong euro. According to the 2002 annual report, after posting a loss in 2001, the Group recovered with a net profit in 2002 of €20.6 million in an industry where chemical companies generally saw sales sink. At the end of 2003, the company employed 15 622 people at its global sites in Europe, the Americas and Asia. The Group tries to remain close to customers worldwide through its global network of 100 subsidiaries and sales offices. The USA and China offer particular growth opportunities, and double-digit annual growth rates are predicted in eastern and South East Asia where the Group is concentrating efforts.

The business strategy is geared to long-term profitable growth and sustained increase in corporate value. Over 10 per cent of sales revenue is earmarked for investment, with 6 per cent of turnover spent on R&D, even in difficult times. In 2003, this translated into €152 million for R&D. Not surprisingly at this level of investment, WACKER ranks among the world's 10 most research-intensive chemical companies. Central to innovation is WACKER's chemical research company, Consortium für elektrochemische Industrie GmbH, whose origins date back to 1896. The original approach of developing a whole family tree of products from one base chemical is still used today at WACKER, although the chemicals have changed over time, from acetylene generated from carbide and ethylene chemistry, to vinyl compounds, polymers and PVCs. Biotechnology is the anticipated focus in the future.

Sustainability features heavily at WACKER, being incorporated into its 10 Group goals. The company's first 'Environmental Report/Responsible Care Report' appeared in 1989, and later editions have been expanded to encompass safety, health and transport issues in addition to environmental protection and social responsibility.

ZF FRIEDRICHSHAFEN: OWNED BY A CITY

Public sympathy following the crash of the airship LZ4 in 1904 heartened Count von Zeppelin to establish a foundation dedicated to the airship industry.

The foundation built up a web of companies making engines, aluminum lattice-work, gear machinery tools and transmissions. In 1916, ZF Friedrichshafen grew out of this enterprise.

Following the Second World War, the Zeppelin Foundation's assets were transferred to the city of Friedrichshafen, in accordance with the deed of the foundation. The deed stated that the foundation's assets should go to the city if the foundation could no longer serve its purpose. Having the city own the business provides an extreme example of the interdependence between a Rhineland business and its local community.

ZF grew rapidly. By 2003, it was present at 119 locations in 25 countries. It is number three among German automotive industry suppliers, and the 14th largest worldwide. ZF's 53 000 employees generated €8.9 billion turnover in 2003. The company is the world's leading supplier of drive line and chassis technology, providing quality, precision internal mechanisms for aircraft, cars, buses, community vehicles, concrete mixers, crane vehicles, lift trucks, lifts, machine tool drives, marine vehicles, off-road equipment, rail vehicles, special vehicles, tourist coaches, tractors, trucks and vans. By 2003, ZF was concentrating on chassis, axles, steering and gears of the highest quality, becoming a systems supplier to car companies, rather than just a manufacturer.

At every step in the supply chain, ZF demands the highest quality, competitive pricing and leading-edge technology. It seeks to set its expectations at the highest level to be able to exceed those of its customers and partners. Zero defects are aimed for, and any failures that cannot be explained are investigated thoroughly.

ZF is a people-focused company, with a long-standing commitment to employees that includes a company pension scheme, company-sponsored health benefits, housing, vacation lodges, holiday pay, Christmas bonuses and employee profit sharing. Even faced with economic recession, it minimized staff cuts and continued to reform work practices, including introducing certification for quality via ISO9001 and environmental standards via ISO14001 and EMAS (EcoManagement and Audit Scheme). The company not only sees that its manufacturing processes need to be environmentally responsible, but works hard to ensure that it is a responsible corporate citizen.

Major challenges for ZF include continuing competitive and pricing pressure, increasing market demands for professional expertise, responsibility, risk taking and maintaining a global presence. Another challenge is being owned by the city of Friedrichshafen, which is seen as a plus. The city does not interfere with the running of the business and, clearly, the city is interested in the long-term sustainability of the company. The city uses dividends for community purposes, and part of management's task is to manage the political side of city ownership by making the public aware of the need to reinvest back into the company.

WHAT MAKES THESE ORGANIZATIONS SUSTAINABLE?

The concept of organizational sustainability has various dimensions to it. Many people think of sustainability mainly as the 'triple bottom line', which includes measuring financial performance, corporate social responsibility and environmental protection outcomes. The organizations featured in this chapter considerably exceed this narrow definition of sustainability, as we will see. Financially they yielded positive growth in revenues during 2002 (wherever figures were available). The two insurance companies were struggling to be profitable in 2003, largely because of world uncertainty. However, even these companies increased revenues and profitability in 2002 and 2003. On rare public comparisons of shareholder-value performance among German companies in 2002, *Manager Magazin* ranked Porsche second, BMW eighth, Munich Re 39th and Allianz 41st.[157] Judging by financial criteria, sustainable people practices, being a good citizen and looking after the environment do not have to come at the expense of growth and shareholder value, but provide the foundation for it.

While delivering strong financial performance, the case study firms generally excel in environmental and social responsibility, as Chapter 5 shows. The featured public companies are generally ranked first or second in their industry on the Dow Jones Sustainability Index. The exception is Porsche, which has challenged the financial markets' requirement for quarterly reporting and is not listed on the major indexes. However Porsche's focus on environmental and social sustainability is clear from its reports. The larger organizations produce sustainability reports, even when privately owned. Many have done so for over 15 years – well ahead of shareholder and regulator expectations.

Sustainability goes beyond the above conventional measures of the triple bottom line. The capacity to endure over time provides another yardstick for sustainability. The founding dates of the case study firms (see Table 2.1) show that the 'youngest' firm is the glass and steel innovator, Seele, founded in 1984. This is followed by Fraunhofer's research institutes (1949). Although founded in 1996, Novartis' origins are much older. Five firms date from before the end of the First World War (BMW, Holcim, Porsche, WACKER and ZF) and three were founded between the two world wars (Kärcher, Migros and Rohde & Schwarz). Five companies were formed in the 1800s (Aesculap, Allianz, Loden-Frey, Munich Re and the three companies that led to Novartis's formation). All are still leading in their fields, which is surely a feat of sustainability.

Displaying sustainable practices does not guarantee an easy existence but may provide the fortitude to recover. All these organizations have endured hard times. Fraunhofer almost went out of business within the early years of its life until it won major government research contracts. Seele has operated in a depressed construction industry throughout its two-decade existence. BMW needed to be rescued by the Quandt family in the 1960s. The founder of Swiss retailing giant Migros was boycotted and ridiculed by competitors and suppliers in his early years. All except Seele and Fraunhofer withstood the 1930s Great Depression and the Second World War. Eleven of the companies survived the ravages of the First World War. Rohde & Schwarz suffered under the dot.com collapse, and both insurance companies weathered global uncertainties following the 9/11 terrorist attacks and the Iraq War. All case study organizations have experienced major changes in the pace and nature of work, globalization, competition, technology, workforce and social expectations, yet they remain at the forefront of their industries.

Sustainability can also be thought of in terms of stakeholders. Bergsteiner[158] proposes that the following laws 'govern' organizational sustainability:

1. an enterprise is not sustainable if it produces negative outcomes for the parties it contracts with; for example, if it has dissatisfied employees, owners and/or customers;
2. an enterprise that produces positive outcomes for voluntary stakeholders, such as satisfying employees, owners and customers, but negative outcomes for non-contracting parties (such as depleting non-renewable resources, or a farmer who uses more water than his legal entitlement), is only sustainable (a) if no-one holds the enterprise accountable for the negative outcomes, and (b) until all the negative outcomes of similar firms eventually combine to undermine the entire industry. An example can be seen in the fisheries industry, where fish are harvested faster than they can grow;
3. an enterprise or business model that produces positive outcomes for contracting parties (such as satisfied employees, owners and customers), but negative outcomes for large groups of non-contracting parties (such as pollution, poverty and social alienation), is not sustainable and should not be sustained;
4. an enterprise or business model that produces positive outcomes for both contracting and non-contracting parties alike is sustainable. This is the objective of the Rhineland model.

Thus, there are many ways of thinking about sustainability. In the following chapters, the 19 elements of the Sustainable Leadership Grid are used to display leadership practices and beliefs found in the 15 European case study organizations. Concrete examples show how these sustainable organizations operate and, where relevant, weather hard times. Chapter 3 begins with the group of management and decision making elements from the grid.

3.   Management and decision making

In this chapter, six elements in the Sustainable Leadership Grid that relate to management and decision making are introduced. Each section starts with a quotation from a prominent US management thinker. The elements are CEO concept, decision making, ethical behavior, taking a long-term perspective, considering a range of stakeholders and valuing a culture of teamwork.

CEO CONCEPT

> The CEO can't be the lonely man at the top. We need a group of people whom we can trust. (Warren Bennis[159])

The Anglo/US and Rhineland models differ greatly in the way in which the role of the top executive(s) is viewed and in the management style expected of such a leader. Even within Europe, expectations differ. UK managers prefer a style quite different from that found on the Continent, but one that is also practiced in the USA (see Box 3.1). From an Anglo/US perspective, leadership often involves a prominent individual who leads from the front, such as Richard Branson at Virgin. This person is typically held accountable for the success of the enterprise. The traditional Rhineland approach is to play down the top person and appoint 'speakers' of the top team instead. The Rhineland model thus de-emphasizes the role of one top person, focusing more on a top team forming the management board. This is reinforced by the 2003 German Corporate Governance Code, which specifies that management board members are jointly accountable for the management of the enterprise. Leadership under the two models would operate on different paradigms. According to Avery,[160] the Anglo/US model would foster classical or visionary leadership focused on the CEO, whereas the Rhineland model would encourage organic or distributed leadership involving more people. Let us look more closely at the Anglo/US and Rhineland concepts of CEO, starting with the Anglo/US view.

Anglo/US CEOs

The traditional Anglo/US view of leaders, as special people who set the direction, make the key decisions and energize the troops, is deeply rooted in

---

BOX 3.1   FOUR COMMON MANAGEMENT STYLES IN EUROPE

Asking how far Europe has begun to unify its management styles, Cranfield University Professor Andrew Kakabadse and his colleagues identified four basic European styles in cross-national teams:[161] *consensus* (executives mainly from Sweden and Finland); *managing from a distance* (French executives only); *working towards a common goal* (Germany and Austria) and *leading from the front* (UK, Ireland and Spain).

Under *consensus*, team spirit is central. These managers emphasize people moving forward together through effective communication and stability, open discussion at team meetings and consensus decision making, as well as attending to organizational detail. The greater the perceived level of consensus, the greater is the job satisfaction.

The *managing from a distance* style displayed by French managers shows a passion for discussion among the managers, but they tend to be left alone to do their work as they see fit, and to pursue their own agendas. A command style predominates here, rather than consensus in decision making. These strategic, conceptual French thinkers understand the need for procedures, but are undisciplined in implementing them. Followers often experience high levels of uncertainty and ambiguity under these leaders, straining internal relationships.

In *working towards a common goal*, German and Austrian executives value functional/technical expertise. Having identified a common goal, the expert contribution of each individual becomes clear, and is integrated to provide the required focus. Executives with this style identify with systems and controls that are seen as leading to success.

The Anglo *leading from the front* style is based on an individual leader's performance. The charisma and skills of particular individuals are believed to lead to either success or failure of their organizations. Relying on the individual's ability above all, this leadership style avoids systems and procedures that might impede the freedom of these leaders to act as they deem fit. US managers may well identify with this style.

Thus, it appears from this survey that management styles typically found in Anglo business cultures are likely to be very different from Rhineland styles, although within each model variations occur.

---

an individualistic worldview. Various writers point out that this heroic notion of leadership is a myth that creates the illusion that leaders are in control of events.[162] Such myths reinforce a focus on charismatic heroes rather than on distributed leadership, leadership as part of a system, and collective learning. That the heroic leader is often a myth is highlighted in a study of successful organizations in Australia. These winning enterprises are characterized by team leadership, not by individual visionary leaders.[163] Interestingly, Harvard Professor John Kotter found that the CEOs he studied in US companies were rarely seen to be making decisions in meetings, but more to be influencing others to achieve consensus.[164]

Underpinning the Anglo/US concept is the view that the CEO alone is heroically responsible for organizational performance, that this performance can be measured (through the share price) and that the CEO is to be rewarded for doing the shareholders' bidding.[165] A focus on shareholder value reinforces the concept of the heroic CEO. This can disconnect the leadership from the rest of the organization and its stakeholders by overemphasizing the contribution of one individual. When CEO performance and pay are tied to company performance, heroic CEOs are placed under enormous pressure to succeed. This can bring them into the temptation to fudge the numbers and cover up mistakes in order to live up to expectations.

Power is largely centralized along traditional hierarchical lines under the Anglo/US model. This often encourages a classical leadership style that concentrates leadership on a single person, rather than having it dispersed throughout the organization.[166] The top person wields power by being able to stop or make possible actions. For example, by setting the mission, strategy and operational goals of the organization, the leader defines how resources will be allocated. The leader gains access to all levels of the organization, can build alliances at all levels, and is centrally placed for access to information and resources.[167]

However, there are limits to a top leader's ability to influence. Limitations stem from boards, threats of legal action from shareholders, product liability claims and disgruntled employees, media scrutiny and government regulations.[168] Thus, despite an acknowledged focus on shareholder value, other stakeholders' interests obviously need to be considered in practice. Furthermore, a lone CEO's knowledge base is limited in a complex global market place and technology-based world, and others' active input is vital.

The role of Anglo/US CEOs is a challenging one. A survey was conducted, among the world's 2500 largest publicly traded corporations, of CEOs who left office in 1995, 1998 and 2000. It reported that today's CEOs are like professional athletes: 'young people with short, well compensated careers that continue only as long as they perform at exceptional levels'.[169] How sustainable this profession has become must be questioned, particularly given that constant growth and exceptional performance are not feasible for all companies. By definition, only a few can be exceptional.

US-based scholars like Nadler and Tushman[170] have long called for a model of leadership that goes beyond the inspired individual. They envisage a model that takes into account the complexities of large, diverse, geographically complex organizations. Extending leadership beyond one individual to a team is one conclusion from this, and an alternative to the all-powerful CEO is the top management team (TMT).

The feasibility of top management forming teams is a moot point under the Anglo/US model. One problem is that building and leading teams is time-consuming,[171] and can be difficult to do within the short time horizons of Anglo/US shareholders. Hambrick[172] and his associates prefer to refer to the 'top management group' (TMG). They believe that this term is more realistic for larger Anglo/US organizations where pressures operate to discourage members from engaging in the internal exchange, collaboration and communication that characterize teams. Despite the emphasis on CEOs in the Anglo/US business world, there is considerable evidence that studying top management groups rather than CEOs alone provides better predictions of organizational outcomes.[173] Perhaps the Anglo/US heroic leader is indeed a myth for all but a few exceptional companies.

Rhineland 'CEOs'

Traditional Anglo/US and Rhineland concepts of leadership differ markedly.[174] First, individual Rhineland CEOs tend not to have superstar status, although in Switzerland this can happen if the leader earns this status. However Rhineland top leadership generally tends to be more low-profile than in the Anglo/US world. It is shared and rarely focuses on one individual. Part of the CEO role is to obtain agreement from the supervisory board, unions, works councils and other parties on major decisions.

Another difference is that day-to-day leadership normally stems from the *Vorstand*, a group of 'equals' that nominates one person to be its 'speaker'. It is the speaker who often appears in public as the equivalent of the Anglo/US CEO. In many European companies, this 'speaker–CEO' is elected periodically by other stakeholders and therefore needs to consider their views when profiling himself (or, rarely, herself). CEOs are expected to make public appearances to serve the company, not themselves. This happens even in large organizations.

Furthermore, charisma and inspiration are not viewed with the same widespread enthusiasm among German firms as in the USA. This is possibly a result of Germany's experiences under Hitler's charismatic leadership. German society has implemented a very contractual form of governance and management in which the rights and duties of each member of society are clearly specified. Rule-bound behavior anchored in firm policies and guidelines forms the foundation for leadership (see Box 3.1). However, while most German corporations allow their top managers considerable latitude,[175] others in the organization have their behaviors shaped by clearly specified rewards and recognitions. This is possible with a highly skilled, team-based workforce that does not need much direction from management. Emotional attachment comes through pride in one's work, long-term employment with the firm, and opportunities for training and self-development, rather than from an inspirational leader.

The Rhineland approach to leadership moves away from the leader-as-person to looking at the whole organization as a system.[176] One way of minimizing the leader's role is to use *substitutes for leadership*. These are features of the workplace that replace or augment the role of leaders.[177] Examples include closely-knit teams of highly trained individuals and professionally educated and skilled workers who do not need to be told how to do a job. Another example is work providing intrinsic satisfaction that can replace a manager's role as motivator. Computer technology can take over many of a manager's controlling and other functions. Expert and other systems provide guidance on tasks and incentives to perform. Detailed workbooks, guidelines, policies and procedures provide important non-leader guidance. Similarly, sharing a clear vision and set of values can substitute for a CEO leading from the front, once people understand the direction they are heading in. Many of these leader substitutes are strong in Rhineland organizations. Thus, it is not surprising that fewer managers are needed in Rhineland firms than in Anglo/US enterprises,[178] which should cut costs and therefore improve profitability.

Another difference is that Rhineland CEOs do not chair the supervisory board, as their Anglo/US counterparts traditionally like to do.[179] This separation reduces the power of the Rhineland CEO compared with CEOs controlling both management and supervisory boards. The CEO and management team are monitored by the supervisory board, whose members closely interact.

An exception to the low profile adopted by a CEO in a Rhineland company, the Porsche president is considered a strong, highly-profiled leader who has become identified with the Porsche brand. Insiders say that he knows what he wants, and may even be too strong and powerful in some eyes. He is also considered very charismatic. However, under German corporate law, the management board is a collective organ and individual members do not act alone. It is worth noting that German law does not allow individuals such as CEOs and chief financial officers (CFOs) to take individual responsibility for the accuracy of a firm's financial statements: this is a top team's collective responsibility.[180]

To be effective, top team members need to feel positive about the quality of relationships, the openness of discussion, commitment to the decisions and discipline to implement them.[181] Again this is easier to do with a long-term perspective than under short-term pressures. Nearly all the organizations in the case studies have long-tenured senior management, who strive to reach consensus decisions.

Allianz, from the finance industry, reflects many of the typical features of Rhineland CEOs. First, it has no star system of individual top managers. Although the previous CEO was very well known in various business spheres in Germany, like most Rhineland CEOs he kept a low personal profile. Not profiling top managers allows them to enjoy a private life outside work. Second, management by consensus is an essential skill in the top team, where the CEO does not stand above the team in decision making or as a hero. Third, board members are integrated up and down the organization, enhancing communication flow and assisting in obtaining the essential consensus throughout the business. Fourth, CEOs enjoy a long tenure.

Migros's central management would generate considerable internal problems if individuals profiled themselves. In this Swiss retailer, decentralized regional units wield enormous autonomy and power, resisting domination from the central management team.

In short, it is unusual for Rhineland organizations to profile a powerful CEO, even if some are well-known. Most operate as speakers of a top team, rather than as heroic decision makers.

DECISION MAKING

> Most people possess far more talent, capability, intelligence, resourcefulness, and creativity than their present jobs require or even allow them to use. We see a profound disempowerment of people. (Stephen Covey[182])

We have seen how widely dispersed power is in Rhineland companies, and this is associated with an emphasis on gaining consensus in making decisions. Valuing consensus-oriented decision-making processes reduces the power of the Rhineland CEO. Power is spread within the management and supervisory boards and to experts elsewhere in the organization. It involves worker participation at all levels. A review of studies on worker participation concluded that an overall participative climate enhances worker satisfaction more than occasional participation on specific decisions or goal setting.[183]

Getting consensus by involving the affected parties can be frustrating, but the process usually leads to rapid acceptance when it comes to action. Consensus need not always be a slow process either. For instance, at Kärcher, decisions are made fast. Senior management of this cleaning systems firm calls the shareholder(s), lobbies, and puts a new proposal to the board. The go/no go decision is fast, despite consultation. Seele also needs fast decisions on construction and other details, and so meetings tend to be informal.

Decisions can occur anywhere – even in the staff kitchen. The readily available directors and constantly interacting teams make mutual decisions quickly.

The Rhineland approach fosters a strongly participative decision-making environment, with operational decisions generally pushed down to the lowest level. A cooperative management style provides a framework for motivated and creative staff to achieve goals. Clearly, those who work directly with any production process or customer will understand the requirements of the job better than those operating some distance away.[184] Therefore, front-line employees are permitted wide scope under the Rhineland model to change their work practices as they deem appropriate. Strategic decisions tend to be made at senior management levels, with operational decisions devolved to the people doing the work. Some Rhineland enterprises also expect workers to develop business acumen. The following examples show how power and decision making are devolved in various ways in the case study organizations.

BMW functions around self-organizing teams at all levels of the enterprise, from top management to the frontlines. These teams of highly skilled employees are empowered to self-organize, make decisions and solve problems. For example, production teams and individuals are authorized to stop the production line if they believe a problem warrants it, a decision with huge financial implications given that downtime is measured in minutes per month. Teams operate under a working structure that blends employee satisfaction with efficiency to suit BMW conditions and culture. The team decides how tasks are rotated within the team and across team products. In addition, BMW has moved away from the classic division of labor to integrating the functions of workers and managers. This reflects a new way of thinking about manager–worker relationships, providing workers with a greater understanding of how the company operates. 'Associates' at all levels make decisions about the work and are expected to think in business terms. BMW's work structures are designed to support responsible, business-focused workers. Self-governing teams make their own decisions and carry responsibility for quality assurance, logistics, production and maintenance. All this had previously been the responsibility of various departments external to the teams.

Fraunhofer, like many geographically distributed enterprises, experiences tensions between the center and the dispersed research institutes, particularly in decision making. At Fraunhofer, the institutes and not HQ make most decisions. This was provided for in the founding guidelines: 'project leaders should have more say than their superiors in the vertical structure' (see Box 3.2). Although Fraunhofer's research is organized around approximately 58 institutes in Germany and abroad, it has to be quite centralized in some respects because the only legal entity is the central Fraunhofer Society, not the individual research institutes. Central management decides strategy and

BOX 3.2   ORIGINAL FRAUNHOFER MODEL

Guidelines for operating at Fraunhofer include the following:

a. *Organization* – dynamic planning and leadership to encourage employee creativity, instead of fixed organizational hierarchy and defined job descriptions.

b. *Management* – matrix structure: vertical institute organization (by discipline) overlaid by horizontal project orientation. Project leaders should have more say than their superiors in the vertical structure.

c. *Geographical distribution and cooperation of institutes* – overlapping activities between institutes are encouraged to stimulate both cooperation and competition between the institutes.

d. *Research planning* – close contacts with universities, industry, public authorities and the market are essential for effective research planning. Networking between these institutions creates a constant stimulus for research.

e. *Personnel* – in attracting good staff, Fraunhofer can offer a great deal of freedom in research (choice of topics, methodology and techniques, choice of client);

   - the most important motivation comes from technically demanding work, a cooperative environment, team spirit and fair payment according to performance,
   - although the tasks of conducting research, initiating projects and bidding for and managing projects can be separated, contract research requires leaders who can bring a healthy balance of all four skills,
   - the intensity and quality of further education given to employees will determine the long-term success of an institute.

f. *Financing* – contract research cannot be self-financing in the long run:

   - the success of a contract research institute must measure up to industry requirements,
   - basic government financing should be related to turnover from private and public research contracts,
   - the volume of industrial contracts is a good measure of performance.

allocates basic funds, maintains government contacts, manages the legal side of staffing and represents Fraunhofer externally. In other respects Fraunhofer is decentralized into self-managing, and at times competing, institutes. Each institute is responsible for its own research emphasis and direction, acquiring and managing projects, negotiating and working within its budget, and achieving results (providing this is done within central guidelines on liability and the Fraunhofer charter). Fraunhofer strives to create self-managing clusters of institutes, allowing them to decide jointly which research areas should have which facilities. For example, expensive clean rooms can only be installed at one or two locations, not at all seven sites requiring them.

Decision making at the top level of Fraunhofer may be changing. The previous president almost always operated as *primus inter pares* (first among equals) within the executive board. However his successor, Professor Hans-Jörg Bullinger, prefers to be the final decision maker rather than *primus inter pares*.

At retailing giant Migros, decision making tends to be decentralized and occurs at various levels. The regional cooperatives and not the central Federation make most decisions, while store managers and staff make decisions about running individual retail outlets. The regional cooperatives are all independent entities that have contracts with the central Federation. However, the stores belong to the regional cooperatives and are independent of other regions. As a result, outlets may look slightly different in each region. One area where the center exerts control is over the price for produce it procures, making such prices consistent all over Switzerland. Although members of regional cooperatives have the power to reject the financial statements of their region and to question management, individual members have little influence in meetings or on the daily business. Each cooperative can decide how to distribute profits. For example, they may lower prices for some or all products, reduce their reserve funds, augment superannuation funds or repay debt. Cooperative members can reject the proposed distribution of profits, although most members tend to accept the recommendations in practice. Tensions can arise between the center and the independent cooperatives, as the center strives to standardize processes, introduce centralized training and rationalize in other ways.

These examples show that decision making occurs at various speeds, and in different ways: by management, teams and individuals. Decisions relating to work practices tend to be taken at the lowest levels; senior management tends to make strategic decisions. However, under the Rhineland model, decision making is typically done in groups reaching consensus, rather than by single manager commands.

ETHICAL BEHAVIOR

A healthy, open, transparent climate – more than anything else – will deter corruption. (Warren Bennis[185])

Ethics is an elusive term that can be difficult to define.[186] Basically ethical behavior involves 'doing the right thing', and is considered essential for organizational sustainability. At the enterprise level, ethics start with distilling the business strategy into a number of desired values and behaviors that can be readily translated into acceptable and unacceptable actions.

Ethics are demonstrably important to leadership. To the ultimate question of 'what is good leadership?' answers show that good leadership is both morally good, or ethical, and technically good, or competent.[187] Singer develops this further and argues that personal ethics are more pivotal and fundamental to good leadership than any learned or formal leadership skills.[188] Sound personal ethics form an inalienable part of an individual's character, and ethics oversee and ensure that technical skills are put to proper use. Thus technical skills are only secondary to personal ethics in a leader.

Ethical behavior seems to pay off. According to American research, leaders perceived as having high ethics have the most success in obtaining employee understanding and commitment to realizing a strategy.[189] There is some evidence that US companies are paying more attention to business ethics than UK organizations but they need to, according to findings that over two-thirds of US citizens polled said that only some, very few or no corporations operated fairly and honestly.[190] US boards appear more involved in creating and implementing ethical standards than they have been in the past. This is partly in response to worker concerns about ethical workplace issues, and to recent exposure of unethical accounting and other practices in public corporations. However, in the UK, SMEs do not appear to be greatly concerned about ethical issues, according to a survey reported in *Management Services*.[191]

German writers on business ethics generally do not share the focus on the individual so prevalent in Anglo/US writing.[192] There is more of a concern with the way the economic order can create incentives for companies and managers to behave ethically than leaving it up to individuals. This requires an expectation that others will behave morally too. Under this expectation, companies with ethical business practices do not feel disadvantaged by, for example, incurring extra costs for offering fair wages and conditions to staff in emerging markets or adopting Rhineland environmental standards in developing countries.

Although ethical behavior is a given for Rhineland organizations, the following specific examples stand out.

Fraunhofer's mission statement clearly declares that principles of good scientific practice will be observed in its research, and suspected cases of scientific misconduct will be investigated.

Holcim, from the cement industry, includes 'business ethics' as one of the strategic personal competencies of its management development program. Business ethics is defined as '[the person] respects and acts according to the values of the company and the cultural environment; keeps the organization's values at the forefront of associate decision making and action'.[193] At Holcim, ethics revolve around the organization's values. Ethical behavior involves an employee in communicating the importance of the values to others, guiding and motivating others to live the values, acting as a role model, and explicitly linking business plans and strategies to organizational values.

At Migros, ethical behavior is a core value. One example is the plethora of ethical added-value labels on store shelves. Migros offers products carrying special labels indicating that the goods have been produced through ethical methods in the emerging world. For example, the Max Havelaar label secures the livelihood of third world producers and seeks to return any surpluses to these producers. A special fish label indicates marine stewardship where suppliers do not overfish. The Eco label signals environmental protection. Migros sells organic cotton because its production is more environmentally sustainable than conventional cotton. A special wood label protects forests, and the Migros Natur line conserves plants, soil and compost.

Unlike some other companies who purchase from, or operate in, under-developed countries, Migros insists on suppliers meeting standards on working conditions for employees worldwide. All supplier employees must be assured of adequate wages and working conditions worthy of human beings. Key standards of the International Labor Organization must be observed. Unions may not be discriminated against and must be given free access to carry out their duties. Equal opportunity must be assured irrespective of age, sex, ethnic origin, nationality, color, sexual orientation, political opinion and social origin. Child and involuntary labor are banned. One day off in seven must be guaranteed and hours worked per week limited to 48. This is set out in a code of conduct that is monitored independently for compliance.

Munich Re refers to its 'corporate integrity'. At this global financial group, integrity includes specific ethical actions of respecting local laws and regulations and using only fair and legal means of competition. All the companies in the Group are bound to standards of corporate integrity for conducting themselves, transacting business and relating to external parties. These standards are also designed to prevent conflicts of interest among the staff. In addition, the Group's ethical principles do not allow investments in industries such as tobacco, alcohol, gambling, armaments and firearms.

The Novartis ethics committee on human stem cell research strives to strike a balance between research freedom and society's demands. Although individual scientists make the necessary decisions, the ethical criteria and procedures help find balance. Novartis's ethical guidelines on stem cell research apply wherever Novartis actively performs research, even where looser legal regulations on using human embryos for research purposes apply.

Porsche, as part of its credibility principle and to boost social acceptance, rejected any form of state subsidy for its new Leipzig plant. This was not done because managers did not know what to do with the money, but in the belief that mature industries like the auto industry should not be given taxpayers' money. For Porsche, credibility refers to a company's willingness to display its views clearly, participate in the public debate, assume responsibility for society and the economy above and beyond its own interests, and take a stand towards politicians and the public if it feels that its arguments are justified.

Seele displays its ethics in various ways, including not 'buying' construction projects through bribery or working in high-bribery cultures. This can be a challenge in many countries.

WACKER'S corporate goals explicitly state that this chemical enterprise will grow by opening up new markets with new products, not by squeezing out other companies.

The above examples illustrate a variety of ways in which organizations display ethical behavior, given that acting ethically is a core value in the Rhineland model.

LONG-TERM PERSPECTIVE

> The emphasis solely on short-term financial results is reckless ... [and] leads to short-term-ism, lying, and scandals. (Warren Bennis[194])

One of the key differences between the Anglo/US and Rhineland models is the time perspective. The Anglo/US model adopts a short-term perspective, whereas the Rhineland model emphasizes the long-term. Kennedy[195] argues that many companies in pursuit of shareholder value have mortgaged their future long-term position in order to achieve higher profits now. He calls for companies to resume a sustainable course and ensure a viable future. Others point out that sustainable prosperity requires a long-term view, showing that companies focused on the long-term outperform those with a short-term focus.[196] Some Anglo/US firms are removing themselves from the stock market because of its short-term emphasis, returning to private ownership.[197]

The long-term view influences nearly every aspect of Rhineland organizations, from innovation and R&D, knowledge management, staff recruitment, retention and development (including CEOs) and investment to strategic management. The following examples illustrate some of the strategic areas to which long-term thinking is applied in European organizations, often contrasting with the Anglo/US model. Areas affecting strategic leadership in particular include the length of CEO tenure; capacity for strategic thinking, planning, investment, growth and reinventing work processes; compensation through stock options; and stakeholder relationships.

Long-term CEO Tenure

In the USA, the median length of CEO tenure in *Fortune*'s top companies is shrinking. In 2000, it was five years among the largest 700 firms, compared with seven years in 1980.[198] In 2000, the tenure of CEOs from large Australian companies averaged 5.1 years.[199] Among the Fortune 700, only 26 per cent of CEOs had remained with their firms for their entire careers, and predictions are that exceeding the average tenure substantially will become increasingly difficult as boards become impatient with a CEO's performance.[200] Many observers are puzzled by the way CEOs are expected to deliver consistent short-term performance under this kind of immense pressure.

According to Finkelstein and Hambrick,[201] the literature is clear on the finding that poor organizational performance tends to precede executive departure. Studies show that, overall, longer-tenure CEOs produce a greater total shareholder return than shorter-term CEOs.[202] Those CEOs who resign through regular transition outperform CEOs who leave for underperformance.[203] CEOs leaving 'normally' beat the market by 1.3 per cent, whereas those resigning for performance-related reasons underperformed the market by 8.3 per cent. This suggests that CEO dismissals can set off a crisis, which disrupts the organization[204] or the CEOs' behavior instigates a crisis which leads to their dismissal.

Both Rhineland and Anglo/US firms prefer recruiting a CEO from inside the organization, 'growing their own' top executives, rather than appointing someone from outside.[205] At Kärcher, the young managing director appointed in 2001 expects to remain for the long term, and the company shares this expectation. He was promoted from within the organization. Aesculap, Porsche, Seele and other firms boast long-term CEOs, some of whom have been 15–25 years in office. In its over 113-year history, global insurer Allianz has changed CEO only nine times. With expectations of a long tenure, a CEO is able to focus on the sustainability of the organization.

A downside of expecting a long stay at the top is that there may often not be a succession plan in place should something happen to the CEO. Fortunately Rhineland companies are typically managed by a team of executives, allowing for continuity of top leadership when another member takes over the speaker's role. This continuity is important for ensuring survival of the strong cultures typical of Rhineland enterprises. Another downside of long CEO tenure is frustration for ambitious lower-level people despairing of ever moving up.

Long-term Strategic Thinking, Planning, Investment, Growth and Work Processes

Under a long-term philosophy, a new Rhineland CEO is unlikely to bring abrupt new changes and strategies. This is because the organization has existing long-term strategies and plans in place that are not greatly affected by short-term decisions and events.

Long-term strategic thinking is typically associated with long-term planning cycles. Porsche's rejection of quarterly reporting requirements was partly based on the argument that it takes the vehicle manufacturer's focus away from long-term planning. Loden-Frey's timeframe for business planning has traditionally been 5–10 years, even though it is in the fast-paced fashion business and cannot predict seasonal fashion trends very far in advance. Kärcher's planning cycle tends to last 30 years, subdivided into shorter cycles. For example, some strategies for this cleaning solutions supplier extend 10 years ahead, certain prognoses are provided for the next five years, while budgeting is done about one year in advance. Rohde & Schwarz wishes to maintain its independence from the financial markets and still meet growth targets in its radio and IT measurement business. Management considers forecasts of at least five years to be essential to achieve these aims. By contrast, Seele does not use formal plans at all because 'everybody in management knows' where this construction firm is going.

Organizations can more readily invest in expensive custom-designed equipment and buildings when able to think long-term. For example, at ZF, specially designed hexagonal buildings linked by bridges are intended to foster creative thinking and communities of practice within this automobile supplier; BMW has a similar cellular arrangement to allow for intensive informal communication flows; Seele has created transparent walls between open design offices and production areas to aid communication and collaboration when creating new building solutions. Even in difficult times, WACKER continues to invest in new chemical research and production facilities required under its long-term plans. The first phase in the build-up of Novartis's US pharmaceutical research center saw nearly 400 scientists working in the new laboratories. This expansion is intended to continue, but it requires large investments now to yield mid-to-long-term returns.

Reaching long-term goals often requires companies to endure fluctuations in growth while investing long-term. For example, Fraunhofer funds basic research into new technologies long before the commercial possibilities have been recognized by its client organizations. Kärcher and Rohde & Schwarz adjust their rate of growth and investment according to the revenues they generate. Porsche claims that its long-term growth strategy underlies its success in the highly competitive automobile market. Shortsightedness and short-term thinking have never been the way for insurer Munich Re. This company tries to create lasting value by systematically building on its strengths. The basic chemical research that WACKER conducts represents a long-term investment in its future.

Work processes can also be thoroughly reinvented under the Rhineland model's long-term perspective. Since 1994, Porsche has completely reinvented all its work processes, claiming that no single hand movement remains from before. Holcim has the capacity to devise organizational structures to integrate and educate its newly acquired cement companies worldwide and thus develop support functions on a higher level.

Long-term Stock Options

Providing stock options to managers and other employees is less widespread in Rhineland companies than in the Anglo/US world. For example, Migros does not pay bonuses to its retail managers, and stock options are frequently not available in family-held or non-profit enterprises. In any case, the appropriateness of using stock options to reward employees, particularly short-term options, is increasingly being questioned. Sahlman[206] warns that any compensation system that is based on performance has the potential to encourage cheating, and only ethical management, appropriate governance, suitable control systems and comprehensive disclosure will protect the investor against disaster. One solution appears to be long-term stock options, and some major US companies are redesigning their stock option plans with the long term in mind.[207] The objective is to drive performance while promoting fiscal responsibility and good corporate governance.

Where they occur, manager rewards in Rhineland organizations are typically aligned with medium- and long-term strategies and outcomes. This encourages managers to take responsibility for their decisions. In 1999, Munich Re introduced a long-term incentive plan for members of its board of management and approximately 80 senior insurance executives globally. The incentives are linked to long-term share price performance. This involves a seven-year plan of stock appreciation rights that may only be exercised under certain conditions. Similarly, in 2001, Allianz introduced its long-term incentive plan for senior managers as an additional incentive to increase the company's market capitalization. The plan rewards distant goals rather than short-term fluctuations in share price. Novartis offers certain pharmaceutical executives a long-term performance plan, a leveraged share savings plan and a restricted share plan. These plans are designed to foster long-term commitment of eligible employees by aligning their incentives with the firm's performance. Long-term approaches to rewards are also taken at Holcim, Kärcher and ZF.

Long-term Stakeholder Relationships

Long-term relationships with stakeholders are highly valued in Rhineland organizations. For example, long-term employment traditions foster a loyal workforce. Even small companies practice loyalty and treat their staff well. Seele's maxim is 'if we do it for our customers then we do it for our own people' in reference to the quality of staff facilities and treatment provided. Loden-Frey's workers tend to join in their youth and remain with the retailer until retirement.

Like many European organizations, Rohde & Schwarz also builds long-term relationships with suppliers, customers and partners, as does Migros with its customers, producers and cooperative members. Munich Re values long-term relationships with its insurance clients. Fraunhofer is pursuing long-term alliances with other European research organizations as part of its growth strategy. WACKER engages in long-term chemical research projects with universities.

Under the Rhineland view, a long-term focus affects an organization's sustainability by reducing disruption when CEOs leave. Through compensation schemes based on the long-term performance of the business, top management becomes committed to the consequences of its decisions, and is enabled to plan and invest for the long term. In the short term, this may involve no growth and re-engineering of processes. Long-term thinking permits long-term investment in expensive facilities, processes, projects and people development. It also supports long-term relationships with stakeholders, and this theme is explored next.

STAKEHOLDERS

> Good leaders achieve results: great leaders achieve sustainable results by serving multiple constituencies. (Kevin Cashman, CEO of LeaderSource[208])

A major criticism leveled at the Anglo/US model stems from its focus on one stakeholder to the exclusion of all or most others.[209] An exclusive focus on shareholders is surprising because it appears that in reality shareholders are unimportant and powerless in influencing large organizations.[210] Shareholders are 'managed' through various tactics designed to minimize their power in influencing a business.[211] In most cases, current shareholders have not even provided the company with capital, but have simply bought the shares on various stock exchanges.[212]

Stakeholder thinking underpins Rhineland leadership. A focus on groups with an interest in an enterprise beyond shareholders is far from new,[213] and US research shows that providing value to multiple stakeholder groups is a key to enduring excellence.[214] This involves recognizing and addressing the interests of a wide range of parties such as employees, customers, suppliers, managers, patrons, board members, the media, firms with which collaborations and alliances are in place, the environment, society at large, local communities and even future generations.[215] Governments, regulators and politicians are also important stakeholders because of the significant effects they can have on the context in which organizations operate.[216] Those representing community interests can mobilize opinion for or against a corporation's environmental and social performance, and should therefore be included among the stakeholders.[217] As a result, corporations need to manage these diverse relationships, which can be quite complex and lead to conflict.

Aesculap builds relationships with a wide range of stakeholders, from employees and customers (doctors and hospitals), to the local community and region, suppliers, regulators, shareholders, employee representative groups, the environment and the young musicians, scientists and universities it sponsors. Like many Rhineland organizations, it also maintains relationships with retired employees.

Why should so many stakeholder claims be acknowledged? A variety of reasons can be given.[218] The first is that managers ought to consider the interests of stakeholders because these parties have legitimate and intrinsically worthwhile claims, an approach that seems to underlie the Rhineland model.

A second reason for considering stakeholder interests is that this can be seen as serving shareholder interests, even if at first glance it might look as if attending to the interests of stakeholders for their own sake could disadvantage shareholders. For example, money spent on environmental protection for the benefit of the community as stakeholders could be seen as lowering profits for shareholders. However at WACKER, for example, environmental management is an essential part of risk management, thereby protecting shareholders against potential damage claims in the event of a chemical accident. At ZF, BMW and other manufacturing companies, environmental protection demonstrably saves money, benefiting shareholders.

Another example comes from customers, who were once not high in stakeholder priorities. It is now widely accepted that, to serve shareholder interests, the interests of customers must also be given priority. Customer interests include the availability and quality of products and services. A study of the privatized water industry in the UK illustrates the importance of satisfying customers. In this case, managers were unable to pursue shareholder interests exclusively because water is a basic community commodity. The researchers found that, despite the costs of improving customer service, overall shareholder value increased after the improvements were made.[219] Other research confirms that high levels of customer satisfaction produce superior economic returns.[220] This is probably because increasing customer satisfaction primarily affects future cash flows, and therefore resources allocated to improving customer satisfaction should be treated as an investment rather than as an expense.

The literature is not clear on whether adopting stakeholder policies always improves performance, despite considerable evidence that traditional performance measures improve under stakeholder policies.[221] Perhaps this depends on how you look at it. Preston and Donaldson[222] make the case that stakeholder relationships can enhance the organization's broader wealth in many different ways, affecting both tangible and intangible business assets. This includes relationships such as alliances and collaborations with other firms, which should be included in a firm's market value along with its physical and financial assets[223] and relationships with long-term experienced employees.[224]

Some people justify taking a stakeholder approach because it protects shareholder interests. For example, shareholders are served by protecting the environment in many ways, including by making environmentally friendly products more attractive to customers, attracting higher-quality staff to work for an environmentally friendly company, appealing to investors in 'green' shares or generating positive publicity for the company. Furthermore, shareholders are forced to live in the same environment as anyone else. They are exposed to carcinogens, give birth to malformed babies and suffer asthma the same as other people. While justifying a stakeholder approach as serving shareholder interests may appeal to some managers, moral philosophers like Singer challenge this rationalization, arguing that a stakeholder approach should genuinely transcend maximizing profits.[225]

Kennedy[226] points out that failing to consider a range of stakeholders has damaged the long-term prospects of many companies. These organizations have alienated core constituencies on whom they will need to rely in the future: stakeholders such as customers, employees and suppliers, not to mention the environment and local communities. Re-establishing relationships with suppliers might mean taking a stake in each other's companies to ensure a longer-term commitment, or issuing fair contracts, as Swiss retailer Migros does. Similarly, re-establishing relationships with customers and important communities like the local town can be done cheaply and easily, through mechanisms such as making corporate training and conference facilities available to the community when the company is not using them, and including citizens in social events (as Kärcher does when it invites senior citizens in for coffee).

Underpinning an organization's sincerity in considering stakeholders' interests is an appropriate reporting system, which should display certain characteristics.[227] These include the following:

- reflecting the views of all principal stakeholders,
- benchmarking against external criteria,
- ensuring that all parts of the business are included in the assessment,
- conducting comparable assessments over time rather than being a one-off exercise,
- embedding the principles of including stakeholders in processes and systems,
- disclosing the results internally and externally,
- continuously improving, and
- permitting external verification of the organization's report.

Under the Rhineland model, managers do not focus on the interests of particular groups, not even when this group consists of shareholders, but act in the long-term interests of the enterprise itself, considering all stakeholders.[228] The 2003 German Corporate Governance Code expressly stipulates that board members and management must operate in the interests of the enterprise.

TEAMS

> If you get the spirit of teamwork, you start to build a powerful bond, an emotional bank account, and people subordinate their immediate wants for long-term relationships. (Stephen Covey[229])

Organizations are rapidly transforming themselves into networked, cellular structures. This is to facilitate speedy responses, enable exchange of knowledge and generate greater flexibility in the event of shifts in the market.[230] Innovative team-based systems and structures are needed to accommodate the new realities of organizations and their markets. Sharing leadership responsibilities and collaboration on projects appears to be the norm in these environments. With increasing use of teams in organizations, many traditional leadership roles are changing, empowering employees to make independent decisions.[231] Self-managing employees are gaining increasing significance.[232]

Teams are designed to complement individual skills and limitations. Self-managing teams become responsible for continuously assessing and improving their own product or service, work design and processes. Leadership is often elected or rotated rather than appointed. However, strong pressure falls on each individual to accept responsibility for his or her decisions and actions, and to become self-influencing and self-managing. Manz[233] argues that Americans are challenged in developing self-influencing employees and other participation practices, compared with Europeans. Perhaps this is because of a strong focus on individual success in the US culture.

To highlight some differences in team leadership, Hackman[234] distinguishes four types of work unit by how much organizational authority is allocated to the unit: (a) a *manager-led unit* in which the members perform tasks as directed by a manager, (b) a *self-managing unit* where the group manages its own performance as well as performing the task, (c) a *self-designing unit* in which members can also modify the design of the unit and aspects of the context in which it operates, and (d) a *self-governing unit* that has all the above responsibilities but also decides what has to be done.

These four kinds of work unit increase in terms of the extent of decision-making the team members engage in, the highest levels being found in self-governing units.[235] Self-governing teamwork requires a highly skilled workforce. This is because these units become involved in organizational strategy, aligning what they do with the organization's strategic direction. They are accountable to all the other teams to which they are linked. Each team is appraised for its quality and timeliness by the other teams it comes into contact with.[236] This puts the focus on satisfying the needs of internal and external customers. Usually the teams are coordinated through extensive communication.

While silos and boundaries do not go away in a team environment, ideas about them can change. Organizations are trying to develop lateral coordination between areas. In doing so, coordination becomes less from manager-to-manager and more from workgroup-to-workgroup. This makes the leadership task significantly more complex and requires an approach to leadership that embraces the differences within and among groups.[237] The role of leader changes in a team environment, becoming that of facilitator and coach.[238] Team leaders are also caretakers, who help their teams achieve goals by providing them with instructions, encouragement and resources as needed. A leader's central role becomes supporting the team, such as helping members develop the necessary skills and resolve conflicts. In between, leaders continue to do 'real' work themselves.

Furthermore, team responsibility requires a collective mind, supported by appropriate organizational culture.[239] In some Rhineland companies, self-governing teams are embedded in the culture, as we see below.

At Aesculap, self-managing teams organize their own roster and flexi times. Team members are expected to learn to think of 'our' machine and not 'my' machine, thus becoming more collaborative in the transition away from managed teams. Production team leaders are not referred to as managers, but as spokespersons. A team leader, specially trained in team-based leadership, looks after three or four surgical instrument manufacturing teams.

Self-governing teams form the backbone of BMW's structure, from the board to factory workers. The 10-member management board forms the highly qualified executive management team, and the next level of management comprises a complex network of interrelated, multi-skilled teams. These teams extend vertically and horizontally throughout the organization, from middle management all the way to the factory floor, and include design, engineering and administration. Not only do employees work in teams, but individual production plants form a comprehensive production network as well. Extensive training helps people work in self-governing teams. BMW teams enjoy a high degree of autonomy as well as group responsibility. They provide a forum for continuous improvement. Each group has a spokesperson who works as a member of the group as well as coordinating its activities, chairing discussions and representing the group to the company as a whole. Elected by the group, the spokesperson does not have the power to give orders or take disciplinary action, but needs to influence others and gain consensus.

The performance management system supports BMW's team-based organization, rewarding individuals for their contribution to the team. Shop-floor staff attend special training weekends designed to promote teamwork on the line. All BMW employees participate in quality circles, and the production line is stopped twice a month for at least one hour per shop for team discussions. Problems, solutions, ideas and learning programs form the focus of these meetings. Groups have a choice of about 35 training modules covering a range of topics related to their work. Things learned from the chosen programs are followed up at the next month's team discussion.

Within its formal structure, Fraunhofer strives to remain sufficiently agile to be able to adapt to changing market and research needs. To achieve this, research institutes are organized largely as 'fractal organizations',[240] where employees form self-organizing, self-optimizing, self-governing project groups or teams. Expertise can be added to or removed from these groups according to the needs of a particular project. Those scientists developing relationships with the customer are assigned the role of project manager within a group, and project managers select and form their own teams. Although teams are expected to be interdisciplinary and range across institutes, in practice fewer than 30 per cent of teams are formed with people from different institutes. Countering this internal focus within institutes may lead to restructuring into interdisciplinary institutes or other units.

Novartis is designing its new facilities in Basel around so-called 'family tables' to support communication among two to three-person teams. Research suggests that this greatly increases innovation and productivity compared with other configurations.[241] 'The management is aware that the only companies to survive in future will be those whose bosses do not have to drive the process of adapting to rapid and far-reaching change in the business environment from above.'[242] This pharmaceutical enterprise is prepared to invest around US$500 million in structures to support new forms of cooperation that will enable teams to reorient themselves quickly and autonomously in response to the outside world.

Thus teamwork is very common in Rhineland organizations, especially self-governing teams and project teams. In some cases, the entire organization is composed of teams, in others teams form for special purposes, while yet other teams are more permanent. Rhineland long-term employment and thinking allows teams the time and stability to develop.

In this chapter we have seen that Rhineland organizations generally de-emphasize their CEOs, who become more of a speaker for their top team. This contrasts with the power of the Anglo/US CEO. Leadership is not sought in one senior person, but is embedded in the entire system in Rhineland enterprises. Decision making revolves around reaching consensus among participating parties, including both internal and external stakeholders. A cooperative and participative style of management results that often involves self-organizing individuals and teams. Ethical behavior is central to Rhineland leadership, as is taking a long-term perspective on most aspects of the enterprise. The long-term view allows investment in people, facilities, processes and systems and enables the vision and strategy to be executed. Of course it needs to be balanced with shorter-term goals. Extensive teamwork, much of it self-governing, characterizes Rhineland organizations. Here the role of the decision-making individual manager is minimal or non-existent.

In the next chapter, we look at some of the many ways in which the case study organizations support and nurture their people.

4. Focus on people

This chapter considers seven elements in the Sustainable Leadership Grid that can be conveniently grouped together because they focus heavily on people. These elements are management development, ensuring a strong organizational culture, making people a priority, retaining staff even in difficult times, creating a skilled workforce, managing uncertainty and change, and fostering cooperative union–management relationships.

MANAGEMENT DEVELOPMENT

> Many people progress up, only to fail at a senior leadership position, for which they are not prepared or well suited. (William C. Byham, CEO of Development Dimensions International[243])

Visionary US companies are six times more likely to promote insiders to CEO than other US companies.[244] It is not the quality of leadership that most separates visionary companies from others, but the continuity of quality leadership. This continuity preserves the core values. GE's celebrated Jack Welch reflected the continuation of GE's 100-year track record of appointing leaders from within. The more common Anglo/US practice of hiring top management from outside the organization makes it hard to become, and remain, a highly visionary enterprise with a cohesive culture.[245] Since a strong culture is central to Rhineland organizations, they prefer to 'grow their own senior management'.

A global study of CEOs leaving office concluded that appointing CEOs from outside the company is a high-risk gamble. The initially high performance of external CEOs slumps during the second half of their tenure and their organizations underperform those led by insiders by 5.5 per cent.[246] The study concluded that over half the turnover among outsider CEOs in 2002 was forced because these CEOs did not live up to their earlier promise. In short, there appears to be merit in developing and promoting senior management from within an organization, which most Rhineland companies do. To ensure that people have the necessary skills, and are not simply promoted to their level of incompetency under the so-called 'Peter principle' requires a strong focus on formal management development processes.

Management education has changed over time in the USA, becoming far more pervasive and less elitist.[247] It has become more integrated into people's actual work and performance management systems. Management development programs are shifting away from simply developing individual skills to being used for strategic intervention. Programs are designed to enable people to identify organizational initiatives that can facilitate and accelerate major strategic change in line with the vision, values and mission of the organization.

During the 1960–1980s, leadership development in the USA focused on functional knowledge, was university (MBA)-based, used case studies and theoretical/analytical techniques and was limited to a few senior executives. In the 1990s, leadership development became almost the antithesis, moving closer to Rhineland practices. It focused on highly specialized knowledge relating to leadership and organizational change and was in-company as opposed to university-based; action learning replaced cases, highly focused content addressed organizational challenges, cohorts of managers were taught in one group and they then passed what they learned onto others. Management development became no longer the preserve of top executives and elite business schools.

Among Rhineland companies, we see the following diverse examples of systematic and thorough management development programs, often linked to succession planning.

BMW rarely hires top executives from outside, preferring to 'grow their own lifelong managers' from within the organization, unless a critical skill gap cannot be filled internally. BMW's active management development process involves three components: corporate development programs (for example on culture, e-commerce), professional development programs (for example skills such as conflict management) and dialogue (communication skills, working cross-functionally and so on). These processes are managed in customized in-house training, facilitated by freelance trainers and business school faculty. In addition, special programs help develop future leaders. One example is providing global managers with opportunities to spend three to five years abroad, after which employees are required to return home. As part of this continuing developmental process, every two years management and others rotate jobs within their areas.

According to Holcim's previous CEO and chairman, Dr Thomas Schmidheiny,[248] 'the ability to develop the potential and enhance the performance of our employees better and faster may be the only sustainable competitive advantage in the future'. This cement manufacturer aims to promote from within, and achieves this in about 75 per cent of cases. The company pays considerable attention to systematic, extensive management development. Holcim's concept aims to have the right people at the right place in each subsidiary throughout the world. People with outstanding talent who demonstrate strong performance are considered for participation in Holcim's International Management Program (HIMP), which provides multicultural experience. International exposure is essential for promotion to senior management and, once uncovered, young talent can progress very rapidly. HIMP is also designed to increase Holcim's competitiveness as employer-of-choice. The management development process at Holcim is described in Box 4.1.

BOX 4.1   MANAGEMENT DEVELOPMENT PROCESS AT HOLCIM

Holcim sees its success as being based on employees with a passion for performance. Making full use of the talents of all employees is a management responsibility, but furthering leadership qualities throughout the group is a responsibility of the top team.

Management development is defined at Holcim as 'the process of selecting and preparing the managers of today to secure the success of tomorrow'.[249] The Holcim process is based on the following principles:

- successful development is the result of an open and collaborative culture that allows employees to assume responsibility for their own future;
- managers are responsible for creating a forward-looking organization through learning opportunities on and off the job. Mistakes are often the best learning opportunities;
- Holcim's managers are measured on both observed performance and assessed potential;
- people development is a crucial task for all top, senior and middle managers and contributes to HR excellence;
- successful development programs require permanent coaching and monitoring;
- Holcim embraces ambitious goals which will lead to challenges and stretching, and expectations that grow with more complex management levels; and
- honest and open feedback to every employee is crucial.

Management development is built around three sets of competencies that outstanding employees develop in professional, personal and social spheres. Professional competencies include technical skills as well as problem solving, planning and organizing, strategic vision, cost/result drivers and customer orientation. Social competencies refer to

---

an effective management style: goal setting and monitoring, team orientation, communication, leadership, walking the talk, selecting and coaching. Personal competencies encompass values and attitudes: open mindedness, motivation, creativity, initiative, learning attitude, self-development, stress resistance, integrity, 'give and take' and business ethics.

The management development process itself involves the following six steps.

1. Relate management development to business plans and group strategies.
2. Review and assess current competencies, performance, potential, readiness and mobility over at least 12 months.
3. Create succession plans for longer-term replacement of current position holders and decide which pool of managers individuals are destined for: plant managers, company managers, CFOs and other positions.
4. Set up individual development plans to add the required competencies and knowledge for a specific management pool. In addition to formal training, methods can include projects and assignments, job rotation, transfers to a culturally different environment, mentoring and joining communities of practice.
5. Implement individual development plans through initiatives such as 'hands-on' experience, people development efforts or attempts to create an open and collaborative corporate culture.
6. Appointments to vacant positions are ideally filled through rotation among existing incumbents, or from the pool of candidates in the succession pool via an appropriate assessment process covering professional, social and personal strategic competencies.

Migros engages in extensive succession planning in its stores and other businesses. Each manager is required to nominate at least two successors for the short, medium and long term, covering various areas. Succession planning is well accepted in some parts of the organization but not in all; some managers have plenty of successors, while others have none. This difference could be related to management style and willingness to share knowledge and power. Therefore, Migros has initiated an internal mentoring and exchange program to allow employees to work with other managers. This is good not only for networking but also for getting around any blocking managers. The explicit succession planning process at Migros requires supporting opportunities for leadership development, which are available from a centralized training department. However, management development faces challenges at

Migros because, to be effective, it needs the support of top management and line managers. This support is difficult to win because of the federal system operating at Migros, and the independence of the regional cooperatives. Management development initiatives are sometimes resisted as centralization attempts and, thus, as an enforced change of culture.

Munich Re prides itself on having many top managers who started as apprentices and worked their way up, showing that 'everyone has a chance to make it' at this insurer. A formal staff potential and development scheme (POE) helps identify talented people throughout the organization using a system of management reviews and discussions, and then directing that potential in a meaningful way. Managers in all divisions are trained before they interview individual employees to identify their potential and development requirements. Processes that help people develop include courses (for individuals or groups) and staff exchanges available to all employees. The POE is a tool intended to align the objectives of the staff and those of the company.

Novartis places great emphasis on leadership development in its pharmaceutical business. It offered over 160 leadership development courses in 2003 for approximately 4000 associates worldwide. The courses are a combination of classroom experience and e-learning before and after. Well-known business schools supply faculty who also come from internal senior management. 'Leading at the Frontline' is the largest formal leadership training program. It is taught in five languages to newly entering or promoted managers. For those who manage managers, the 'Role of the Leader Program' links business strategy to leadership skills. The 'Business Leadership Program' at Harvard Business School is aimed at the most senior managers, enhancing their as long-term visionary thinking and ability to develop operational processes and drive performance in line with the firm's longer-term strategy. The 'Senior Leaders Mentoring Program' demonstrates top management's commitment to building future leadership among high potentials. Not everyone wants to become managers, so Novartis offers dual career paths for scientists and business people. The company also enables its associates to make radical internal changes in career paths.

Growing your own managers is also a Porsche principle, and management development programs are widely available. The process starts when the automobile manufacturer fosters graduate entry as part of its junior management program. After a suitable period of training (tailored to each individual), graduates are immediately assigned significant tasks within the Research and Development, Production and Logistics, Finance and Business Administration, Human Resources or Marketing/Sales departments. Trainees work closely with colleagues who support them in their role and share their work experience, thus quickly introducing them to the world of Porsche.

Porsche, an employer-of-choice, is usually ranked in the top 10 employers among university graduates. It takes in 60–80 of the 600 graduates interviewed annually. Faced with a shortage of qualified junior staff, particularly in engineering, Porsche devised a professional university marketing campaign and rethought its leadership and management requirements. Requirements for recruits include general management ability, particularly entrepreneurial behavior; process and cross-functional thinking and acting; ability to lead and motivate employees; team and project orientation; communication and conflict resolution skills; quality management; and intercultural competency. Succession planning is given considerable attention, and all positions are filled with potential successors, in some cases with up to three names.

The above examples illustrate some of the systematic approaches Rhineland organizations take to developing managers internally, starting with young entrants, developing regular managers and accelerating the development of high potentials.

ORGANIZATIONAL CULTURE: VISION AND VALUES

The work of leadership is to ensure each person has the same commitment to common vision, purpose, and principles. Leaders give people a sense of purpose. (Stephen Covey[250])

Culture can be defined as 'basic assumptions that people in an organization hold and share about that organization. Those assumptions are implied in their shared feelings, beliefs and values, and embodied in symbols, processes, forms and some aspects of patterned group behavior'.[251] Organizational culture provides clues to the 'soft rules' of an enterprise and is an instrument for managing communication, behavior and relationships.[252]

Some authors propose that culture consists of several levels.[253] Edgar Schein defines culture on three levels: artifacts, values and basic assumptions.[254] *Artifacts* include tangible reflections of the culture such as physical layout, language, stories, ceremonies and how people behave. Although easy to observe, artifacts are not particularly helpful in understanding why people behave in certain ways or hold particular values. Many researchers prefer to define culture in terms of *shared values* or beliefs.[255] This corresponds to Schein's second level of culture. Values and beliefs provide the justification for people behaving the way they do and help identify desirable behaviors. Often people can articulate these reasons and values. At Schein's third level of culture, *basic assumptions* are usually not explicit. They are more difficult to articulate, and people may be unaware of their influence. Assumptions are important because they drive people's behavior. According to Schein, these basic assumptions are at the core of culture, even if they conflict with stated values. Sometimes basic assumptions are referred to as 'core values'.[256]

Many organizations manage their culture through statements of vision, values and/or philosophy designed to express core beliefs and the informal rules that guide the behavior of organizational members. Vision is equivalent to clarity about an organization's purposes and direction.[257] Although some people dismiss visions as irrelevant to organizational performance, businesses need a purpose. Charles Handy argues that the purpose of a business goes beyond making a profit, to something 'better', a higher-level purpose: 'Owners know this. Investors don't care.'[258]

Considerable evidence suggests that organizations with clearly articulated vision statements tend to perform better than those without.[259] Indications are that visions tend to be more effective for leaders who have a high level of discretion or control within their firm.[260] On the surface, Anglo/US CEOs would be expected to wield significant discretion and control. However these CEOs are often measured on short-term criteria, and can be easily removed. This dilutes the CEO's overall discretion and control. The long-tenured leaders in Rhineland organizations with their patient shareholders should be able to exercise more discretion. This long-term perspective allows Rhineland organizations more time for a vision to be communicated and take effect. Thus they ought to display and implement visions with more follower buy-in than Anglo/US organizations.

Interestingly, not all Rhineland organizations have articulated vision statements. For example, automobile manufacturer BMW did not have an explicit vision statement for many years. Rather, the vision appeared to stem from the brand, driving employees to maintain the high quality and excellence associated with it. BMW's key message of enjoyment, quality and high performance seems to apply to employees as much as to products. Nonetheless vision is important at BMW, as former chairman of the board Joachim Milberg indicated when he said that the CEO must be someone with vision and the ability to turn this vision into reality together with his or her team. Note that this statement focuses vision at the top, and places more emphasis on the CEO's role than the typical Rhineland idea of the CEO merely as elected speaker of the top team.

Values are also important to organizational culture. They provide the common standard by which people can calibrate their decisions and actions. Both research into best employers[261] and the findings of academic researchers,[262] show that performance is enhanced in organizations with higher-order purposes and organizational values that align with individual members' values. Shared values make a difference in work attitudes and performance, particularly shared core values. By keeping their core values and ideals, visionary companies strive for progress that enables them to change and adapt while preserving their basic ideals.

It is a myth that visionary companies are great places to work for every-one.[263] Only those employees who fit extremely well with the core values, beliefs and demanding standards of a visionary company will find it a great place to work. 'Visionary companies are so clear about what they stand for and what they're trying to achieve that they simply don't have room for those unwilling or unable to fit their exacting standards,' as researchers Collins and Porras wrote.[264]

Loden-Frey looks for people with radiance (first), then technical skills. Store managers interview people three or four times before appointing them, to ensure organizational fit. Aesculap places social skills, teamwork and communication ahead of technical skills, arguing that people can acquire technical competency in making surgical instruments, but not social skills. Automobile supplier ZF also spends time interviewing potential employees, often for one whole day, to make sure the chemistry is right. Novartis also preselects people on the basis of how they match the pharmaceutical compa-ny's values during interviews.

Organizations need to build connection and commitment based on free choice, rather than coercing people.[265] By selecting and then retaining people who share the core values, managers do not need to control or mold them. However, a shared corporate culture and values can be difficult to establish in fast-growing organizations because of the time and effort required to align the different value systems of the individuals within them.[266] Furthermore, focusing on short-term success does not give individuals time to integrate their own values with those of the organization; nor does it communicate consistent organizational values to members.[267] For these reasons, developing a strong culture in organizations can be particularly challenging where staff turnover is high and individual and organizational values are not aligned.

We see many examples of shared vision, values and corporate philosophy operating among Rhineland companies. The examples below are character-ized by strong, but very different, cultures. The cultures reflect an overarching purpose and core values that go way beyond simply making money.

All it takes to operate' is Aesculap's philosophy, reflecting its strategy of providing everything required for the core processes in operating theaters and specific medical procedures. Part of its mission is to become an irreplaceable partner for the surgical treatment of patients in hospitals, helping hospitals to perform better. This brings a need for people to think in terms of relation-ships and processes. Constant R&D and innovation in product and service is part of the firm's philosophy. Aesculap envisions a completely new future involving a radical Office 2010 project and leasing surgical sets.

Corporate guidelines serve as a basis for the broader B. Braun Group's desire for a uniform global corporate identity, including Aesculap. The guide-lines are as follows:

- being a competent and reliable partner for clients, achieved through professionalism, seriousness, willingness to make decisions and performance;
- aligning the understanding and application of all employees with the company's aims;
- recognizing that every member of the organization makes a valuable contribution to the company's development;
- demonstrating active concern for the responsible treatment of the environment;
- maintaining the Group's independence, with innovative power and single-mindedness.

Fraunhofer faces daily challenges of managing innovative professionals from a wide range of backgrounds in its commercial research context. Fraunhofer scientists are expected to be outstanding researchers, inventors and business people. A fundamental objective has been to create a culture so that 'by granting them [employees] a free hand, more self-organization, more autonomy and responsibility of their own, we can trigger new surges of achievement'.[268]

Holcim's vision is to 'help build the foundations for tomorrow's society'. In an environment that encourages employees to be curious and expand their knowledge, this global cement manufacturer supports qualities such as initiative, team spirit, a sense of responsibility and a willingness to learn. Fair play and an appreciation of different national cultures are basic to the organizational culture.

Migros's defining culture stems from 15 principles laid down by its founder, Gottlieb Duttweiler. Strongly powered by history and tradition, the retail-based organization is values-driven rather than profit-driven, yet it is highly 'profitable'. Duttweiler believed in the family as the cornerstone of life, and consequently Migros considers itself a family – the largest in Switzerland. Migros's vision is to be a cooperative, achievement-oriented community. Duttweiler believed in a moral market parallel to the goods market, which influences many of Migros's business dealings today, with unions, customers, members of cooperatives, the wider community and employees. Stakeholders in Migros are considered social partners. Organizational policies, particularly employee policies, generally reflect these values. An uncompromising customer orientation is a core value at Migros. Duttweiler started with the view that customers were paying too much to middlemen, and he set out to provide 40 per cent lower prices. He continually sought to give customers what they wanted, and so the business grew. Today, this has resulted in what Professor Werner Müller from the University of Basel calls a 'make it happen' for the customer culture.[269] This culture can be so strong that it overrides other initiatives that potentially compromise it. Orders from head office or supervisors can be ignored, and employees are even admired for doing so if they end up 'making it happen' for the customer. Other strong values at Migros include admiring endurance, individual fighters and a high level of professionalism and performance in workers.

Novartis provides its employees with a higher-order purpose through its mission to discover, develop and successfully market innovative products to cure diseases, ease suffering and enhance the quality of life. At the same time, it aims to provide a shareholder return that reflects outstanding performance and adequately rewards those who invest ideas and work in the company.

Porsche's core competence is not just its excellent engineering, or its pride and passion for perfection and high quality. Rather Porsche sells enjoyment in driving from point A to point B. The philosophical legacy of the company founder, engineer Dr Ferdinand Porsche, strongly influences the Porsche Group to this day. In addition to its engineering values, Porsche deliberately goes against the trend whenever feasible, as it did in rejecting quarterly reporting and refusing government subsidies. Its character is derived from a desire for independence and freedom. The president asserts that this valuable and rare blend of factors inspires the high level of motivation and creativity in Porsche staff, not to mention the inspiration derived from their product, and the fact that about 75 per cent of Porsche cars ever made are still drivable today.

Rohde & Schwarz's corporate purpose is to 'contribute to advancing the quality, efficiency and security of information and communication'. The mission statement emphasizes innovation, precision, long-term relationships and quality. Over a two-year period, Rohde & Schwarz aims to involve every employee in continuous improvement programs. Top management actively reinforces the corporate values, which are articulated as follows:

- we will continue to be an independent, autonomous company;
- motivated, efficient, qualified and empowered employees are the foundation for our success;
- in addressing the market, we rely more on speed and flexibility than size and assets;
- significant contributions to the market by our own products and services guarantee our profitability;
- we cultivate direct contacts with our customers and rely on long-lasting, trustful partnerships;
- we are recognized as a high-quality corporation.

At Seele, knowledge permeates the entire organization. Constant communication is essential to achieve the high level of quality, innovation and customer service the company strives for. People are expected to tell each other what they think about problems and be performance-oriented. The focus is on transparency of people, process and product, as well as on quality and creativity. This is reflected not only in the firm's transparent glass buildings, but also in its business operations. The culture is highly relationship-focused and centered on providing meaningful, creative work for employees. Seele values toleration of, and cooperation with, others in an honest and transparent way. This requires that people get to know each other so that they can communicate better.

WACKER's strategic philosophy in the chemical industry is explicit in the following extract from the 10 Group goals.

1. Customer focus: the WACKER Group gears all its activities to meeting customer needs and goals. Customer satisfaction is the measure of our success.
2. Employees: the WACKER Group's greatest assets are its employees and their technological expertise. We want to attract top employees around the world.
3. Sustainable management: all WACKER Group employees know they have to use resources responsibly. Strongly committed to sustainability, they always strive for a balance between economic, environmental and social goals.
4. Integrated silicon-based production: the WACKER Group's integrated silicon-based production system offers a unique competitive advantage. It is the basis of our expertise and production efficiency.
5. Market share: each WACKER unit should rank among the top three suppliers to its markets. This ensures the production volumes needed to be cost-competitive.
6. Sales/growth: the WACKER Group wants above-average growth in its markets. Growth is the starting point for meeting the expectations of shareholders, employees, customers and suppliers.
7. Innovation: 10 per cent of consolidated sales should come from products developed within the previous five years.
8. Cash flow: the WACKER Group aims to generate sufficient cash to self-finance growth and produce an attractive rate of return.
9. Profitability: WACKER seeks an average return on sales (EBIT) of 12 per cent to sustain its growth and innovative strengths.
10. Value creation: the WACKER Group's top priority is sustainable value creation. Long term, every WACKER business must generate earnings that exceed capital costs.

Many Rhineland organizations proudly refer to themselves as 'special', reflecting pride in the organizational culture, products or services and achievements. Yet the nature of this 'specialness' varies considerably in the details of the specific organizational culture, values and philosophy. Although Rhineland organizations can be distinguished by their strong individual cultures, many values recur: innovation, customer focus, remaining independent, high quality, excellence, achievement, respect for traditions, learning, protecting the environment, moving forward and valuing their people.

PEOPLE PRIORITY

If you distance yourself from your people – refusing to cultivate meaningful relationships with them – you are destined to fail. (Margaret Wheatley[270])

The catch cry, 'people are our greatest asset' is rather inconsistent with actual people practices in organizations that 'downsize' to make financial statements look better. This practice needs to change in companies whose value lies largely in intellectual assets, brands, patents and the skills and experience of their workforce. Assets that stem from the knowledge of the workforce can no longer be treated as the disposable property of investors. As Charles Handy wrote,[271] 'a good business is a community with a purpose, and a community is not something to be "owned".' Best employers also focus strongly on people compared with other employers.[272]

Thirteen people practices have been found to promote strategic advantage for firms.[273] Pfeffer[274] and his colleagues point out the difficulty (at least in the Anglo/US world) of finding a single company that does all of these things, or does them equally well. Interestingly many of these practices are found in Rhineland companies:

1. employment security,
2. selectivity in recruiting,
3. paying high wages (this is not always necessary, Pfeffer *et al.* concede),
4. offering incentive pay such as bonuses,
5. employee ownership,
6. information sharing,
7. participation and empowerment,
8. self-managed teams,
9. training and skill development,
10. multiskilling and cross-training,
11. a relatively egalitarian culture,

12. compressing wage differences to make people's remuneration more even, and
13. promoting from within.

Pfeffer and his associates acknowledge that achieving competitive advantage from these practices requires a long-term view, as well as a broad management philosophy underpinning them.[275] These recommendations reinforce the alignment evident between the people practices and Rhineland values. Of the 13 practices, only employee ownership has generally lagged in Rhineland enterprises. Perhaps employee ownership is not critical in a culture that still values trust and loyalty between employer and employee because the long-term interests of both parties coincide.

It is difficult for Anglo/US companies to treat workers as Pfeffer and his associates propose. One reason is that US corporate law has ignored workers, focusing on shareholders, managers and the board.[276] A second reason is that maximizing shareholder value requires treating employees as an expense, which is reflected in terms such as 'human resources' and 'human capital'.[277] Costs, capital and resources need to be monitored and controlled, reduced where possible to maximize quarterly returns. This makes workers vulnerable to 'downsizing' and reduces their commitment to their employer, especially when their work is outsourced.

The German literature is becoming more critical of US human resource models, assessing traditional German approaches more positively than in the past.[278] Companies operating in Germany have tried many US techniques, but labor market differences require these methods to fit the local context. In Germany, the HR debate has centered on three issues: shifting from collective towards individual labor management, linking business and HR strategies, and devolving HR issues and responsibility to line management.

Some US writers[279] are calling for the human and emotional side of organizations to emerge, in which humanistic practices and policies form an integral part of an organization's daily operations. A simple example of this is reflected in Seele's belief that a very clean environment enhances work quality, exchange of ideas and learning between workers. Accordingly, the company sand blasts raw steel before workers handle it, out of respect for employees as human beings (despite the extra cost). Another example is that apprentices are given challenging and stimulating learning projects to work on at Seele.

Kennedy[280] argues that a strategic focus for Anglo/US corporations will need to be on investment in people. Good people will have been lost (together with the knowledge in their heads) during 'downsizing', and survivors will be frightened. Employers need to build an attractive workplace, and this can be done in part by rebuilding an appropriate corporate culture. Making the workplace community inviting to all employees and putting a meaningful human dimension back into it is a good start. Among Rhineland companies, retrenchment is relatively rare because the companies realize that, as soon as the economy recovers, they will need labor that is not only skilled, but fits the corporate culture.

People are clearly a priority in all the case study organizations. This is evident in many ways. For example, European workers tend to enjoy considerably longer annual leave than in the Anglo/US world. Handy[281] argues that Europe's five to seven-week annual leave, parental leave for fathers and mothers, working weeks of fewer than 40 hours and other social benefits for the employee signal that long working hours are not necessarily good. He argues that the organization is serving its own sustainability when it protects employees from overworking. The following examples illustrate various other ways in which Rhineland organizations focus on their people.

Aesculap claims never to have sacked a person in its more than 136 years of existence as a surgical supplier. Employees unwilling or unable to embrace change are at times allowed to continue using old processes and technology, even after new technology has been introduced elsewhere. Alternatively, introducing new processes or technology may be delayed until the affected employees retire or become ready for change.

At BMW, people are regarded as the main factor in this automobile company's success. Since 1983, people have no longer been viewed as a cost, but as an investment. The human resource policy is integrated into the overall corporate policy in making both strategic and operational decisions. Work/life balance is important and BMW has hundreds of flexible working time models. This variety is driven partly by consideration for employees. It is also driven by the need for efficiency in managing an expensive workforce and seasonally induced short working times, while running expensive production machines. At the Munich plant, associates work four days a week, while in Regensburg employees enjoy five consecutive days off every three weeks to compensate for working nine-hour shifts at other times. The Dingolfing plant is located in a rural area. It normally closes in August to enable the staff to bring in the harvest from their working farms. The Berlin motorcycle factory irons out peaks and troughs in demand for its products by having employees work longer hours in summer and fewer in winter. Working hours and operating times are oriented towards market demand to meet customers' needs quickly and enhance employees' work/life balance. In 2001, about 600 BMW employees took sabbaticals and almost one-third of the workforce availed itself of flexi time.[282]

Fraunhofer's success in contract research depends largely on treating its people well. Research students are paid double the university stipend, making Fraunhofer a financially attractive place to undertake a doctorate. For graduate scientists, Fraunhofer tries to compensate for its government-induced low pay rates with good working conditions, international activities, research freedom and extra resources or special arrangements. Despite paying relatively poor salaries, Fraunhofer is the number 16 employer-of-choice in Germany for engineers. People are attracted by the fun of working on varying projects, in teams, and by relatively easy access to funding for new research projects.

Migros's corporate philosophy is to focus on its 80 000 plus retail and other employees. Staff share in the organization's profit under a collective agreement, reviewed every four years. Employees are also provided with good social security benefits, often beyond those available to most other workers. For example, they enjoy between five and seven weeks' annual leave, increasing with age. Normally women work until 63 years of age in Switzerland, men to 65, but, at Migros, employees can either take early retirement from age 57, or they must retire at the latest at 62 (women) and 64 (men). The organization provides other employee benefits including 14 weeks' paid maternity leave, continuing training, free whole life insurance, pension funds and financial rewards for long service. In addition, Migros takes greater care of alcoholic employees than many other companies tend to do. Relevant employees are interviewed, with a focus on their performance first, and only by the third interview is there talk about alcohol. Alcoholic employees are provided with the option of being sent to a clinic for two or three months on paid leave or leaving Migros. So far, all counselees have chosen the clinic. Migros's representatives visit the employees at the clinic, and the organization provides them with a job on their return. This is important, given that about 75 per cent of reformed alcoholics stay clean if they have a job. This compares with 13 per cent staying clean who do not have a job when they come out of a clinic.

Despite its renowned focus on people, in dealing with a labor dispute over wage increases in 2000, Migros appears to have adopted an adversarial approach towards employees. It appears that strict cost control won that day over Migros's socially-oriented philosophy.

An example of global insurer Munich Re's people orientation is an employee-initiated kindergarten for 30 children, which receives company sponsorship. Although both men and women benefit from the kindergarten, it is company policy to foster women. The objective is to double the number of women in managerial positions (from 7 per cent to 14 per cent) over the next five to ten years. Although women comprise 50 per cent of Munich Re's intake from universities, retention is poor. The company is investigating the causes, but argues that low female retention seems common in the insurance industry.

At construction specialist Seele, performance is reviewed weekly in small meetings. If someone appears to be underperforming, open discussions take place, between individuals and in the team. For example, the issue might be that someone is not willing to work weekends when the team is under pressure, or is producing poor design work. Other employees expect the directors to talk with poor performers. Discussions take place in a closed but transparent room, enabling others to see that the discussion is occurring but not to hear. Two written warnings precede termination as the law requires, but the objective is to raise performance rather than terminate. For outstanding performers, rewards include larger projects, more responsibility, company cars and special gifts or bonuses.

That people are a priority in Rhineland organizations is evident in various ways, including focusing on employee needs and benefits and seeking to provide conditions that help people develop on the job and balance their working and personal lives.

RETAINING STAFF

> Every organization is becoming a 'talent-based enterprise'. Talent becomes the be-all and the end-all (Tom Peters[283])

In 1999, US employers discharged 1.2 million workers, the highest number of layoffs since 1995.[284] Layoffs have continued, particularly in the Anglo/US corporate world. A consequence of these layoffs is that they break the implicit agreement between employer and employee, namely security in return for loyalty. This silent agreement still survives in many traditional European organizations. In a 1997 OECD *Employment Outlook* survey of employment mobility and earnings that also included the UK and USA, Germany stood out as having the lowest staff turnover rates. The report concluded that German workers were less likely than people in other countries to change industry and occupation. This was probably because of their greater investment in developing specialized skills, including company-specific skills. Poaching within an industry is further inhibited by an industrial system that equalizes wages for particular skill levels within an industry.[285] Thus the Rhineland system keeps staff turnover low.

Does staff turnover matter? Hodges and Woolcock[286] note that the advantage of the Anglo/US hire-and-fire employment market lies in being able to shed costs quickly. The growing popularity of employing casual staff does this too. These practices provide employers with considerable flexibility, which in turn enables their firms to meet price competition more easily than Rhineland enterprises can. However, price is a significant factor mainly in commodity items. In most other sectors, speed of innovation, product quality and adaptability to market demand are more important than price in international competition. Taking a hire-and-fire approach and employing more casual staff are incompatible with retaining a highly-skilled workforce. In times of crisis, Rhineland firms tend to adjust through internal flexibility (such as reorganizing and training) rather than external flexibility (hiring and firing).

A long-term US study into the effects of 'downsizing' on both individuals and corporations concluded that layoffs rarely lead to increased profitability, and sometimes they achieve the exact opposite as a Dutch study also found[287] This is because the hidden people costs are not recognized by the financial system. For example, across-the-board cuts, or those that are not perceived as being related to individual performance, leave a traumatized surviving workforce behind. The survivors are reluctant to take the risks an organization often needs to get back on its feet after massive layoffs, such as risking new markets, products or customers. Similarly, following layoffs, a company often redistributes the same amount of work across fewer employees, raising their stress and sickness levels.[288]

Layoffs should be a last resort and not a first reaction.[289] When they are unavoidable, advance warning to employees benefits both those who go and those who stay behind. *Fortune*[290] reports that employees at Agilant Technologies were highly productive and devoted to the company even while they were living under the cloud of massive layoffs and had already accepted 10 per cent pay cuts. This shows that by putting people first, even major layoffs can be handled to the benefit of the enterprise. However, Rhineland companies try many creative alternatives before laying people off, as Box 4.2 shows.

Dess and Shaw[291] examined the relationship between voluntary staff loss and organizational performance. This is important because 'talent' will continue to be in short supply into the foreseeable future. From a cost–benefit perspective, losing underperformers would probably be beneficial to an organization but losing talent would be a net cost. In a growing knowledge economy, intellectual activities are central to adding value to manufacturing and other industries in areas such as R&D and process and product design. Another perspective is that advantages accrue to organizations from the creation of unique sets of resources that competitors cannot emulate. This occurs when links form between various employees, allowing sharing of ideas and skills in unique ways. In this way, individuals combine resources to provide competitive advantage for the firm. Retaining staff capitalizes on these linkages.

Staff turnover is comparatively low in Rhineland organizations, reinforced by the role that unions, legislation and valuing skilled staff play in the economy. Employee turnover is under 3 per cent annually at cleaning systems producer Kärcher, under 2 per cent at chemicals giant WACKER and close to

---

BOX 4.2   AVOIDING LAYOFFS IN RHINELAND COMPANIES

Rhineland enterprises place great emphasis on developing and retaining a skilled workforce. In difficult economic times, they strive to avoid laying off highly qualified and motivated employees. According to Böhmer and Reuss,[292] the longer a recession lasts in Germany, the more reluctant firms are to let more people go. Managers assume that they will only need to rehire again soon, once the economy turns around. The sooner managers anticipate an economic upswing, the more creative the firms become in finding ways to retain their staff.

Hiring out employees to competitors is one of these solutions, as is collaborating with unions in offering shorter working hours for the same wages to buy time in advance. Devices like time banks, sabbaticals, reducing salaries, working fewer hours and a shift to casual employment are used to avoid losing talented staff. BMW is clearly well positioned to do this, with hundreds of flexible working models, which it uses even in good economic times. In difficult times (in 2001) and with the Chemical Union's agreement, WACKER arranged for each of its 16 000 employees (including managers) to take about a 5 per cent reduction in salary to help the firm survive, effectively raising an unofficial employee loan. This loan was based on a verbal agreement, not a contract. The resulting solidarity drove performance sufficiently high for, two years later, the company to repay half of the forgone salary to its staff, with the rest to follow.

The creative approaches many Rhineland organizations adopt in their endeavor not to lose staff reflect the long-term thinking of staff and management, the heavy investment in staff development and the cooperation of unions in protecting their members' jobs.

---

zero at surgical instrument manufacturer, Aesculap. The annual turnover rate for the first three management levels at Porsche is 1.2 per cent. Cement manufacturer Holcim reports that the rate of managers leaving its business is about 2–3 per cent. Despite Fraunhofer's avowed mission of training scientists and then releasing them into industry after five years, annual staff turnover is only about 12 per cent.

To ensure that they retain people, Rhineland organizations often offer diverse career paths. For example, at Porsche, three equal development paths can be taken: the specialist, project management and company management alternatives. Each development path offers career opportunities, and support is geared towards extending the necessary competencies and preparing for the next step.

HR at Aesculap is very strategic because this surgical supplier is dependent on its highly knowledgeable, stable workforce for innovation in surgical supplies. It fosters an organic, autonomous team culture, especially in R&D, production and customer relations. Given stiff competition for recruiting top talent, Aesculap's management believes that its culture provides a competitive edge, particularly in the way the firm takes care of its existing employees. The company trusts its workers to an extent that could make it quite vulnerable. For example, the blacksmithing is still done by hand by one critical specialist on whom the company depends. When this smith is away, the furnace stands idle. People refuse to undertake this dirty, hot, noisy work, apart from this one man, and no successor is in sight or can be attracted. Although this dependency makes the company quite vulnerable, the company trusts this loyal worker, rather than changing its processes or outsourcing the work.

Holcim has integrated recruiting, retaining and developing employees into its corporate strategy. This policy is crucial to realizing the corporate vision of 'laying the foundations for the society of the future'. This cement manufacturer applies high standards in recruiting staff. It explicitly works towards creating a climate that ensures employees have a long-term commitment to the company.

When Munich Re restructured its Munich office in 2001/2002, this global insurer promised the affected employees that not a single person would lose his or her job as a result of the change. The promise was kept.

Novartis's innovative redevelopment of its office sites in Basel into village-like environments surrounded by art and parklands is designed to attract and keep the best scientists and managers in a worldwide competition for talent.[293]

Rohde & Schwarz illustrates how, even during economic downturns, Rhineland companies seek to retain their staff. During the hard times following the end of the dot.com era, this radio and communications company did not reduce permanent staff. The firm's objective is to strengthen its position even in difficult times and to emerge from a recession in good shape. By forecasting years ahead, the firm realized that the telecom demand would have to fall, and so was prepared for that situation: people just did not know exactly when it would happen. To cope with the predicted hard times, the company issued flexible six-month contracts in production so that it could react very quickly and not affect permanent staff. Furthermore, Rohde & Schwarz maximizes output by empowering employees, giving them freedom and autonomy in executing their work as long as quality is not lowered. The company encourages togetherness and offers family support to help propel the team building necessary for future success. This develops a sense of belonging, important because it is the commitment and people's motivation that contribute to the firm's sustainable achievement.

WACKER is ranked second employer of choice among German chemical companies. Its largest cost item is people. In difficult times the company seeks to redeploy its employees between the various divisions within the company to avoid layoffs. This helps retain the very core of the company and its expertise: the employees. It means that, once a crisis has been weathered, the company is ready immediately for the next upswing. Not only is redeployment in the interests of employees and the company, it is regarded as a more socially responsible solution to cost cutting than letting staff go. This strategy is attractive when some divisions are performing well while others are not, but provides tremendous challenges when all divisions are underperforming. Staff loyalty is enhanced through profit sharing and extensive benefits, including unlimited paid sick leave for managerial levels and above. Other employees receive six weeks paid sick leave in accordance with German law, after which the employees' health insurance provides a portion of their salary.

The above examples illustrate the high value Rhineland organizations place on retaining staff and the lengths many will go to in order to avoid 'downsizing', even when circumstances are sufficiently serious for them to do so legally. Working with long-serving employees requires considerable commitment to staff development. This theme is expanded upon next.

SKILLED WORKFORCE

> Whether you work in a public, private, or non-profit organization, developing the skills and abilities of your people is paramount to your success. To sustain a competitive advantage, you must invest in your people. (Tina Sung, CEO of the American Society for Training and Development[294])

A major incentive for investing in training is to enhance the business. OECD evidence suggests that training tends to increase productivity, wages and profits.[295] A skilled workforce is not only central to the Rhineland model, but is also essential to Anglo/US companies, as a report on the UK automobile industry concluded:[296] 'High levels of skills are essential if manufacturing firms in high wage areas of the world are to compete in the long term. This is an area where the UK automotive sector continues to lag and measures to raise skills at all levels of the UK workforce must be at the center of any strategy to enhance the industry's competitiveness. It is clear from our discussions that these will need to go beyond the traditional focus on shopfloor skills, important though this is.' However, research suggests that UK small businesses, which account for the majority of enterprises in the economy, are reluctant to engage in external training activities.[297] This is despite EU programs designed to help develop the workforce.

The Anglo/US approach discourages employers from investing in training for a workforce that may have short tenure, throwing this responsibility onto employees. This leads to a system based on generic training of skills that can apply at different firms but employees can take with them when they leave.[298] Examples include vocational and managerial education gained from technical colleges and universities. From an Anglo/US employee's perspective, it is advantageous to invest in skills and acquire certificates that can be taken to a range of future employers, rather than developing company-specific skills. However, research into Anglo/US public companies shows that businesses that invest in training and developing their workforce perform better financially than firms not investing in employees. For example, US companies that invested extraordinarily in employee development outperformed the Standard & Poor index on the stock market by 17–35 per cent in 2003 alone.[299]

Many European companies prefer to 'grow their own' workforce, from apprentices and young graduates to senior management. Some observers worry that this could increase wages. Interestingly, the OECD reports that firm-specific training does not normally result in higher wages because the resulting skills are not readily exportable to other firms, thereby removing a potential disincentive to provide training.[300] Rhineland HR goals are often based on the premise that people will not leave, but will develop by moving to other positions within the organization.

Growing the workforce begins early, with apprentices. Apprentices gain practical experience by working in a company while learning the theory in a vocational school.[301] Training apprentices is also seen as a form of social responsibility. BMW, Migros, Munich Re, Seele, WACKER and ZF, like many other Rhineland organizations, train apprentices and then employ some of them upon graduation. In countries where apprentice training is not widespread, it is uninteresting for a firm to train apprentices. This is because competitors who do not invest in such training can poach the trainees. The Rhineland system avoids this in various ways, such as fostering a culture of long-term commitments, encouraging widespread vocational training, developing company-specific skills and using industry-wide wage setting.

University graduates are also put through extensive development programs. Allianz, BMW, Holcim, Munich Re, Novartis, Porsche, ZF and others have created systematic, company-wide management development programs as part of a strategy to remain successful and competitive. At Fraunhofer, by contrast, the objective is to train scientists to think and act commercially, and then move them out of the organization into industry or their own businesses within about five years. Fraunhofer's aim is to bolster national industrial

R&D by releasing trained researchers into industry. In a sense, this is society's return on the modest public funding that Fraunhofer receives.

Rhineland organizations tend to invest considerable sums in developing a skilled workforce, sometimes supported by the state. For example, in 1998, German organizations invested about €17 billion in employee training and education. Despite the massive economic upheavals in Germany at the time, this was €250 million above their 1995 level.[302] In 1995, 75.9 per cent of employees participated in in-house training, rising to 100 per cent in 1998. The average number of hours spent in training increased from 14 hours per employee in 1995 to 20 hours in 1998.

There was no union or legal pressure behind this increasing Rhineland investment in across-the-board employee education. It appears to stem from within the businesses themselves. This contrasts with approaches often adopted in the Anglo/US world, whereby the bulk of training focuses on management and technical personnel, and is much rarer for manual workers. This lack of training for production workers reflects a short-term perspective that regards investment in staff as uneconomic.[303]

However, staff development can be viewed as part of organizational learning, a principal way of achieving the strategic renewal of an enterprise and gaining competitive advantage.[304] Renewal places organizations under tension. It requires them to experiment with and learn new ways, while simultaneously exploiting what they have already learned. Considerable learning occurs as part of work itself, altering the old model of 'first learn, then work', and making learning a continuous part of working.[305]

Professionalism seems more highly esteemed in Germanic areas than elsewhere.[306] Consumers expect high-quality products from the Rhineland,[307] which is easier to ensure with a highly skilled and motivated workforce. Not surprisingly, enterprises nurture their people and take pride in employees' work. Internal mechanisms that create these social factors rest on Germany's public education and apprenticeship systems: its skills training and technical education.

It is the goal of many Rhineland organizations not only to develop their employees' technical skills, but to create self-managing workers. The need for managers is reduced when staff have the necessary skills and knowledge. At Kärcher, having skilled employees enables management of this cleaning system supplier to operate in a 'hands-off' style. Only subsidiaries that do not meet budget are called to account, otherwise they are left alone to manage themselves. Here self-management does not mean operating without management altogether, but implies self-responsibility, self-motivation and self-accountability among the workforce.[308] Of course, it is important that self-management is not just espoused but is implemented instead of controlling employees.[309] Let us look at some examples.

The role of HR is strategic at Aesculap, where people need to achieve goals. Achieving this in an innovative environment often requires changing people's skills and qualifications, for example in computer-assisted surgery or in using new surgical implants. Aesculap needs people who can handle the new technology it generates, so the company trains them. The Aesculap Academy offers over 130 courses annually for 3000 participants, investing over €4 million annually in training and further education. It extends training to customers such as doctors, nurses and hospital managers. As a result of globalization, Aesculap also trains employees in intercultural and language skills.

Allianz invests about €375 million in career training measures for its employees every year. The Allianz Management Institute provides leadership-oriented qualifications for the entire insurance and finance Group, collaborating with international universities and research centers.

BMW spends the equivalent of an average-sized German university's annual budget each year on training and developing its employees; in 2000, for example, this totaled almost €100 million. Training is extensive at BMW, with 45 000 employees attending training courses in 2000, including training for entire teams. Over three years, every team attends a three-day workshop, allowing the company to enter the next phase of teamwork training. Lifelong learning at BMW enables employees to keep up to date, contribute to the process of change and capitalize on opportunities. The company offers a wide range of training in different professions and trades, using various learning and teaching methods. BMW claims to have had the highest proportion of trainees in the German car industry in 2000, at 5 per cent of its workforce.

Fraunhofer starts with highly skilled professional researchers recruited mostly from universities and colleges. However, the ideal Fraunhofer employee is a scientist with business know-how, and universities usually do not produce such employees. Therefore, Fraunhofer has to train staff to understand how industry representatives think, and how to negotiate on research contracts with their industrial counterparts. Fraunhofer prefers to develop its own people, beginning with doctoral students from local universities under the guidance of a director–professor, using largely learning-on-the-job and mentoring.

At retailer Loden-Frey, continuing learning is encouraged in various ways. For example, store employees are highly trained in service, and at least one of the most senior managers in this relatively small enterprise devotes one day a week to reading the latest management literature.

Migros subsidizes employees in undertaking training and further education. In Migros-run schools, the base subsidy for employees is 70 per cent of course fees for attending any course at all, including language, knitting or tennis classes, rising to a 100 per cent subsidy for work-related courses.

Novartis invests considerable effort in recognizing and responding to its highly qualified and motivated associates' needs. It uses a broadly based range of programs for developing associates and helping them fulfill their career goals. The 'Pathways Program' uses defined competency profiles. It sets clear performance expectations within a consistent framework for individual development. This program ensures that associates will be supported in developing their skills throughout their careers with this pharmaceutical company.

Porsche's entire workforce is highly skilled. Apprentices are trained for three years in a separate area before being allowed to work on the vehicle production line. This area is equipped with state-of-the-art technology and is continually optimized to match current needs. After an initial training period tailored to individual requirements, selected young professionals take on future tasks targeted at their individual development goals as part of a two-year program. Core elements of this program are joint workshops, individual training modules, a three-month project in another department, presentation events and regular round-table discussions. Every employee has the opportunity to engage in lifelong learning. Individual learning measures are based not only on the current needs of employees and their managers, but also on Porsche's strategic HR needs. In 2000/2001, Porsche registered over 9000 participants in courses relating to personal, social and methodological skills as well as technical measures.

ZF's trainee program has existed since 1990. Its success is gauged by the satisfaction both candidates and ZF departments all over the world express. About 70 per cent of trainees remain with this automobile supplier, demonstrating considerable loyalty and company-specific skills built up during the training process. Trainees participate in four different projects during the 15-month program, at least one of which is abroad. A fifth project lasts for the entire 15-month period. Projects cover logistics, cost controlling, benchmarking and communication systems, as well as some technical topics.

The high value placed on continually updating workplace skills in Rhineland organizations is evident from the above examples, with training a major budget item. Skills are enhanced for employees across the organization, not just for elite groups. Even highly educated employees are supported in developing their skills in areas such as management and new technology. From this it is clear how Rhineland enterprises value and develop a skilled work force.

UNCERTAINTY AND CHANGE

To survive and succeed, every organization will have to turn itself into a change agent. (Peter Drucker[310])

As everywhere else, companies in Europe are subject to changing markets, technology, globalization and world events. Peter Drucker[311] calls upon organizations to promote change and continuous innovation, recognizing them as opportunities and not as threats. In Rhineland organizations, change is generally a considered process, but how change is handled varies from enterprise to enterprise. Let us consider how four organizations have managed change: Allianz's Office of Integration (discussed in Box 4.3), reinventing top team behavior at Loden-Frey, Munich Re shaking a conservative giant, and Rohde & Schwarz's change factory. In all cases, we see the vital commitment and involvement of senior management, along with communicating a vision and strategy.[312]

At Loden-Frey, the top managers reinvented themselves. Major behavioral change occurred at the very top of the organization among the family members. Originally, two brothers and their sister ran the store. Employees described the situation then as top management being so focused on their infighting that the business started to decline. In order to increase harmony within the family and rescue the business, one of the brothers brought in a psychological coach. He also bought out his siblings. His brother remains as an executive. The coach continued to work with the brothers for about six months until they learned to trust each other. Thus, the family members reinvented themselves and their working relationships. Leadership now depends heavily on effective communication between the brothers, and in turn on their communication with the rest of management. The brothers want to be seen as unified and, to ensure this, they always attend meetings together. Admitting being wrong and needing help takes courage, especially within a family enterprise.

Munich Re's former CEO, Dr Hans-Jürgen Schinzler, described as a cautious executive in charge of a conservative insurance company, led a wave of change and transformation. He turned the reinsurer into a diversified financial services group with plans to cross-sell banking and other insurance products. Change at Munich Re is driven by the business environment rather than cost cutting, and is preceded by intensive planning to improve operations continually. Change is not an end in itself or a 'knee-jerk' reaction to events.

In 2001, a major restructuring was led by an internal team of four people, one of whom was a member of the Munich Re management board. The organization's old structure of a product/regional matrix led to deep market/product know-how, but did not result in a holistic approach to the client. With the company now reorganized into operational units geared to client segments, the talk is no longer about markets and products but about clients and solutions. The new structure was not designed around individuals and it even reduced the number of senior management positions. However, a core promise was kept that no-one would lose his or her job or take a cut in salary. The

BOX 4.3   ALLIANZ AND DRESDNER BANK MERGER

Allianz admits that it suffers from being a multinational giant that can lapse into complacency and be difficult to change other than when in a crisis. However, fast-paced change is affecting this global insurer, which absorbed one of Germany's four major banks, Dresdner Bank, in 2001. During the merger, Allianz paid particular attention to the 'soft' side of the integration, especially communication, cultural differences and employee commitment.

Changes in the market place were the driving force behind the €24 billion acquisition of Dresdner Bank by the Allianz Group, according to the Group's Infobook aimed at investors. Clients want top advice and a wide choice of products from companies they trust with their savings. Together Allianz and Dresdner were expected to benefit from the growing private pension market in Europe, providing first-class advice and using multiple distribution channels (bank branch, insurance agency, Internet, telephone and home). Merrill Lynch analyst Brian Shea is cited in the Infobook as saying that the Dresdner alliance would strengthen Allianz's sales in Germany, unravel relationships with German banks, reduce Allianz's excess capital and break up cross-shareholdings in different companies, among other advantages.

To achieve the transition smoothly and rapidly, Allianz established an Office of Integration and gave it the total support of the top management team. The Office of Integration was created with a young team of 10 employees from diverse professional backgrounds within Allianz and Dresdner, who were released from other duties for about six months. Half the team was female, an unusually high proportion of women for both organizations. The Integration Office was also supported by experts from McKinsey and IBM and reported to an Integration Committee that made strategic decisions for the entire process. Some 20 teams were responsible for each integration step, facilitating and organizing the process in each department. Each integration team was headed by two project managers – one from Allianz and one from Dresdner; two sponsors took responsibility for achieving the defined team goal and a Communication Committee supported the process. Dresdner began to turn around in 2003 after overcoming the effects attributed to poor decisions and risk management in the past.[313]

change affected 2500 employees at the Munich head office first, before being rolled out globally. The new structure received a baptism of fire when the 9/ 11 terrorist attack in the USA occurred in the midst of the change, but has been well received overall by clients and staff.[314]

This was a fast, transparent six-month change process to minimize clients' inconvenience. All employees initially lost their old roles and reapplied for new ones throughout the organization. Interviews and selection processes for each position were held over weekends. It took 5500 person-hours to realign IT systems and 100 workshops to form new teams at the Munich office. The project was immense because of the need to reform physically and electronically at least two files per issue or client as the matrix system was dissolved. Moving people around created logistical problems as basic as working with limited elevator capacity. Immediate communication and symbolic celebrations were important. For example, a Christmas speech from the chairman began the process and, after the restructure, the company held a celebration ball. During the process, top management was seen to be unified and committed throughout the company.

However, this change at Munich Re was not without its problems. Not everyone supported the new structure and about 15 managers who did not change were assigned to special projects. Some people needed more skills to be able to cope with the responsibility suddenly thrust upon them, such as underwriters creating new products.

In 1999, Rohde & Schwarz CEO Friedrich Schwarz initiated 'a process of continuous transformation and improvement that creates the prerequisites for attaining our corporate objectives'. This radio and IT communications company chose evolutionary change, modifying only parts of the organization at any one time. By taking small continuous steps, managers believed that they could take the people with them. In a special area called the 'change factory', a group of 20 process moderators worked with employees to help them adapt. They began by telling people what change is, and then went into specific change projects. The program's objective was to promote annual growth of 15 per cent and increase market share. This was based on the following six 'pillars', which are totally integrated and not seen as independent: process of agreeing on objectives, teamwork, balanced scorecard (called a Pentathlon), cross-organizational project work, visualizing results and team communication. The change process emphasized that even a company already doing well can only continue to do so if every employee contributes.

These examples show that major change is occurring in Rhineland organizations, from mergers and acquisitions, restructuring the business, transforming business operations and reinventing the top team. Change tends to be approached in a considered way, but implementation may vary from being incremental to fast, in small sections of the business to the entire business, or with high or low intervention, including leaving change to occur at its own pace.

UNION–MANAGEMENT RELATIONS

[Top management] will represent the corporation to the outside world and maintain relationships with governments, the public, the media, and organized labor. (Peter Drucker[315])

Collaboration is a significant part of the industrial relations system in Rhineland countries where trade unions and worker representatives are socially legitimate.[316] The unions receive protected status under the law and rights to codetermination in larger organizations. In return, unions are committed to an offer of industrial peace, using strike action as a last resort only. Unions and management tend to regard themselves as social partners under the Rhineland model, allowing dialog and consensus to dominate their relationships.[317] Key features of the collaboration include a relatively centralized and coordinated form of collective bargaining via a small number of unions, the integration of labor at enterprise level through codetermination mechanisms such as works councils and the clear separation of functions between external unions and works councils inside the enterprise.[318]

Collective bargaining and codetermination are organized through a massive array of national, regional and plant-level associations in most of Europe. These organizations thus gain an institutional stake in maintaining the industrial relations system in Rhineland cultures. Lane concluded, contrary to some alarmists, that this industrial relations system is not on the verge of collapse.[319] This is largely because employers are still reliant on the cooperation of their skilled workforce. Economic analysis suggests that employment protection and a high participation in unions by OECD member countries do not adversely affect national unemployment figures – providing there is strong coordination between unions and employers, as in Rhineland companies.[320]

Although Rhineland trade unions are powerful, Albert[321] argues that they tend to use this power for the good of the community. The unions typically adopt moderate positions that they then defend vigorously. German trade unions 'show a greater sense of economic responsibility towards the nation as a whole than many of their counterparts abroad'.[322] This contrasts particularly with unions in the Anglo/US world.[323] German trade unions tend not to impose unreasonable and immoderate demands on management as a general rule, realizing that consensus and compromise pay off. This applied to German workers who were once amongst the highest paid employees in the world.

Relations tend to be collaborative rather than adversarial under the Rhineland model, although major strikes do occur when negotiations break down. In practice, German unions generally focus on the needs of their members more than broader social concerns.[324] However, the Rhineland trade union sector is comparatively well educated and well intentioned. Maintaining their own social and economic research centers keeps unions informed on various fronts, including providing them with data to support their demands.

By contrast, Anglo/US unions are usually less powerful than in Rhineland areas.[325] Unions in the USA take varying approaches to union–management relations. Sometimes union leaders regard employee involvement as undermining the union's influence and allowing management to manipulate workers. Others are optimistic that joint management–employee involvement benefits members and brings about more constructive union–management relationships in large companies.[326]

Rhineland workers have additional powers. Laws require all companies with five or more employees to have a works council, if workers ask for one. Works councils have veto powers over many personnel decisions, and members are expected to participate in developing strategies that will make the company more competitive and sustainable. Swiss-based cement manufacturer Holcim reported that, because of its size, it has been forced to create an extra layer of worker involvement with a European works council, but that no decisions are taken at that council. However works councils usually enable Rhineland workers to participate at the company level rather than just at the broad industry level where unions operate.[327] Anglo/US enterprises have no obligation to provide a voice for employees by establishing works councils.

Labor is also involved at supervisory board level in Rhineland companies. Under a 1996 German codetermination law, the *Mitbestimmungsgesetz*, companies with more than 2000 employees were required to fill 50 per cent of the seats on the supervisory board with employee representatives.[328] Under the 2003 German Corporate Governance Code, public companies with more than 2000 employees in Germany should fill between one-third and one-half of supervisory board seats with employee representatives. In either case, the chairperson retains the casting vote. However, all members are obliged to act in the best interests of the enterprise. While bargaining at the plant level is common in American industrial relations, American unions often perceive a conflict of interest in workers participating at board level. Unions prefer to be free to criticize the company and fight for workers' rights. This reinforces the adversarial relationship with Anglo/US unions, who could fear losing bargaining effectiveness by sharing responsibility.

Interestingly, a major contribution of worker participation in Germany seems to be that it promotes industrial peace, acceptance of change and social stability.[329] One European company contrasted its experiences with US unions thus: 'In New York, unions are like a Mafia, and so they can double the costs of [doing business] there. The rest of the US is somewhat better.'

The Rhineland system of codetermination has also adapted to globalization, new technology and the ever-increasing influence of international capital markets. Some writers fear that the Anglo/US adversarial approach to labor relations will erode the Rhineland system as US influence and shareholder value ideology spread throughout the world.[330] However, the Rhineland model contains some inbuilt resistance. For example, labor's representation on Rhineland supervisory boards inhibits adoption of a hire-and-fire policy, so, in practice, only a few European firms could implement a strategic management plan based purely on shareholder value, even if they wanted to.[331] Changing from the Rhineland system is also made difficult because employer associations and trade unions strongly support the collective bargaining system, although modest reforms have been introduced to allow more flexibility.[332] Similarly, many firms feel that welfare provisions help maintain the labor–management cooperation on the shop floor, and this generates high productivity growth. Thus, major dismantling of the social partnership approach to codetermination and unions is unlikely in Rhineland countries. The following examples illustrate some Rhineland approaches to labor relations.

Allianz's 2001 annual report clearly identifies the members of its supervisory board by name and position. Included are captains of industry as well as Allianz employees, most of whom are identified simply as 'employee'. However, one identified himself as 'janitor' of an Allianz subsidiary, showing that employees at all levels sit on the board at this insurer.

Migros protects union membership among its product suppliers in other countries as well as in Switzerland. Unions may not be discriminated against by suppliers to Migros, and must be given free access to carry out their duties.

Seele is currently non-unionized in its home state of Bavaria, and employees there have chosen not to have a works council. This construction design company pays above the wage level agreed with unions and ensures comparable rewards for employees doing equivalent work. Thus, people see no role for unions. However, if any one employee asked for a works council, Seele would have to install one.

At chemical conglomerate WACKER, the works council is consulted on matters of environmental protection and occupational health and safety as part of the sustainability process. The council monitors environmental protection measures, collaborates with various experts and participates in HR and organizational measures related to sustainability. It also provides suggestions and advice on WACKER's approach to responsible care. Costs of the works council are borne by the company. While the company estimates that about 10 per cent of its employees belong to the chemical industry union, employees do not have to inform management of such membership. Relations with the union are considered good.

ZF managers point out that codetermination requires employees to take responsibility for company decisions at this automobile supplier. Employee representatives come to accept the economic reasons for these decisions and in turn convince their colleagues. This process gains employee acceptance from understanding each other's point of view. Supervisory board representatives and works council members help make difficult decisions acceptable to employees. Here these representatives consider, not only economic factors, but also the human side.

In summary, Rhineland labor–management relations are designed to promote harmonious, stable conditions in which enterprises can operate while looking after the well-being of the workforce. Arrangements under the Rhineland's codetermination principle allow for some flexibility: enterprises can be unionized or not and have works councils or not, depending largely on employee wishes. Certainly there are additional direct costs to an enterprise running works councils. This often involves paying some employee representatives solely for that purpose. However, employee representation on supervisory boards and other forms of employee contributions to management also bring benefits, such as helping staff to understand the firm's strategic thinking and circumstances, as well as making an input into major decisions.

This chapter has shown how the case study organizations approach seven people-centered elements in the Sustainable Leadership Grid. They focus heavily on growing their own managers via structured management development programs and strategies. They typically demonstrate a strong organizational culture, built around a vision and set of core values. Cultures are valued but take time to develop. Making people a priority and retaining staff even in difficult times, as Rhineland organizations do, assist in maintaining strong corporate cultures. We have seen that these enterprises go to great lengths to treat their employees well and avoid retrenching people. An economic reason for this is that the enterprises have invested considerably in creating a skilled workforce which possesses company-specific capabilities and knowledge. Like all organizations, the case study firms need to manage change, and we have seen various ways in which they do this. Finally, the Rhineland organizations are required by law (and also encouraged by the ensuing benefits) to foster cooperative union–management relationships. This extends to significant employee membership on the supervisory boards of large companies.

In the next chapter, we examine how some of the elements in the Sustainable Leadership Grid affect systems and processes in the case study organizations.

5. Systems and processes

This chapter covers the elements in the Sustainable Leadership Grid that broadly affect systems and processes. It shows how the following elements operate in the case study organizations: attitudes towards the financial capital markets, innovation, knowledge management, quality and corporate sustainability in the sense of both social and environmental responsibility. At the end of the chapter, we see how even the publicly listed companies among the case study organizations display most elements of Rhineland leadership. The chapter concludes with a summary of the ways in which all the elements in the Sustainable Leadership Grid highlighted in Chapters 3, 4 and 5 interact to form a self-reinforcing system. But first, let us look at some systems and processes in the case study organizations.

FINANCIAL MARKETS

> One of the most important tasks ahead for top management will be to balance the conflicting demands on business being made by the need for both short-term and long-term results and by various constituencies. (Peter Drucker[333])

A 2004 World Economic Forum survey of the world's 1000 leading global companies revealed that 38 per cent of CEOs responding considered the financial capital markets as the leading threat to their corporation's brand.[334] They were concerned that short-term views may be distorting the accurate valuation of their companies. Unlike many Anglo/US corporations, most Rhineland public companies watch their share prices but do not allow them to drive the business.[335]

A comparison of US and European ownership and control has highlighted some of the differences between the Rhineland and Anglo/US models on important investment criteria.[336] For example, an 'insider' and an 'outsider' system can be distinguished. Under the outsider system, ownership of a corporation is dispersed among external financial institutions such as pension funds or individual shareholders, as is common in the USA and UK. Large holdings of shares in one company are rare, and consequently shareholders exert little direct control over corporations. Here, ownership and control are separated.

In many European countries, the insider system prevails. Few companies are listed on the stock market, and those that are listed tend to have a high concentration of shares in few hands.[337] In Germany, for example, single shareholders often own share parcels of 25 per cent or more, creating a single majority shareholder.[338] Concentration of share ownership is much higher on the Continent than in Anglo/US countries. European ownership is often solidly in the hands of families (Quandts at BMW, Porsche via the Porsche/Piëch family with its written voting pact; WACKER through the Wacker family holding) or other companies (Allianz's and Munich Re's cross-holdings). Cross-shareholdings, that is, complex webs of shareholdings among companies, have been relatively common in Rhineland countries, although this is changing under new taxation laws. Sometimes the government owns shares in a corporation, as at ZF.

Both advantages and disadvantages arise from large shareholdings. The interests of large shareholders can offset personal agendas in management. However, they may lead to larger investors, who may have different priorities from small investors, exerting influence instead. Long-term, committed investors tend to arise from insider systems and may be appropriate where the long haul is valued. Other situations may call for dispersed ownership, particularly where short-term investments require greater flexibility and commitment. As Becht and Mayer expressed it, 'dominant owners are able to retain control over long periods whereas managers facing markets in corporate control with dispersed ownership are subject to short influence periods'.[339]

According to Hodges and Woolcock, 'Germany remains to be convinced that it should adopt a model of industrial finance and corporate governance that has failed to prevent the progressive decline of British and US manufacturing.'[340] However, the insider system in Germany is beginning to change as large firms adopt the dispersed ownership model. This brings with it pressures to grow. However, continual double-digit growth is not sustainable just by using production, factories, facilities and working capital in conventional ways.[341] As a result, growth figures have often been bolstered by acquisitions, international expansion and other one-off or short-term 'tactics' rather than by core growth, particularly in the Anglo/US world. Without questioning the need for such growth (which Rhineland companies often do), US-based companies try to prolong growth by leveraging 'hidden' assets. Hidden assets include a wide array of underused, intangible capabilities and advantages such as relationships, market position, networks and information.[342]

Independence is a core value among most Rhineland organizations, including SMEs.[343] Closed systems of ownership and financing have protected many from the short-termism of the financial markets.[344] Being independent of the financial markets does not mean being anti-growth. WACKER seeks an average return on sales of 12 per cent to sustain growth and support investment in innovation. It aims to generate sufficient cash to finance growth from its own resources. Rohde & Schwarz adopts a similar strategy.

Increasingly, public companies are beginning to counter the power of the analysts. For example, the luxury goods firm LVMH reportedly demanded €100 million in compensation from Morgan Stanley because it believed that Morgan Stanley analysts were biased against LVMH in ranking it.[345] LVMH claimed that a relationship between Morgan Stanley and the Italian firm, Gucci, influenced the analysts' ranking. Other Rhineland firms are refusing to comply with capital market listing requirements or to deviate from their long-term plans, as we see below.

Reinsurer Munich Re's share price was severely affected by the 2001 terrorist attacks in the USA. Ever cautious, but never imagining the nature of the attacks, its scenario planning had included assumptions about severe loss events. This meant that Munich Re had prudently made capital provision that ultimately proved sufficient even to cover the exceptional 9/11 losses. Some analysts had criticized the company for not distributing its US$2 billion reserves to shareholders prior to 9/11. The analysts changed their assessments in the days following 9/11, when they demanded to know how high Munich Re losses would be. Like others involved, Munich Re was unable to provide an instant answer, and speculation led to what the company describes as a 'negative fantasy' in its annual report. The share price of €285 tumbled to €207 on 12 September: within 24 hours. The company responded immediately by announcing its initial estimate of its share of the claims burden, which eventually set the share price back on an upwards course. Reinsurance is a long-term business, incompatible with the short-term focus of the financial markets. Munich Re knows its business, and will continue to set aside provisions for the unknown in defiance of some analysts.

Porsche rejected the need for quarterly reporting in 2001, and was not dissuaded by having its shares deleted from the stock exchange for medium-sized companies in Germany (the MDAX). The Frankfurt Stock Exchange is reported as saying that its officials know of no other listed company that declines to report on a quarterly basis,[346] but resistance is growing.[347] Porsche was convinced that such reports do little more than inflate internal bureaucratic expenses, without making the picture any clearer for investors. Furthermore, such valueless reports serve to fuel the volatility of capital markets in an already nervous investment environment. Porsche's president claimed: 'The stock exchange is on the brink of becoming a game of roulette that unfortunately diverges all too frequently from economic reality.'[348] In addition, quarterly reports interfere with pursuing long-term strategies, which not only adversely affects the company but also disadvantages shareholders. In 2002, the company decided not to list on the New York exchange. This was because the US requirement for CEOs to attest personally to the accuracy of financial statements conflicts with the Rhineland approach of spreading this collective responsibility across the members of the management and supervisory boards.[349] Porsche is determining its own speed of action, has taken back the initiative and does not take orders from anyone.[350] Instead Porsche reportedly fought back by suing the Frankfurt Stock Exchange that changed its rules to require quarterly reporting.[351]

Kärcher, Loden-Frey and Rohde & Schwarz have independence from the financial markets and growth from their own financial resources as one of their core values. These companies refuse to issue public shares in order to preserve their independence, even though this could stifle growth and postpone investment because of insufficient capital. Loden-Frey is content to remain a single-store business rather than go to the equity markets in order to raise the capital to grow. Rohde & Schwarz has developed its own forecasting system, which managers believe is superior to those the market analysts rely on.

Kärcher regards always having to grow as unnatural even though it exhibits substantial growth. At cleaning systems provider Kärcher, development takes place in 30-year steps, which is incompatible with capital market reporting requirements. Kärcher has never really considered going public, partly because remaining a limited shareholder company has taxation advantages as long as individual shareholders in public companies continue to be taxed as well as the company itself.

Rohde & Schwarz has a strong growth objective to expand its market position in its various fields of business worldwide, to develop new market segments and to update its line of products, thereby enabling the company to grow faster than the market. The executive board's minimum requirement is to gain market share over competitors in times of economic recession, including in a climate of negative market growth. This enables the firm to emerge stronger from a recession especially as high expenditures for R&D and innovation largely remain unchanged even in these circumstances.

Privately-owned Seele is cash-rich and invests back in the company in technology and training, thereby creating a virtuous, upwards cycle of success. This is uncommon in the long-depressed construction industry. Seele's objective is not to increase turnover, diversify or grow any further, but simply to increase profitability with the workforce and size it currently has. Growth is not on the planning horizon, and management voluntarily chose to scale operations down slightly in 2001 to achieve a comfortable size. The senior management and owners chose quality of life over growth.

Allianz, as both vendor and consumer in the financial markets, has a special challenge. In common with many financial sector organizations, it derives much of its business from investment banking and the stock market. It will be interesting to watch how the company blends its traditional Rhineland values with the Anglo/US model's demands in relation to the capital markets.

Most Rhineland organizations are resisting pressures from the financial capital markets one way or another, except those inextricably linked to the markets. Retaining independence ranges from challenging the analysts and stock exchange requirements to focusing on growing from their own revenues – or deciding that they do not need to grow. Public companies need to strike a balance between the needs of shareholders and other stakeholders.

INNOVATION

Going forward, your only weapon is systematic, radical innovation – making innovation an all-the-time, everywhere capability. (Gary Hamel[352])

There is wide consensus that innovation is one of the main sources of technological progress and economic growth.[353] A debate has arisen about which model of capitalism better supports innovation. Hall and Soskice throw some light on this debate by distinguishing between *radical* and *incremental* innovation.[354]

Radical innovation refers to major shifts in product lines and processes or developing entirely new goods. This kind of innovation tends to characterize Anglo/US firms, as examples from the IT, biotechnology and other high-tech industries demonstrate.[355] Anglo/US companies support radical innovation because their top management can respond quickly by shedding staff or taking over other companies to change direction quickly. Larger Anglo/US firms tend to be more innovative than smaller enterprises, possibly because they have more resources.[356] Although the Anglo/US model tends to be associated with radical innovation rather than continuous improvement, this does not preclude continuous improvement in Anglo/US countries, as a study of successful Australian organizations shows.[357]

Incremental innovation entails continuous, small-scale improvements to processes and products to enhance quality. This form of innovation characterizes Rhineland enterprises.[358] The reason for this may be that Rhineland labor policy restrictions on hiring and firing employees make radical innovation difficult where restructuring or new skills are suddenly required. Rhineland enterprises address this by 'up-skilling' the existing workforce and managing the innovation system within the organization.

Others point out that, in general, the Anglo/US short-term approach does not foster an innovation culture designed to increase the long-term wealth of companies.[359] This is despite innovation and change becoming the preferred, and perhaps the only, strategy in an increasingly boundaryless and interconnected world.[360] Cutting R&D and change budgets to meet quarterly growth targets makes long-term innovation particularly difficult. International R&D figures support this with the finding that US firms tend to invest less in long-term projects compared with Rhineland countries.[361]

Despite their reputation for incremental innovation in products and processes, Rhineland enterprises are also involved in radical innovation.[362] In-company innovation is supported by a wider system in Germany and Switzerland. This includes industry association research networks (*Verbundforschung*); an elaborate system of research institutes and technology transfer institutes (such as Fraunhofer); a bank-based system of long-term finance; and a steady supply of highly trained, loyal and educated workers. While this complex system slows down radical innovation, it does not preclude it, as Fraunhofer's invention of the MP3 technology and Seele's blast-proof glass show.

Innovation is a key theme running through many of the case studies in this book. All the Rhineland case study organizations endorse and actively support innovation. Innovation drives the strategy for new pharmaceutical products at Novartis. About 75 per cent of Kärcher's cleaning products and systems are less than four years old. Aesculap derives 25 per cent of its turnover from surgical products invented in the previous three years. For Seele, every building project is unique, requiring continuous R&D and innovation. Fraunhofer's core business is innovation. It addresses a strategic need for growth in R&D by encouraging long-term alliances with other research institutes. Representatives scour the world looking for new ideas at Loden-Frey, which constantly needs to innovate in its wares and store displays, as well as in its operating systems and service. At Rohde & Schwarz, each employee's job is defined in general terms only so as not to stifle their creativity and entrepreneurial behavior. The onus is on each employee to personally determine how to achieve goals and not rely on inflexible rules, including job descriptions. The company invests 12–13 per cent of turnover in R&D. The following examples illustrate in more detail the strong focus on R&D and innovation in Rhineland organizations.

Aesculap's strategy is to be an innovation system provider for operating theaters, attained through extensive R&D. It engages in continuous dialog with physicians and clinical staff as it seeks to expand its range of services. Internally, the company operates a suggestion scheme for improving the production process. It rewards employees with money for suggestions that are implemented. The company receives about 600–700 proposals annually, which have led to substantial increases in profits. The company hosts a special event each year to celebrate the people with the most suggestions. The winner's achievement is rewarded with €2000, decided through a special committee process. The downside to this system is that it tends to lead to many frivolous suggestions as people try to win money.

BMW regards R&D as a 'step into the future', and includes innovation as part of its sustainability focus. With its reputation as a technology leader, BMW invests in wide-ranging R&D projects, particularly those that help meet the demand for sustainable mobility. The objective for R&D at BMW is to create advanced automobile design with minimum environmental impact, and without limiting the quality of human life. BMW has developed a Research and Innovation center in Munich, architecturally designed to stimulate creativity in automotive research. Another 100 employees form a think-tank that lays the groundwork for other innovative concepts. BMW captures its broader employee experience through the i-motion suggestion program, under which employees continuously improve the firm's performance. I-motion enables and encourages associates to influence the workplace and receive rewards of up to €15 000 for good ideas reflecting engagement, quality and cost savings. Team leaders score ideas with points reflecting how much value the idea adds to the workplace. This is intended to be a rapid, direct and non-bureaucratic decision-making process. Even during the trial run, around one suggestion for every second employee was submitted, resulting in direct cost savings of €50 million.

Kärcher is very serious about R&D, going against the trend at many of its cleaning system competitors by spending a higher percentage of sales revenue on innovation. This is part of a strategy to increase R&D revenues by 5–10 per cent annually over the coming decade. In 2003, the company already owned 268 patents. To maintain this level of innovation, the process is managed. First, idea competitions, workshops and other initiatives are used to generate ideas. Examples of three kinds of workshop are as follows:

- market awareness workshops – looking at future markets and requirements using both external experts, such as cleaners, and internal staff;
- application-oriented workshops – very practical and 'hands-on', about carpet cleaning and other tasks. Internal and external experts attend, plus some householders. Kärcher once held a competition to clean a real house;
- technology-oriented workshops – developing the ideas emerging from the other two workshops, and examining the functions of each product/idea.

Ideas are put through two filters at Kärcher. The first filter takes about 10 minutes to qualify an idea as worth looking into. Ideas that pass Filter 1 go through the second, lengthier filter , and both evaluations are sent to Kärcher's innovation board. The innovation board consists of three managing directors, the division managers and the product managers. It meets three to five times a year to discuss the new ideas and detailed implementation plans that accompany them. These plans may be prepared internally or by university staff. The board considers factors such as costs, benefits, risks, time and priorities. At a typical meeting, the board might discuss 10 ideas from Filter 2, plus 10 more advanced projects. Top management needs to give the final approval because innovation involves risk on behalf of the company. Risk associated with projects can sometimes be reduced, but the effort invested in a project depends on its importance rather than on risk alone. Thus, the company engages in some risky projects because of their potential payoff

Novartis's strategy revolves around innovation and maintaining a full pipeline of innovative products. Reflecting this, investment in R&D increased from about 13 per cent in 1999 to over 15 per cent in 2003. Seven major drugs were approved during 2003 and 11 new medicines have been launched in the USA since 2000. Novartis is living up to its aim of building the most competitive, innovative research organization with the most promising pipeline in its industry. In view of its 79 projects in clinical development or registration, financial analysts rated Novartis's rich pipeline as one of the industry's strongest. In its Campus Project, designed to stimulate innovation, Novartis is reinventing the office workplace to achieve 'friendly informality' built around small teams. The campus borders onto large public parks that entice people to work outside the office under trees or in coffee shops. The Basel headquarters are being transformed from an industrial complex to a place of innovation, knowledge and encounter.

Porsche regards innovation and renewal as fundamental to its business, has totally reinvented all its processes and technologies since the early 1990s, and continues to innovate in its vehicles through huge investment in R&D. It employs about 3000 researchers. Porsche's innovations in operational processes have been so successful that the company has set up a separate profit center to sell this know-how.

WACKER's business revolves around innovation through both basic and applied R&D in the chemical sector. Maintaining the research budget during difficult economic times in 2002–3 underscores the key role innovation plays in sustaining success. The oldest part of the business is the research arm, the *Consortium für elektrochemische Industrie*, which is responsible for basic R&D, and new product and application concepts. The Consortium's success is evident in the 850 plus national and international patent applications submitted. Commitment to R&D is supported by a culture of team spirit and creativity. Its flat structure locates researchers close to research directors to promote teamwork and speed project development. A Group-wide innovation management process covers several stages from idea generation to the final development outcome to solve customer problems. The innovation process involves (a) identifying mega-trends in institutional and university research, and (b) employing strategic marketing to find out what customers are researching. This information enables WACKER to define significant research areas that match its core expertise. Projects are then refined in terms of their economic attractiveness and the chances of patenting the intellectual property.

R&D development tends to be centralized in WACKER's research consortium, where research projects are conducted for the various business areas. Once commercially promising developments have been patent protected, the relevant business division takes over the project. Although the focus is on developing marketable projects, WACKER researchers can use 15 per cent of their time to follow their own research ideas as opposed to working on assigned projects. The Group also engages in collaborative research with universities and shares projects with organizations such as Fraunhofer. Innovation is not restricted to formal research groups. In 2002, the company suggestion scheme received several thousand ideas from employees. About 70 per cent of the ideas were implemented, saving the company millions of euros, and providing generous bonuses to the innovators.

At ZF, R&D in both automobile components and people is considered vital for driving value internationally. The company invested around 6 per cent of total sales in its 2003 R&D budget of €524 million. Approximately 600 of the 3000 employees in ZF's development team work in corporate R&D, augmented by another 1500 people elsewhere. Not surprisingly, ZF is among the 50 largest patent applicants in Germany. The company acknowledges that its very significant technical advantages have not been taken up to best advantage because of too strong an intellectual focus on R&D and production process engineering. A more structured approach to R&D aims to harness the innovators' visions better to meet the commercial needs of the group without stifling people's pioneering spirit. The company proposes that developing the whole person within the workplace will create more effective self-management and greater entrepreneurship, aiding the uptake of their inventions.

Clearly Rhineland organizations invest both financial and human resources heavily in R&D. Even in difficult times, the commitment to continuing R&D and innovation rarely falters.

KNOWLEDGE MANAGEMENT

Quality relationships make for better knowledge exchanges. (Margaret Wheatley[363])

Early on, people believed that knowledge could be 'managed' as a way of enhancing efficiency. Increasingly, people are realizing that the real value for corporations and society will be generated only by developing environments that enable people to create and share knowledge through their relationships.

This means that the core of value creation is people, not IT systems. The effort of creating a knowledge-centered organizational culture brings benefits. These include greater cooperation and learning, which in turn enhance knowledge sharing; and an increased quality of work life that helps retain the people who own the knowledge.[364] Realizing these benefits depends on employees being given autonomy and an opportunity to experiment and make mistakes. It requires an organizational culture that values knowledge sharing and learning.

'The knowledge-focussed [*sic*] manager creates learning opportunities, encourages knowledge sharing, sees staff turnover as loss and considers recruitment too important to be delegated to the HR department', wrote Karlerik Sveiby.[365] Knowledge-focused managers manage the environment in which knowledge is created, sharing information and knowledge and encouraging trust.

An emphasis on knowledge is not exclusive to either the Rhineland or Anglo/US enterprises. However there is a risk to organizations working on a short-term basis that organizational knowledge will get lost through high staff turnover. Employee turnover, while bringing fresh knowledge from newcomers, endangers organizational memory as individuals take their knowledge with them.[366] This applies to everyone, from CEO to skilled workers. Since Rhineland labor practices encourage long-term employment, employees tend to develop firm-specific knowledge. A hire-and-fire culture encourages employees to develop more generalized knowledge so that they are attractive to a wider pool of potential employers.[367] Thus, retaining experienced staff helps preserve organizational knowledge, even though it needs continual updating through development opportunities. It also minimizes the risk of ex-employees taking in-house knowledge to a competitor. The following examples show how knowledge is shared and dispersed within Rhineland organizations in different ways.

For Holcim, knowledge management is a fundamental part of being a learning organization. The aim of this cement manufacturer is sharing knowledge and promoting collaboration globally. It employs a framework consisting of five elements. These include information content, people, processes for creating and disseminating knowledge and an exchange platform along with infrastructure to provide data and information services. These four are clustered around the fifth element, structuring knowledge. Structuring knowledge is a challenge because just putting information into databases does not work. Knowledge islands have been developed at Holcim, clustered in specialized areas such as IT and mill operators. The islands try to share knowledge among about 40 communities of practice who bring the people and content elements of the model. The communities of practice involve people in a managed process for creating, sharing and re-using knowledge, supported by appropriate infrastructure. Communities of practice provide the day-to-day social context in which knowledge can actually be managed.

Holcim believes that corporate knowledge is best managed by the people who own, need, create and use it. Communities of practice are fluid; they form and disband according to the need for them to share knowledge. Holcim uses various devices to create and share knowledge, including corporate learning events. Another example is that the firm collects experience accumulated over the past 20 years of managing projects. Debriefings highlight the lessons learned from every project and at the beginning of a new project, people are required to consult the debriefed lessons.

Munich Re argues that the decisive qualitative difference in the insurance business is the risk carrier's knowledge potential. This arises from the combination of experience, expertise, innovation and the productive transfer of this through discussions with clients and other partners. The capacity of the company to retrieve and assess information across different fields and locations gives it competitive advantage. Munich Re undertakes its own research in a wide range of sectors, thereby collecting considerable formal knowledge in addition to its tacit employee know-how and accumulated experience. The company is developing ways of displaying and structuring the accumulated knowledge in a globally dispersed organization.

For pharmaceutical giant Novartis, knowledge management is a core concern, particularly getting associates to share knowledge across organizational boundaries. Instead of managing knowledge, the focus at Novartis is on sharing knowledge and developing networks of people. This is done in various ways, including use of research advisory boards, knowledge fairs, networking communities and electronic platforms and conferences. In addition, Novartis is developing new kinds of buildings with the specific intention of encouraging people to meet and interact, thereby sharing knowledge.

Rohde & Schwarz maintains that communication is the key to ensuring that knowledge is available to the people who need it in its radio measurement and testing business. Teamwork helps share knowledge when all those involved work together. Rohde & Schwarz holds several 'show and tell' fairs internally to encourage engineers to communicate their results. Regular communication is encouraged across the entire organization to share open information on targets, customers, employees, processes and structures, products and services, competitors and project debriefs. This enables employees to pursue their targets. Since organizational figures and data help drive results, they are available on a 'need to know' basis.

WACKER's research consortium holds a traditional, compulsory 'Friday colloquium' at which the heads of the various research groups meet under rotating chairmanship to present their projects and the interim results of their working groups. This is an efficient way of exchanging information and ideas among chemical and other scientists.

Knowledge is managed in different ways in Rhineland organizations, but the various processes are supported by long-term employment, innovation systems, highly-skilled and trained employees and creative venues for sharing knowledge. A major strategy is to provide opportunities for people to communicate.

QUALITY

> Pick your own measures that have meaning, and recognize that results may not be the point of it all. The integrity and whole-heartedness of your actions may be the final measure. (Peter Block, director of the US Association for Quality and Participation.[368])

A 2004 survey of the world's 1000 leading global companies revealed that 27 per cent of the CEOs responding considered the quality of products and services as their most important measure of corporate success.[369] Notions of achieving the highest quality possible and promoting excellence permeate Rhineland company cultures,[370] although excellence is often expressed in very different ways. Much has been written on quality procedures such as total quality management (TQM), the details of which are beyond the scope of this book.

Empirical evidence suggests strongly that improving and maintaining high quality pays off in terms of customer satisfaction and superior economic returns, but requires a long-term perspective.[371] In a study of US Fortune 1000 companies, larger companies tended to be more likely to adopt TQM.[372] Among the European case study organizations, both large and small firms strive for high quality, including firms in the services sector. Those involved in manufacturing are ISO9001 certified in production as well as in other areas of business, including BMW, Kärcher, Porsche, Novartis, Rohde & Schwarz, Seele, WACKER and ZF.

Interestingly, people are replacing machines on tasks where manual work can be more accurate. For example, Seele employs an operator to straighten steel tubes manually because humans can achieve 98 per cent or greater accuracy. This is better than a machine. Aesculap's surgical scissors are hand-finished and fitted because machinery cannot provide the guaranteed precision of 100 per cent accuracy and fit. Windscreens at Porsche are inserted into the cars by hand because the windscreens form a structural part of the design, and robots are not sufficiently accurate on the production line.

Noticeable in Rhineland companies is that pursuing the highest quality is not a matter for debate; it is a given for most of them: 'no compromise on quality' paraphrases the sentiment. However, different organizations ensure their quality in diverse ways, as the examples below illustrate.

Fraunhofer's quality can present a challenge to measure because, as a research institution, it works with innovation and intellectual property rather than with tangible products. Measures of Fraunhofer's quality lie partly in the level of scientific publications and prizes, along with its own and its customers' commercial success. Continued growth in contract research speaks for Fraunhofer's enviable commercial success, especially when about 75 per cent of research contracts are repeat business from existing customers. Informal feedback from industry representatives and the media yields mostly glowing reports. Evidence of Fraunhofer's success in commercially viable research also comes from its patent applications. In 2000, Fraunhofer was ranked 24th in Germany in the number of national patent applications, registering 507 German patents in that year in addition to many international ones. By 2001, it held 1372 active national patents.

Holcim is highly focused on quality. This cement manufacturer employs 'communities of practice', akin to quality circles, to involve its people in enhancing quality, by creating, sharing and re-using knowledge. In particular Holcim monitors the quality of leaders in terms of their professional, social and personal competencies, and ability to motivate and lead a team.

Kärcher pays cleaning product teams a quality bonus, with payment going to the whole six-person team for the quality the team produces. If faults are found, the team is required to pay the person who fixes the faults from the team's own quality bonus.

Loden-Frey's customers return to the Munich store because of the high-quality, consistent service that is ensured through company-wide service standards and training. This is also reflected in letters of appreciation.

At Munich Re, quality control takes different forms. As an insurer, Munich Re is in the risk business. The company adopts strict risk management processes in all parts of its business, including underwriting, investment and operational areas. A quality control unit interfaces with all other divisions and some global clients.

Novartis refers to its most important mission as discovering, developing, sustainably producing and distributing high-quality medicines that address unmet medical needs. In a 2003 leadership survey, Novartis's leadership style was seen as having become more participative, persuasive and motivating, bringing with it a higher perceived competitiveness of associates, product quality and product development. In addition to voluntary adherence to the ISO9000 series and TQM, Novartis follows the pharmaceutical industry's regulatory quality systems, namely good manufacturing practice, good laboratory practice and good clinical practice.

Porsche's quality is evident in everything it does, starting with the beautifully produced annual report, its renowned vehicles and finally the company's reputation as Germany's leading organization. The company regards its outstanding quality as a crucial success factor in international competition, and designs everything itself to ensure the right quality. Top quality in production is safeguarded through a systematic quality management system, coordinated by a central department reporting directly to the CEO. Continuing improvements to internal structures and processes help the organization maintain its production standards at the highest level.

Rohde & Schwarz commented on its excellent quality record in the radio communications industry thus: 'nobody's perfect and we have to work continually to maintain our standards. It is true, however, that quality and reliability alone are becoming [taken for granted as something] that every vendor has to deliver. Success in the future will depend more than ever before on anticipating the customer's needs through good marketing so that we can deliver a complete solution rather than just boxes ... Not to forget: pushing limits contributes to customers' progress.'

Seele engages in many practices designed to enhance the quality of its glass and steel products, including finishing the insides of parts that are not visible. Quality signs are posted everywhere: 'Seele ... ein Qualitätsbegriff' (Seele ... a quality concept). Drawings and samples are checked at all stages of the process, as are samples of suppliers' products. Prototypes of Seele's own end product are made, against which on-site quality is checked. Furthermore, the company values a clean environment because it enhances work quality. Seele strives to provide quality facilities for its people, including state-of-the-art technology for everyone and a luxurious staff kitchen. This attractive environment encourages informal communication among employees that promotes open knowledge transfer within the firm with the aim of enhancing quality.

Through its chemical products and processes, WACKER is engaged in preserving the world's cultural heritage by placing conservation on a scientific footing. It has established a special department to manage this process.[373] Collaborating with technicians, scientists and skilled tradespersons, WACKER develops chemical products and processes for restoring historic buildings and monuments. By 1997, it had over 2000 restorations to its credit. Well-known examples include Berlin's Brandenburg Gate, Michelangelo's Pieta in Rome, Mozart's birthplace in Salzburg, the Venus de Milo in Paris, the Capitol and the Steuben monument in Washington, Crete's statue of Hadrian, the Moais of Easter Island and the mosaics of Ephesus, Antakya and Istanbul. Clearly, systematic quality assurance measures are essential for handling these world treasures, and WACKER's standards are based on the ISO9000 series. In addition, meticulous planning and the right materials are essential to successful restoration. Silicones, which WACKER started producing over 50 years ago, and their modern derivatives provide masonry protection and strengthening. This is enhanced by specially developed paints to prevent moisture and polluting gases from permeating buildings. In other cases, the decision is taken to replace the original with copies created from WACKER's special molding compounds.

The above examples reveal a strong focus on quality among manufacturing, service and research enterprises. How quality is measured varies, but, where relevant, the Rhineland organizations meet or exceed the relevant ISO standard. Patents, prizes and customer and competitor feedback provide additional quality indices.

SOCIAL AND ENVIRONMENTAL SUSTAINABILITY

The aim is sustainable, competitive organization. (Warren Bennis[374])

It is a tautology to say that, in order to have a future, an organization needs to be sustainable; that is, to survive and prosper over time. However, not all organizations do endure, so it is useful to look closely at those that do. Sustainability requires pursuing economic, ecological and social goals with equal vigor, so that organizational needs align with the needs of the market and society in which an enterprise operates. After all, impoverished, degraded markets offer limited opportunities. This means paying attention to more than financial metrics. It includes measuring long-term success through customer satisfaction ratings, employee morale and turnover, employee skill sets, feedback from suppliers, community and other stakeholders, and environmental impact.[375] It also means measuring organizational renewal and adaptability, along with other key measures. Applied research organizations like Fraunhofer explicitly embrace the mission of working towards the sustainable development of society, industry and the environment, embracing many of these factors.

The concept of corporate social responsibility is still rather vague, with no agreed global standards apart from the Global Reporting Initiative.[376] It appears to cover a wide constituency, emphasizing the welfare and prosperity of stakeholders, including society. However, some argue that the environment should be viewed as simply another stakeholder, while others distinguish environmental responsibility from other forms of social responsibility, as this books does.

The Anglo/US shareholder value approach has been extensively criticized for failing to extend its concept of profits to include social and environmental measures, and for the ruthless approach taken to pursuing myopic financial gain by, for example, lobbying regulators to relax environmental standards.[377] Worryingly UK firms employing fewer than 500 people ranked social and environmental responsibility ninth and tenth, respectively, in a list of 10 issues affecting their businesses.[378] Employee retention, new product development and competitive advantage topped the UK list instead.

Although some Anglo/US organizations do focus on corporate social responsibility and protecting the environment, these considerations become easy targets when cost cutting is required. In a sense, this is 'cheating' society. Sacked employees fall onto social welfare (in countries where it exists). Pollution has to be cleaned up by the community, not the profit-making polluter. Not training young people and not employing older people creates social crises for groups in the community. All become 'someone else's' problem. This is short-sighted because being socially responsible appears to pay off, as Box 5.1 shows.

BOX 5.1   FINANCIAL BENEFITS IN BEING SOCIALLY RESPONSIBLE

Clearly social responsibility 'pays' in many feel-good ways, but does it pay off financially? Is there a business case for companies and investors to engage in socially responsible management and investing? Research from around the world is showing that there is. Being socially responsible brings financial benefits to an organization and its investors. For example, numerous studies show that socially responsible European, UK and US firms match or outperform their counterparts commercially.[379] Socially responsible firms are associated with improved shareholder value among 500 Standard and Poor firms and have been found to outperform their class financially against other indices.[380]

Why might sustainable practices and financial performance be linked? Many reasons can be given, including that sustainable practices reflect good management, often lower costs, and enhance reputation and brand.[381] Sustainable practices can lead to better management of business risks and opportunities that also benefit investors and may make the enterprise less vulnerable to the effects of adverse events. Designing products and operations to be more sustainable also often increases profits and can generate savings through improved processes.[382] These effects create a virtuous cycle in that better performing companies have more resources to invest in sustainable practices, which in turn should make them more robust to external events and more attractive to long-term investors and customers, and hence their market value rises.

About half the top 250 UK companies report on social responsibility. However it is not clear how much of this is genuine as opposed to lip-service. About 75 per cent of employees in these organizations reported not having sufficient opportunities to become involved with charities at work.[383] In a 2004 World Economic Forum survey of the world's 1000 leading global companies, only 6 per cent of CEO respondents perceived sustainability as the most important measure of success for their corporation.[384] It seems that many CEOs are so preoccupied with quarterly returns that they may have relegated the future to the 'too-hard' basket. However, more than 70 per cent of the CEOs surveyed believe that mainstream investors will become increasingly interested in corporate citizen issues.

Sustainability reporting has been more widely accepted in Europe than in the USA.[385] It is common for Rhineland organizations to use a form of balanced scorecard, in which organizational success is measured by indices beyond the mere financial.[386] Communication measurement specialist Rohde & Schwarz, for example, has developed its own expanded balanced scorecard based on six measures relating to products and services, growth earnings, structures, teamwork, customer markets and staff potential. Progress towards these goals is made highly visible to all employees. At BMW, the triple bottom line for measuring its success includes economic, environmental and social goals.[387] Interestingly, high-quality reporting through expanding stakeholder dialog to include many groups is included under economic goals. Another 'economic' goal at BMW is to support sustainability issues.

Some writers question whether financial, environmental and social responsibility go far enough as measures of sustainability. Additional measures could include social inequality, average life expectancy, crime level, population growth rate, consumption of fossil fuels per capita, energy consumption, share of renewable energy resources and access to information.[388] Some of these metrics represent values and objectives consistent with some corporate objectives. Other measures, particularly those in the social equity area, represent quite a stretch for corporate consideration, even in Rhineland countries.

Under the Rhineland model, social and environmental responsibility form basic elements of sustainable development, as does the positive treatment of employees. These elements are only gradually becoming part of the Anglo/US way of doing business, even though heated debate about corporate social and environmental responsibility has been going on for decades. Looking back to the 1970s, Ladd[389] argued that organizations would not go out of their way to avoid environmental pollution unless law, public opinion or other external pressures forced this issue into the organizations' rational decision-making process. Ladd argued that organizations cannot have moral obligations and, hence, cannot have moral responsibilities. He called for finding a third way out of the dilemma between organizational rationality and the need to operate morally within a society.

At the same time, in the USA, Rockefeller was espousing the need for business to balance making a profit with dealing with society's problems. In Rockefeller's view, 'we American businessmen have allowed ourselves to become too absorbed in the problem of learning how to manage and control the awesome technology that has been created by our national genius. We have turned our backs on the larger environment, both physical and social'.[390] Nothing much seems to have changed since the 1970s in this respect, except that the fascination with technology has been replaced by a focus on shareholder value.

Handy[391] argues that the majority of Anglo/US companies perceive environmental and social responsibility as goals for rich organizations only. But all enterprises benefit from a healthy social and environmental context. Supporting Handy's observation is a study showing that few US firms have embraced the principles of sustainable development, leaving a large gap between what society says it needs as sustainable development and how organizations actually practice it.[392] This reticence was evident in the way firms adopted ISO14001, an international environmental management standard aimed at advancing sustainable development in organizations. Interviews with US managers indicated that they resisted the standard because they did not see the benefits outweighing the costs, and believed that their existing environmental systems were adequate.[393] Interestingly, conforming to ISO14001 is widespread among Rhineland organizations, including Allianz, BMW, Kärcher, Munich Re, Novartis, Porsche, Rohde & Schwarz, WACKER and ZF. The US study concluded that most US firms do not know how to respond to sustainable development as a societal issue and US managers will use sustainable practices only when stakeholders insist on sustainable development as the norm.

Pressure is mounting in the Anglo/US world, however. Calls for increased social responsibility are coming from mainstream customers, some business leaders, investors and academics.[394]

The calls are for organizations to embrace social responsibility as part of their overall strategy rather than simply providing lip-service to skin-deep ethics and social values.[395] Irrespective of whether environmental management is part of, or separate from, corporate social responsibility, it has entered the reality of business practice as a silent stakeholder more than broader forms of social responsibility.[396] The environment's rise in importance is linked to the declining quality in air, water and land, and in people's quality of life.[397] The growing importance of the environment is also evident in Anglo/US countries.[398] This is despite a strongly held belief among managers there that they need to pollute and consume diminishing resources to produce their products efficiently.[399]

What defines environmental problems and what the appropriate solutions are have changed over time. The 1970s concept of ecology evolved into modern ideas of waste minimization and management, recycling, pollution protection, product stewardship, eco-efficiency and environmental strategy in the USA and Europe.[400] However, critics argue that just regulating pollution rather than eliminating environmentally damaging behaviors has failed to help the planet much.[401]

Pressures for an increased focus on the environment have come from many sources. In Europe, government regulations and the threat of further legislation have led companies, particularly in Germany, Switzerland and Scandinavia (and also in South Africa), to focus seriously on the environment. This also reflects pressure from society, customers and employees in those countries. In the early 1990s, Germany, a world leader in environmental protection, introduced laws and guidelines banning use of polluting substances and materials, and requiring manufacturers and retailers to take back all packaging. Manufacturers of electronic and electrical goods have to take back and recycle products at the end of their service life. Guidelines also govern factors such as environmental auditing, site registration and the certification of companies involved in disposal or recycling. Much of the compliance with the environment is still voluntary, but many Rhineland companies strive to exceed these obligations in environmental management.

Pressure to focus on the environment in the USA now comes from the financial sector. Some investors make financial decisions based on studies suggesting that environmentally friendly companies perform better financially.[402] Environmentalism is becoming a question of risk management and credit rating. For example, insurance companies put environmental pressures on clients; banks and other financiers impose environmental conditions on firms seeking loans; some consumers consider environmental issues in purchasing decisions. In these and other ways, the trend towards greater emphasis on the environment is translating into more traditional corporate terms of risk management, meeting consumer demands and the cost of capital. This makes it less an external environmental issue than a strategic part of the business.

Despite calls for environmental and social responsibility, many business leaders are unsure about which programs and processes to engage in to benefit society and shareholders.[403] Dunphy[404] has defined six successive phases through which many organizations pass in moving towards sustainability.

1. Rejection: corporations flout government sustainability regulations or mobilize against sustainability initiatives.
2. Non-responsiveness: enterprises focus on short-term profitability, regarding sustainability as irrelevant to their activities.

3. Compliance: the corporation complies with legal requirements and community expectations about employee relations, environmental protection and corporate social responsibility.
4. Efficiency: an organization will pursue opportunities offered by a sustainability focus to create significant efficiencies, such as saving water and energy in production.
5. Strategic proactivity: sustainability is central to business strategy, differentiating a producer from its competitors by acquiring a reputation for excellence in employee management or environmental protection, or by investing in local education to ensure a future supply of educated workers for the business.
6. The sustaining corporation: in addition to providing adequate returns to investors, corporations pursue initiatives designed to create a sustainable world because this is the right thing to do.

The following sections illustrate a range of approaches taken by Rhineland companies to corporate social responsibility and environmental protection. Many of the examples fall around stages 5 and 6 of Dunphy's taxonomy.

Corporate Social Responsibility

Aesculap, the part of the B. Braun Group involved with surgical services and supplies, keenly embraces its responsibility in the area of corporate citizenship. As part of a family-owned enterprise it sees itself as firmly entrenched in, and connected to, society. In the first instance, it articulates a concern to be professionally responsible for customers, employees and the regions in which it works. An example of its commitment to culture and society is the B. Braun Foundation, which fosters events to promote young musicians and sponsor science and universities. The company's Asclepius Museum serves to keep surgical history alive with its impressive collection of over 5000 surgical and medicotechnical items. These include items showing the development of modern medical technology.

Allianz strives to integrate sustainable practices into the core of its insurance business. This includes underwriting, and managing assets and risks. Top management provides active support for this strategy. The company makes the following commitments regarding sustainable approaches to business:

• to support private and business customers in managing risks and making use of technical improvement options,
• to offer staff a healthy working environment,
• to exert its influence as a financial institution operating on the international stage,

- to be the role model for sustainable development among its stakeholders,
- to act as a dependable and fair partner in business,
- to develop into a guarantor of sustainability on the international stage.[405]

For many years, Allianz has made major contributions to the arts, culture, social debate, economic debate, education and science, and historic reconciliation. Visible manifestations of these commitments include the Allianz Environmental Foundation, Allianz Cultural Foundation and a foundation formed to support victims of the holocaust. The company's archivist manages Allianz's museum dedicated to holocaust victims, making explicit its own unsavory role during the Nazi era. Furthermore, senior executives are actively involved in supporting and participating in the reform process in Germany and more broadly in Europe.

BMW's thought and action in all departments is informed by responsibility towards humankind and the environment.[406] Its corporate vision is that of sustainable mobility on a global level, based on the use of hydrogen as a fuel source. This is in addition to sustainability within its local community and plants. BMW seeks transparency and openness with its various stakeholders, making its progress in sustainability visible to all via its sustainability reports. Concrete examples of social responsibility in action at BMW are exemplified by its operations in Thailand. Here its 700-strong protected workforce enjoys health insurance plans, a pension fund, medical treatment facilities, BMW's worldwide standards for industrial safety, shuttle bus service to work and an on-site Buddhist temple. In South Africa, BMW takes an active part in combating AIDS/HIV, including supporting a community counseling center available to all residents near its Rosslyn plant.

Cement manufacturer Holcim asserts its strong commitment to being a global leader in sustainability, including acceptance of social responsibility. A member of the World Council of Sustainable Corporations, in 2002 Holcim prepared its first sustainability report to include such topics as education, hospitals, healthcare and food in emerging countries. Holcim also concerns itself with occupational health and safety as part of its social responsibility. This includes zero tolerance for fatalities at its cement manufacturing sites. Sometimes local partners resist investment in safety because the partners do not share the same vision. Holcim's concept is based on the idea that it has a role within its sphere of influence, mainly in rural communities, and it wants to influence education and health in the neighborhood.

Migros takes its social responsibilities very seriously indeed. This retailer invests 1 per cent of its surplus (about CHF120 million annually) in social activities, running cultural events to benefit the entire community. As part of this, it runs the largest public adult school in Switzerland, charging students only modest fees. It also organized a National Feel Good Day based on fitness, wellness and nutrition as a broad public experience held in many Swiss cities. The objective was simply to promote well-being in the wider Swiss community. Migros sponsors all manner of projects that it sees as socially relevant (dance, film, drama, theater, literature), helping to shape the future. Projects are expected to be flexible and complex, to communicate energy and provide platforms for knowledge to be passed on. Examples reflecting the variety of projects include Think Quest, an internet competition for youth; Sabmeet, presentations from young creative people bridging art and commerce, and concerts for the over-50s. Migros's social responsibility extends to the origin of its products and method of production of goods it sells. The organization's involvement with production allows innovation and sound environmental policy to meet social and environmental objectives.

Pharmaceutical giant Novartis supports a number of foundations, including the Novartis Foundation for Sustainable Development. This promotes autonomous development as a way of improving economic, social and environmental living conditions among the world's poorest people. It supports the Novartis Foundation, a scientific and educational charity, formed in 1949 and located in central London, that promotes scientific excellence; the Novartis Foundation for Gerontology to support healthy aging; and the Novartis Foundation for People and the Environment to improve people's health and to protect the environment. The Apica Foundation is active in Switzerland and supports charitable causes that benefit the general public. Novartis strives to operate in a manner that is sustainable – economically, socially and environmentally – in the best interest of its long-term success. To monitor this, in 2003, over 18 000 associates around the world were surveyed on their opinion and information about compliance with the firm's code of conduct and corporate citizenship policy.

One of chemical concern WACKER's top 10 goals is sustainability, and accordingly the firm is compiling new, binding principles for all employees. The principles not only reflect the three basic pillars of sustainability (social, economic and ecological), but integrate them firmly into company policy. This places the firm at Dunphy's stage 6 of sustainability. WACKER's integrated management system regulates all workflows, competencies and responsibilities for methods and processes under guidelines for quality, environment, safety and health. These certified management systems apply to every business division, and are based on legal regulations, WACKER's voluntary commitment to responsible care and its adherence to global and European standards such as ISO14001, ISOTS16949, ISO9001, QS9000 and SA8000. The integrated environmental management system at WACKER is dynamic, seeking continuous improvement, and is subject to external and internal audits.

Environmental Responsibility

Aesculap regards environmental protection as part of its corporate identity and responsibility to the region, town and future generations. Annually it invests about €500 000 in environmental measures and produces an environmental report. This award-winning manufacturer of surgical instruments has been active in environmental protection since 1987, ahead of government regulations. It has employed a full-time environmental protection officer since 1988. Aesculap's environmental management system provides a tool for executives not only to prevent environmental problems from arising, but to optimize environmental protection by managing risk, costs and benefits, involving cooperation among all parts of the company. Practical examples include the following:

- adoption of a building process-control technology that reduces the peak energy load, leading to energy savings of over 10 per cent;
- cleaning installations converted from chlorinated hydrocarbons to water-based cleaning agents, with no harmful emissions into the air;
- using micro- and nanofiltration and vacuum evaporators, the volume of waste water from plating processes has been reduced from 1500 cubic meters to 420 cubic meters a year;
- reusable packaging for deliveries to and from Malaysia and England has reduced packaging waste; and
- at the Benchmark Factory, environmentally protective measures include less waste through reprocessing and recycling, rationalized use of energy through heat recovery, reduced energy use through regulating energy consumption of installations, and using rainwater and grassing over the external site (to prevent water runoff).

Allianz, a service-oriented insurer, does not affect the environment greatly through its direct operations, but, ISO14001 accreditation standards are met by the various businesses in the German Group. Allianz implements many individual environmental initiatives, including application through the Allianz Environment Foundation. This fund is endowed with over €50 million and, since 1990, has allocated about €35 million to environmental projects. At the local level, Allianz has achieved measurable reductions in heating energy of 10 per cent and in electricity consumption of 13 per cent in some of its offices. E-mail reduced paper consumption in one of its subsidiaries by 22 per cent.

BMW's commitment to the environment is extensive, ranging from reducing or eliminating noise and environmental pollution sources within and outside its various production plants, to enabling its vehicles to be easily recycled at the end of their serviceable lives. Furthermore, BMW assists the environment by product design: for example, changing its products from dependency on fossil fuels to hydrogen fuels, and using lighter-weight materials in its vehicles. Examples of voluntary environmental actions include using sulfur-free fuel in BMW fleet cars, exceeding government requirements for recyclability of its products and using rail transport wherever possible. Recycling is enabled by BMW's network of recycling firms established since 1991, with recycling at BMW assigned only to certified contract partners. All BMW production sites are certified to comply with ISO14001 standards (or the equivalent), ensuring uniform environmental management globally. Approximately 70 employees are involved with environmental management, and annual audits are conducted at each site, yielding an input/output balance. Suppliers are required to adhere to international environmental guidelines as well as to BMW regulations.

Wherever possible, Holcim takes its Swiss environmental standards into all countries in which it makes cement, finding that this improves efficiency and attracts workers, and hence enhances the bottom line. Many environmental measures are in place at this organization. In Switzerland, Holcim dispatches 63 per cent of its products by rail. A major objective is to use by-products or waste from other industries as alternatives to fossil fuels. The extremely high temperatures in cement kilns allow Holcim to make environmentally efficient use of products such as used tires, thereby consuming waste. Cement production requires considerable energy, and Holcim creates 24 per cent of its energy via alternative fuels (thermal and electrical energy, as well as plastic, animal fats, waste oil, tires and dry sewage sludge). Another environmental objective is to use more alternative raw materials, such as materials with natural binding properties, to reduce the proportion of clinker in cement and thus the energy consumed.

Kärcher's attitude towards environmental management forms part of the overall corporate ethos. The company not only sees that its cleaning products need to be environmentally friendly, for example by consuming less water and power, but it actively pursues opportunities to reduce any negative impact on the environment from production. Since 1996, the firm has complied with the requirements of DIN ISO14001 for production, R&D and distribution. The aim is to mitigate and continuously improve the firm's operational impact on the environment and the impact of its products. Water is recycled, waste is reduced and materials are recyclable. In the production plants, the focus is on saving energy, recycling paper and CDs, as well as handling hazardous substances. A new building incorporates a solar power plant in the roof, which contributes 28 000kWh of electricity per year to the national electricity grid, simultaneously reducing an estimated 14 tons of CO_2 emissions. Employees who come to work by train receive 50 per cent of the fare back from their employer; Kärcher provides a battery-charging station for employees' electric cars and holds an annual bicycle competition, in which those who ride to work take part in a year-end draw for a first prize equivalent to the cost of a bicycle. Kärcher provides an environmental information service, which reports on current environmental developments at work and in the home, and provides employees with advice on how to live in an environmentally conscious way. In-house environmental training courses give all employees an opportunity to inform themselves during working hours about the environmental impact of their workplaces. The managing director emphasizes that, even if management were not proactive about environmental protection, the people would create pressure for it, and so at Kärcher there are recycle bins at every workplace.

Munich Re embraces sustainable development as an important issue throughout its insurance business. This is done as part of a belief that investing in environmental protection and other forms of sustainability is a by-product of financial success. Furthermore sustainability reduces legal risks and future litigation costs. Munich Re actively passes on its know-how to clients, politicians and the public as a means of positively influencing risk behavior. The company's shares have been included in the Dow Jones Sustainability World Index and the FTSE4Good index since 2001, and its business operations were accredited under well-known environmental criteria such as those of ISO14001. In addition, the company's own assets are invested primarily in shares or bonds that are represented in one of the leading sustainability indices.

Porsche strives to develop the cleanest possible products and manufacturing processes with a view to their future environmental compatibility. The main objectives are to conserve resources and use them in an economical way, and minimize harmful effects on the environment. The company is ISO14001-certified and has agreed to be audited regularly on a voluntary basis. Annual environmental audits reveal that Porsche's stringent corporate environmental protection has resulted in cost savings per vehicle produced. For example, between 1990 and 2000, water consumption was halved, electricity consumption was reduced by 23 per cent and energy use fell by 36 per cent. During the same period, paint shop emissions were cut by 71 per cent and 83 per cent of total waste was recycled. Export products are transported by rail rather than road, and the Leipzig plant was designed to maximize environmental protection.

WACKER has a long history of environmental monitoring and protection in the chemical industry. It takes a proactive stewardship role in trying to ensure that all its products and production processes conserve raw materials and energy, and minimize emissions, solid waste and wastewater. These environmental standards are applied worldwide because 'environment is environment and we have to look after it'. Suppliers are audited for their compliance with similar standards. The company focuses on the recyclability and biodegradability of its products. Silicone, for example, degrades over a period of 10 years and further research is needed into the impact of silicone on humans and the environment. WACKER actively participates in the Global Silicone Council, sponsoring silicone research and on-going events for researchers worldwide to exchange views. The company's first environmental report was issued in 1989, making it one of the first 10 companies in the world to do this. The company asserts that, because it competes mostly against public companies, its customers expect an equivalent level of reporting.

ZF is regarded as a leader in environmentally responsible operating methods. In 2003, the company spent approximately €60 million on investment and operational measures aimed at reducing this automobile supplier's environmental impact, which it says not only led to cost reductions, but also provided competitive advantage. ZF exceeds legal environmental requirements. Environmental protection is embraced through adherence to ISO14001 certification and the expectation that suppliers and partners will also adhere to these standards. ZF holds staff training in environmental protection measures and every two years publishes an environmental report. ZF's environmental department is located at Head Office and employs two people.

The evidence above shows that environmental and social responsibility play a central role in many Rhineland organizations. Environmental measures provide both competitive advantage and cost savings, in addition to 'being the right thing to do', corresponding to Dunphy's stage 6. Social responsibility is displayed in diverse ways, but is well entrenched in these Rhineland organizations.

This chapter has shown the strong emphasis many Rhineland companies place on their independence from the financial capital markets, particularly the short-term aspects which detract from the long-term perspective that is so central to the Rhineland model. Innovation in products, services and processes is a prominent feature of the case study organizations. Renewal is driven internally with ideas gathered from a wide range of stakeholders: from employees to customers and suppliers. Continuing formal learning gathers the latest information from outside the organization. Developing and retaining its knowledge has a core place in a Rhineland organization. Many of the case study organizations have formal processes in place to capitalize on their people's know-how, experience and learning. Moving away from formal IT management systems, there is a trend towards supporting communities of practice and informal opportunities for employees to share their experiences. Some organizations have specially designed facilities to stimulate this sharing and creativity. Quality is also a core process in Rhineland organizations, be it in services, products, processes or corporate identity. Where relevant, all comply with ISO9001 standards. During visits to these organizations, quality is evident virtually everywhere, but tends to be taken for granted rather than made a feature of, perhaps because quality is central to Rhineland organizations and does not differentiate one from another any longer.

Corporate sustainability in the sense of social and environmental responsibility probably most immediately springs to mind when reading a book on sustainability. We have seen the many different and serious ways in which the case study organizations are approaching their corporate citizenship, and that this brings both financial and non-financial benefits. The relationship between the community and the organization is fundamental to the Rhineland model and is expressed in a variety of ways. Most public companies are ranked at or near the top of their industries on the Dow Jones or other sustainability indexes. However private organizations also display corporate social responsibility, as we have seen. Environmental responsibility is strongly emphasized in all the case study organizations, with formal adherence to ISO14001 standards only part of their response. Office-based and service enterprises as well as manufacturers have implemented a wide range of environmental measures, which bring financial savings and help manage risk – as well as being the right thing to do.

Clearly the elements of the Sustainable Leadership Grid covered in Chapters 3, 4 and 5 do not operate in isolation. The final section in this chapter shows how these elements interact to form a self-reinforcing system.

SELF-REINFORCING SYSTEM

The examples provided in Chapters 3 and 4, together with the elements discussed above in this chapter, show that Rhineland organizations are far from being clones of each other in their leadership, culture or business operations. Yet they have common features that distinguish them dramatically from the Anglo/US approach based on shareholder value.

Looking more closely at the 19 elements in the Sustainable Leadership Grid suggests that these features align to create an overall system. Key elements are the long-term perspective, broad stakeholder focus and, commonly, a fierce desire to remain independent of the financial markets. In such a context, corporate social responsibility and environmental protection emerge as serious concerns, along with developing long-term relations with customers, suppliers, the local community and broader society and, above all, with employees. This focus becomes associated with ethical beliefs, developing and retaining a highly-skilled workforce and a need for innovation and knowledge-sharing processes within a strong culture and shared values. In turn, teams support these sharing processes, as does investing heavily in developing managers from within the organization. Teamwork and retaining staff support knowledge management as well.

All this requires a strong vision and strategy, preferably with stable senior leadership supported by the input of many experts throughout the organization. With Rhineland CEOs being just members of management teams, the elected speaker of the group, it is difficult for CEO leadership cults to develop. This speaker often has a finite tenure and, in any case, is expected to adopt a consensual decision-making style with his or her peers. Given the expertise and knowledge dispersed throughout the organization, consensual decision making is likely to enhance the quality of decisions. The downside is that consultation takes time, although this is not inevitable. Under their long-term planning horizon and conditions of workforce stability and stakeholder support, Rhineland organizations allow time for consultation and careful consideration before making major changes. They also strive for high-quality outcomes, necessary to satisfy their customers and fuel employee pride in their workmanship.

Quality outcomes in turn improve the firm's innovativeness and competitiveness, and hence its reputation. To achieve all this, a basic tenet of the Rhineland model is making people a priority, which with a trained and loyal workforce enhances the sustainability of the enterprise by, for example, making mutual sacrifices in difficult times.

In a similar way, the Anglo/US model also forms an integrated system aligned with a focus on short-term shareholder value. It becomes difficult to invest in long-term strategies, plans, projects and people when most of the effort is going into the next quarterly profit. Not having long-term investments and obligations to staff enables rapid reorienting of the enterprise in response to changed environments. To achieve this flexibility, CEOs need extensive solo power, and using this power supports a hero cult at the top. Stakeholder relationships are difficult to maintain when decisions need to be made in favor of shareholders, and when organizational members come and go. Importing managers and new staff brings new ideas, along with the skills of newcomers at no cost to the employer.

However, importing too many outsiders makes it difficult to establish and maintain a strong vision and set of values. This also undermines development of a strong culture and a pervasive sense of ethics throughout the organization. High quality and excellence are difficult to maintain with staff coming and going and not being committed to the organization. It is difficult to achieve excellence with a non-loyal and often poorly educated workforce that possesses generic skills, but not necessarily those directly related to the firm's needs. Exercising corporate and environmental responsibility is often seen as deflecting an enterprise from short-term goals and decreasing shareholder value. However this becomes more relevant when recast in rational terms of risk management and attracting staff and investors. An antagonistic relationship with unions is considered the price of being able to 'downsize' and cut costs quickly. All this is reinforced by manager rewards tied to short-term stock performance. As we have seen, many executives and academics are recognizing the pitfalls in the Anglo/US system and calling for change.

Given the Rhineland model's effectiveness in underpinning sustainable organizations, and the solid support its principles enjoy from leading researchers, thinkers and practitioners, why is it not the center of attention? One reason could lie in the fact that the elements in the Rhineland and the Anglo/US models align to form two separate systems. As the above examples show, the elements within each system reinforce one another, making it seemingly difficult for individual elements to operate alone. This could make it hard to change isolated parts of either system. We are stuck in the system we have inherited.

Yet, as we have seen at the beginning of each of the previous sections in Chapters 3, 4 and 5, Anglo/US management writers are calling for companies to adopt each of the elements of the Sustainable Leadership Grid. Are they just ivory tower philosophers divorced from reality? Is it something for businesses in the control of founding families rather than for public companies? Let us take a closer look at the case study organizations that are not family-owned to see how closely they conform to the Rhineland end of the Sustainable Leadership Grid.

RHINELAND PUBLIC COMPANIES

Major challenges in adopting Rhineland principles confront public companies that operate under pressure to please analysts and external investors. These organizations rarely have the benefit of patient shareholders, as private businesses do. This section examines European enterprises that are owned by outsiders and are not family or founder-influenced.

Table 5.1 summarizes where the non-family Rhineland businesses (Allianz, Fraunhofer, Migros, Munich Re, Novartis and ZF) stand on Rhineland criteria. Three of these enterprises are publicly listed global corporations: Allianz, Munich Re and Novartis, long since removed from their founders. The table shows that these firms conform to the Rhineland model, ranging between 16 and 19 elements. Munich Re provides an example of a publicly listed corporation that conforms to *all* the Rhineland criteria in the Sustainable Leadership Grid.

On 14 dimensions, all six non-family companies conform to the Rhineland model. They deviate only on the CEO concept, challenging the financial markets, having a strong organizational culture, self-governing teams and

Table 5.1 Non-family Rhineland organizations compared with the Sustainable Leadership Grid

Rhineland elements on the Sustainable Leadership Grid	Allianz	Fraunhofer	Migros	Munich Re	Novartis	ZF
CEO concept: top team speaker	✓	—	✓	✓	?	✓
Decision making: consensual	✓	✓	✓	✓	✓	✓
Ethical behavior: an explicit value	✓	✓	✓	✓	✓	✓
Financial markets: challenge them	— balance	NA	NA	✓	?	NA
Innovation: strong	✓	✓	✓	✓	✓	✓
Knowledge management: shared	✓	✓	✓	✓	✓	✓
Long-term perspective: yes	✓	✓	✓	✓	✓	✓
Management development: grow own	—	✓	✓	✓	✓	✓
Organizational culture: strong	✓	✓	✓	✓	✓	✓
People priority: strong	✓	✓	✓	✓	✓	✓
Quality: high is a given	✓	✓	✓	✓	✓	✓
Retaining staff: strong	✓	✓	✓	✓	✓	✓
Skilled workforce: strong	✓	✓	✓	✓	✓	✓
Social responsibility: strong	✓	✓	✓	✓	✓	✓
Environmental responsibility: strong	✓	✓	✓	✓	✓	✓
Stakeholders: broad focus	✓	✓	✓	✓	✓	✓
Teams: self-governing	✓	✓	✓	✓	✓	✓
Uncertainty and change: considered process	✓	✓	?	✓	?	✓
Union–management relations: cooperation	✓	✓	✓	✓	✓	✓
Total elements in conformity	18	17	17	19	16	18

Note: ✓ = conforms; — = does not conform; ? = not known; NA = not applicable.

145

union–management relations. Most of these deviations occur through inapplicability or lack of information. However, Allianz's merging with Dresdner Bank and other firms would account for some dilution in its culture, although insiders say that the gap is narrowing. No information was available on self-governing teams at customer-owned Migros. Challenging the financial markets was not relevant to the three organizations 'owned' by their members or a city. For Allianz, conformity to the capital markets no doubt grew out of the fact that much of its business derives from these markets. No information was available for Novartis on CEO concept, financial markets or union–management relations.

Of the remaining non-family enterprises, ZF started as a family business and, although no longer influenced by the founding family, it displays all relevant Rhineland characteristics. The financial markets criterion does not apply because the company is owned by the city of Friedrichshafen. Although Fraunhofer's origins are not rooted in a founding family, it still reflects all but one relevant Rhineland element. The exception relates to the CEO concept, because the current president has stated a desire to operate more as a decision-making CEO rather than as the speaker of the top team. Structural constraints within Fraunhofer and the independence of the many research institutes may make it difficult for him to do so.

From the above, it is clear that some public companies in Europe reflect Rhineland leadership practices. This shows that it is possible to combine being publicly owned with sustainable leadership practices. The next chapters continue this theme, showing how Rhineland elements work in both public and private organizations based in countries outside Germany and Switzerland, including the Anglo/US world.

PART III

Beyond the Rhineland

European capitalism has a vitality and dynamism wholly disallowed by the con-servative consensus ... as capitalist enterprises they conduct themselves very differently from their American competitors (Will Hutton[407])

6. Scandinavian, South African and family businesses

The Sustainable Leadership Grid was derived from German and Swiss organizations, where even publicly owned companies display many of its elements. However, Rhineland leadership is also found in other parts of the world. This chapter begins with examples from public corporations in Scandinavia and South Africa. Then the focus shifts to family businesses in different parts of the world. This is because many of the Rhineland organizations described in Part II are fully or partly owned by the founders or their descendants. Could the involvement in corporate decision making of the founding family make a difference to the way an enterprise is led? Evidence presented in the second part of this chapter suggests that it does. The case of SAS, the largest privately held software company in the world, illustrates a close fit with Rhineland leadership principles.

SCANDINAVIAN COMPANIES

This section describes companies from two Scandinavian countries: Finland and Sweden. To place the discussion in context, Box 6.1 provides some background on these two countries.

BOX 6.1   BACKGROUND ON FINLAND AND SWEDEN

Together with Denmark, Norway and Iceland, Finland and Sweden are often referred to as the Nordic lands or Scandinavia. All five countries have a largely common history and identity, which includes strong collective and egalitarian values. Nordic countries are said to be struggling to reconcile their national identity, in which they see themselves as being better (and richer) than Europe, with becoming members of the EU.[408]

Quality of life is higher in Nordic regions than in most other countries when measured by wealth, political stability, generous social welfare

---

and foreign aid programs, low crime and high standard of living. According to *Forbes Magazine*,[409] in 2003 a United Nations survey ranked the Nordic countries the best places to live in the world, on the basis of factors like education, democracy, income and public health. As a group, Nordic people are the happiest in their jobs and women enjoy more equal treatment with men than women anywhere else.[410] However, this idyll is being challenged. The populations are aging because of high life expectancy and low birth rates, which is expected to strain the highly successful Nordic social welfare states. The homogenous culture is also facing social changes due to an influx of immigrants.

Sweden retains a low-key monarchy. Home to 9 million people and a member of the EU, Sweden has resisted adopting the euro. The government plays a major role in the economy. It employs about 34 per cent of the workforce and accounts for 55 per cent of GDP. The slow growth of the Swedish economy has been partly attributed to high government involvement.[411] Gradually the official unemployment rate has fallen to 4 per cent. Germany and the USA are Sweden's largest export markets, but services form the major growth sector in the economy. The Wallenberg family, a powerful industrial dynasty in Swedish business, controls corporations with a combined market value of over US$100 billion. Wallenbergs hold over 40 per cent of the market capitalization of the Stockholm Stock Exchange through their main industrial holding company, Investor.

The Republic of Finland has a population of about 5 million. Finland was an early member of the EU and has adopted the euro. Its economy is considered the most competitive after America,[412] but reducing the 9 per cent employment rate is crucial to preparing the Finnish economy for the impact of an aging population. The economy depends largely on its information and communications technology sector, thanks to the world's leading mobile telephone handset producer, Nokia, and related companies.

Atlas Copco: First in Mind: First in Choice[413]

Founded in 1873 as a railway equipment manufacturer and seller, Atlas Copco AB has grown into a global industrial group. Headquartered in Stockholm, Sweden, it operates in over 150 countries. Sweden's Wallenberg family has been associated with Atlas Copco since its inception, with Peter Wallenberg chairman of the board until his retirement in 1996. Wallenbergs are still represented on the board of directors via their holding company, Investor. Although no longer in management roles, Wallenbergs control 21 per cent of voting rights and represent 15 per cent of capital. However, at the end of 2003, this public company was owned by over 37 000 other shareholders.

Revenues for 2003 exceeded US$6.1 billion, reflecting over 13 per cent annual growth generated by about 26 000 employees.[414] While seeking to become the preferred company for investors, Atlas Copco does not perceive any significant pressure or conflict from the financial markets in achieving its long-term perspectives. It aims to create and continually increase shareholder value by delivering innovative and competitive solutions to customers.

The Group develops and manufactures electric and pneumatic tools, compressed air equipment, assembly systems and construction and mining equipment. In addition, it offers equipment rental and service. Atlas Copco's vision is to be a leader in each business. It wants to be first in mind and first choice for customers because customers perceive the best value at this company. Three strategies help realize this vision.

- *Growth* secures long-term profitability and is achieved through new products, new market niches and creative use of products. The company strives for 8 per cent annual revenue growth, an operating margin of 15 per cent, and continuous enhancement of its efficiency.[415]
- *Development* through continuous improvement in operations and products, as well as innovative business concepts and technologies.
- *Multiple brands* that differentiate Atlas Copco products and services using market and customer needs. The Group owns over 20 distinct brands, each adding to revenues and profit.

Operations revolve around three core values of interaction, commitment and innovation, which have formed the company's past, created the present and help guide its future. For Atlas Copco, the core values provide a competitive advantage in maintaining its leadership position, even in changing environments:

- *Interaction* refers to listening to the needs of customers and other stakeholders (including the environment), thereby leading to innovative solutions. Interaction requires knowledge, presence, flexibility and involvement in stakeholder processes. One reason rentals are valued is that they allow employees to get close to customers.
- *Commitment* includes making people a priority and promoting long-term relationships, thus adding value to customers' businesses. Atlas Copco is committed to staying in long-term relationships with customers and business partners in its markets. This drives its focus on high-quality products and keeping promises.

- *Innovative* spirit is central to the Atlas Copco way of doing business. The firm regards innovation as the ultimate driver of long-term profitability and growth. For example, Internet technologies now support all business areas in matters related to people, products and customers.

The Group strives to lead in environmental protection in its industry. All processes, including administration, distribution and production, take account of environmental preservation. In this way, the Group believes it is best serving the interests of customers, employees, shareholders and the communities in which it operates. The firm aims to have all relevant subsidiaries ISO14001-certified, in addition to requiring them to comply with all local environmental legislation and regulations. This commitment extends beyond words. It includes training all employees in environmental impacts and practices, designing products to minimize impact on the environment, advising customers on the environmental effects of Atlas Copco products and services, monitoring suppliers in this regard and producing an annual sustainability report, which is sometimes included in the annual report.

At Atlas Copco, social responsibility refers to the impact of a company's activities on society and stakeholders, including employees, customers, business partners and local communities. In the absence of internationally accepted social indicators, Atlas Copco measures social performance in its own way. Social measures include employee mobility and performance, occupational health and safety, and reaching its goal of 40 hours' training and development per employee per year (the average was 37 hours in 2003). The Group is strong on other forms of social responsibility as well, typically conducted at the local level. For example, in Sweden, employees collect funds to support drilling for, and providing, clean drinking water in parts of the world where this is a problem. The Group then matches employees' donations. In Zambia the local sales company supports various school programs, and in South Africa the company sponsors university students and an extensive HIV/AIDS program for employees and their spouses. Atlas Copco is consistently represented on the Dow Jones Sustainability World Index.

Although strongly decentralized, Atlas Copco ensures that new employees Group wide receive a solid orientation to their job, team, company, business area and the Group itself. Employee development includes on-the-job experience and being given real responsibility from day one, continuing feedback and training, and opportunities to work on local and international projects. Job mobility is actively encouraged because it allows people to develop over the longer term, and all vacant positions throughout the Group are advertised internally. About 1200 salaried employees have taken advantage of this opportunity since 2000.

As an employer, Atlas Copco promotes itself as an over 125-year-old company with brand-new ideas for helping customers achieve results. The firm strives to be an attractive workplace through its core values, especially innovation, as well as its focus on leading edge technology, customers and ambitious growth targets. Achievement and performance are rewarded, and employees have considerable freedom to perform, while being held account-able for their actions. Creativity is valued along with pragmatism, openness, fairness and honesty, and a balanced lifestyle within a professional and caring family culture. Relationships with unions vary from country to country, but are generally regarded as constructive. In Sweden, relationships are consid-ered very cooperative, and four local union representatives sit on the Atlas Copco board.

Knowledge sharing is regarded as a key part of personal development and is rewarded. The Group fosters a learning environment, and supports this through extensive training and international opportunities, and by aiming to promote 80 per cent of managers from inside. In 2003, 10 per cent of staff appointments were from outside the Group, and 9 per cent left the Group.

The decentralized culture pushes decision making down to the local level. It encourages managers to delegate to employees wherever possible, includ-ing delegation to teams. However, whether the teams are manager-led or self-governing depends on the location. This local focus means that the firm is continually adapting to changing environments and making improvements. The culture requires that radical change is carefully considered.

Atlas Copco's close fit with the Rhineland model is shown in Table 6.1, where it conforms broadly to 16 criteria. The company regards the CEO as the ultimate decision maker who leads by example and takes an active and visible role in promoting the culture to employees. Team leadership varies from country to country and the company takes a balanced approach to the financial markets.

Nokia: Connecting People[416]

The origins of Nokia date back to 1865, first in the forest industry and later in rubber and cable works. In 1967, the three businesses merged to form the Nokia Corporation. From the early 1980s, Nokia gradually shifted into the telecommunications and consumer electronics markets, becoming the largest Scandinavian company in that branch by the 1990s. It focused on telecom-munications and divested itself of its other industry operations. The rest is history, as this Nordic company became the global leader in manufacturing mobile phones and aims for the top of the mobile Internet market.

Speed and flexibility in decision making are enhanced through a flat, networked organizational structure. Nokia has four main divisions: mobile

Table 6.1   Nordic and South African companies compared with Rhineland criteria on the Sustainable Leadership Grid

Rhineland elements on the Sustainable Leadership Grid	Atlas Copco	Nokia	Alexander Forbes	SABMiller
Country of headquarters	Sweden	Finland	South Africa	South Africa
CEO concept: top team speaker	—	?	?	?
Decision making: consensual	✓	✓	?	?
Ethical behavior: an explicit value	✓	✓	✓	✓
Financial markets: challenge them	— balance	✓	?	?
Innovation: strong	✓	✓	✓	✓
Knowledge management: shared	✓	✓	✓	?
Long-term perspective: yes	✓	✓	✓	✓
Management development: grow their own	✓	✓	✓	?
Organizational culture: strong	✓	✓	✓	✓
People priority: strong	✓	✓	✓	✓
Quality: high is a given	✓	✓	✓	?
Retaining staff: strong	✓	✓	?	?
Skilled workforce: strong	✓	✓	✓	✓
Social responsibility: strong	✓	✓	✓	✓
Environmental responsibility: strong	✓	✓	✓	?
Stakeholders: broad focus	✓	✓	✓	✓
Teams: self-governing	— varies	?	?	?
Uncertainty and change: considered process	✓	?	?	?
Union–management relations: cooperation	✓	✓	?	✓
Total elements in conformity	16	16	12	10

Note: ✓ = conforms; — = does not conform; ? = not known.

154

phones, multimedia, networks and enterprise solutions (wireless systems for business). The year 2003 was a record one for the mobile phone industry with volume growth of 16 per cent. Nokia achieved record profits and sales volumes from its 51 359 employees. Net sales turnover in 2003 was over €29 billion, down slightly from 2002, but yielding a 5 per cent increase in profits over 2002. Its one-year sales growth was 17.5 per cent.[417] Nokia innovates constantly while maintaining its stable culture, investing €3.76 billion in R&D in 2003. This was 23 per cent more than in the previous year.

Although Nokia publishes traditional financial measures, it focuses heavily on three success factors: customer satisfaction, operations efficiency and engaging its people. It is noteworthy that the long-serving top team does not receive excessive salaries and benefits.[418] Employee engagement is a vital factor for the company. Nokia's Employee Value Proposition contains four elements designed to motivate, engage and maintain employee satisfaction and well-being: Nokia way and values, performance-based rewards, professional and personal growth, and work–life balance.

The 2003 measurement system for monitoring company culture included employee opinion surveys, focus groups and gathering employee demographics. Diversity, occupational health and safety, and equal employment opportunity are all features of the program, along with opportunities for health and fitness, and personal and professional growth.

The strong culture is characterized by good communications embracing a shared vision and goals, shared knowledge, openness, speed and integrity. Nokia's four corporate values are as follows:

- *customer satisfaction* – anticipating customer needs and providing high-quality solutions, products and services;
- *respect* – for one another and stakeholders, open communication;
- *achievement* – performance starts with individual professionals who care;
- *renewal* – continuous willingness to change, passion for innovation, looking for new ideas and ways of working.

According to the chairman and CEO, Jorma Ollila, 'by conducting business in a responsible way, Nokia can make a significant contribution to sustainable development, at the same time building a strong foundation for economic growth'.[419] Corporate responsibility at Nokia involves acknowledging that the business has an impact on society and the environment, and responding appropriately. The company has adopted common reporting criteria for its many social and environmental activities. Nokia actively supports projects designed to bring mobile communications to emerging economies, such as Russia, India and the Philippines. Over 100 000 young people have participated in Nokia's 'Make a Connection' program in 16 countries, which aims at improving life skills amongst youth. Volunteering among Nokia employees grew from 23 to 28 programs in 2003. Environmental factors are integrated into programs that cover the entire Nokia product life cycle from design to disposal. Nokia was ranked first in its industry sector on the 2003 Dow Jones Sustainability Index, is listed on the FTSE4Good index, and has received a wide range of awards for social and environmental responsibility.

The aim is to make communication with stakeholders part of everyday Nokia business. Stakeholders include consumers and network operators, partners and suppliers, employees, shareholders and investors, academics, the media, non-governmental organizations, consumer associations, governments and authorities. The company is proactive in communicating with different interest groups. For example, suppliers undergo a development process that includes training in ethical issues and attending 'Supplier Days' to meet senior management. 'Investor Days' are held twice a year, when senior management communicates extensively with investors. Union membership tends to cover about 95 per cent of the Finnish workforce, which makes cooperation with unions an essential part of corporate behavior.

The company has been recognized for its ethical performance. For Nokia, ethics make business sense by helping to minimize risk, ensure legal compliance, increase efficiency and build its reputation among stakeholders. Business units are encouraged to discuss the firm's code of conduct, which complements the Nokia values.

Nokia's distinctive management and leadership approach 'creates commitment, passion and inspiration through collaboration and coaching, and ensures focus and efficiency by setting targets, fulfilling goals and reviewing results. Personal growth through self-leadership provides the foundation for successful management and leadership practices. Employees are encouraged to be responsible for their own development and to take advantage of the various development opportunities available'.[420] The firm provides extensive management and leadership development programs.

Nokia's fit with 16 elements of the Rhineland model is shown in Table 6.1. No information is available on three criteria: the CEO concept, attitude to radical change and self-governing teams. However the emphasis on self-leadership at Nokia suggests that this leadership style could extend to teams. Regarding change, Nokia is a telecommunications company in a fast-paced industry. This fast pace is likely to require Nokia to have a culture of rapid adjustment to its environment. Many proponents of the Anglo/US model would be surprised to learn that it is possible to lead the world in this sector while operating on Rhineland principles.

SOUTH AFRICAN COMPANIES

South Africa provides what for some people is a surprising example of the way companies operating there are expected to consider social justice. Directors are expected to balance the interests of shareholders and other stakeholders as part of their corporate governance. The reasons for this are explained in Box 6.2, which provides a brief political and economic background on South Africa, and then describes the King Reports on corporate governance. Alexander Forbes and SABMiller show how two public corporations in South Africa conform to the Rhineland model.

BOX 6.2   SOUTH AFRICA: BACKGROUND AND KING REPORTS

The 45 million people in South Africa enjoyed full democracy in 1994 when they held the first all-race elections. The ruling African National Congress (ANC) won its third five-year term in the April 2004 general election. President Thabo Mbeki has expanded the Mandela government's market-oriented policies, implementing more privatization, public sector restructuring and economic growth. Government policy focuses particularly on black economic empowerment, correcting social imbalances and job creation within a disciplined financial framework.

Unemployment is high, officially around 30 per cent in 2002, but unofficially estimated at 40 per cent, according to the Economist Intelligence Unit. This has contributed to South Africa's being one of the most unequal countries in the world in terms of how income is distributed. Incomes range from the high affluence comparable to anywhere else in the developed world to levels of poverty associated with developing countries. Well known for its precious metals, fruit and wine, South Africa's traditional economy dominated by mining and agriculture has shifted. Manufacturing and financial services now contribute the larger share of GDP. However gold still accounts for over one-third of exports. Services contribute most to GDP, particularly in the financial, tourism and retail sectors.

King Reports: South Africa is regarded as a leader in corporate governance, that is, in the way corporations are run and how the balance between the interests of the organization and its various stakeholders are managed. In 1994, the first King Report on corporate governance appeared, incorporating a code of corporate practices and conduct. The report was named after the former High Court judge, Mervyn King, who headed the committee that produced the report.

The committee aimed at promoting the highest standards of corporate governance, and in many ways it set a benchmark for the rest of the world. The report advocated that companies should take a balanced approach to the interests of a wide range of stakeholders. In 2002, this ground-breaking report was updated in a second report, known as King 2.

King 2 moves away from focusing on profit for shareholders to a triple bottom line, covering the economic, environmental and social aspects of a company's activities. The report recognizes that the relationship between a company and its stakeholders should be mutually beneficial, while acknowledging that a company needs to make a profit to be of interest to many of its stakeholders. The report points out a growing recognition that developing an atmosphere of trust will enable companies to survive crises better through enhanced goodwill from stakeholder groups. Among other things this requires transparency, fairness, taking responsibility and being accountable for actions.

The King report also acknowledges that corporate governance reflects the values of the society within which it operates. South African values include collectivism, consensus and consultation, humility and support towards others, coexistence with others, trust and belief in fairness, and a high standard of ethics. These values underlie Rhineland societies as well.

Adherence to the King 2 corporate governance code is essentially voluntary, except that, since 2003, the Johannesburg Securities Exchange requires all companies listed with it to comply with King 2, as well as disclosing their social and environmental performance following Global Reporting Initiative guidelines.

Alexander Forbes Group Pty Ltd: Investing in the Future[421]

Alexander Forbes is a leading provider of financial and risk services to specialist groups and individual clients. With over 6000 employees active in more than 30 countries, South-African based Alexander Forbes is the world's tenth largest insurance broker. This public company also has considerable operations in the UK. The company brokers insurance and reinsurance, manages risk and insurance programs and claims, and provides healthcare and asset consulting, along with other financial services. Clients come primarily from small and medium-sized businesses, specialist groups and individuals.

The company aims to be an independent, fast-growing provider of services in the business area. Financial results support its fast growth. In 2003, operational revenue was US$610.6 million, up 15 per cent from the previous year. Operating profit (US$61 million) increased by 19 per cent over 2002. This performance was achieved across all regions and businesses in a difficult business environment for the insurance industry.[422]

The board subscribes to ethical principles and good business practices, as contained in the 2002 King 2 Report (see Box 6.2). Company philosophy is to conduct its affairs with uncompromising honesty, integrity, diligence and professionalism. Staff at every level are expected to adhere to the highest ethical standards.

The firm's 2003 Sustainability and Corporate Social Investment report focuses on the South African operations and is based on international best practice. The board is responsible for ensuring that sustainable economic, social and environmental practices are incorporated into all parts of the business. Being a knowledge-based firm, the environmental impact of Alexander Forbes's business is relatively limited. However, facilities management and cleaning contracts require compliance with best practice environmental standards. Further environmental measures include recycling paper and printer cartridges, and donating unused furniture and obsolete computers to educational institutions or community groups for re-use.

The firm invests widely in social projects. Through various trusts, it assists organizations working with elderly women, children, people suffering from life-threatening diseases such as HIV/AIDS, and those who require healthcare assistance.

A broad range of stakeholders and long-term relationships play major roles at Alexander Forbes. The firm's mission is stated thus: 'We build long-term relationships with clients, with insurers, with reinsurers and with investment managers. In every relationship we act with honesty and integrity.'[423] The company describes itself as passionate about its customers, to whom its members listen carefully. Staff are expected to commit themselves to excellent client service and this is continuously monitored. Other objectives include building long-term relationships with clients, suppliers and industry regulators, and delivering sustainable superior returns to shareholders, with whom the group regularly communicates. In 2002, Alexander Forbes won the Investment Analysts Society award for reporting and communication.

The firm employs professionals whose skills are shared worldwide using leading-edge technology. Employee remuneration is performance-based, and the human resource (HR) systems enable employees and their managers to take responsibility for personal growth and development within the organization. The firm strives to exceed legal requirements when investing in employees' development. Innovation is encouraged through the firm's focus on 'innovative, fast, and efficient service by empowered local management in every region in which we operate'.[424]

Alexander Forbes conforms to 12 elements in the Sustainable Leadership Grid (see Table 6.1). No information was available about the other elements: CEO concept, consensual decision making, attitude to the financial markets, staff retention, self-governing teams, radical change management or union–management relations. Given the investment in developing people at Alexander Forbes, it is likely that the focus is on retaining staff, although staff turnover figures were not available.

SABMiller plc: Brewing Corporate Values[425]

Founded in 1895, South African Breweries (SAB) was listed on the Johannesburg Securities Exchange as the first industrial share in 1897. One year later, it was listed on the London Stock Exchange. Over 100 years later, it was a FTSE 100 stock, renamed SABMiller plc. In 2002, SABMiller plc was formed after SAB plc acquired the Miller Brewing Company, the USA's second-largest brewery by volume. The acquisition made SABMiller the second-largest brewer in the world. The company has ventured into diverse businesses over the years, but in 1997 it sold off or closed non-core operations in order to brew beer and make wines, spirits and fruit drinks, as well as bottle Coca-Cola and Schweppes drinks. It also retained strategic investments in hotels and gaming.

In 2003, turnover was about US$8.3 billion, an increase of 18.2 per cent on 2002.[426] Earnings per share were up 11 per cent. International operations accounted for 42 per cent of group turnover by 2001. Employees numbered over 42 400 in 2003, working in 40 countries.

SABMiller's mission is to meet the aspirations of customers through quality products and services, and to share the wealth and opportunities generated fairly among all stakeholders. In this way, the Group fulfills its goals of growing and maximizing long-term shareholder value while behaving in a socially responsible and progressive manner. In 1998, the company's first corporate citizenship review was published, reflecting a serious commitment to the natural environment and HIV/AIDS sufferers. Independent assessors have judged SAB sustainability reports as among the top 10 sustainability reports in the world, although assessors commented that training, diversity and occupational health and safety needed improving in 2003.[427] Nonetheless, that year, SABMiller ranked equal first in the beverages industry on the Dow Jones Sustainability Index. During the financial year ending March 2003, SABMiller companies invested US$13 million (1.7 per cent of pre-tax profits) in local communities.

The Group's non-negotiable values and principles include integrity, honesty, responsibility to society and ethical corporate governance. Individual operating companies may specify additional standards, but the following agreed company principles govern relationships with stakeholders:[428]

- conducting business with integrity,
- supporting mutually beneficial and enduring relationships with stake-holders,
- seeking to be open and accurate in dealings and communication,
- respecting the rights and dignity of individuals,
- optimizing wealth creation to provide fair reward and recognition for stakeholders,
- meeting the changing needs of customers and consumers by providing consistently high-quality brands and services,
- being a responsible corporate citizen,
- respecting the values and cultures of the communities in which it operates.

The principles address different stakeholders. For example, for shareholders, SABMiller is committed to increasing long-term shareholder value, exceeding that achieved on comparable investments. It is committed to an open governance process, which protects the sustainable value and reputation of the company by managing the business effectively, complying with legal requirements and best practice in governance. The company seeks to maximize total shareholder return and to communicate with all its investors regularly and openly, providing reliable and timely information about the company. It seeks business partners who share the firm's values. Another example relates to customers/consumers, for whom SABMiller provides brands and services of consistently high quality and value. It is also committed to providing products that are safe for their intended use, and to advertising and promoting its products in an honest and ethical manner, respecting local social values.

The company aims for continuous improvement by encouraging employees at all levels to be creative, innovative and open to new ideas.

SABMiller's relative fit with the Rhineland model is shown in Table 6.1, where all 10 elements for which there was information correspond. The unknown elements are: CEO concept, consensual decision making, attitudes to the financial markets, knowledge management, management development, staff retention and skilling, self-governing teams and change management.

Summary

The above examples illustrate how large, successful corporations from different sectors and countries reflect many Rhineland leadership values and behaviors, based on available information. The two Scandinavian enterprises, Atlas Copco and Nokia, each reflect 16 of the Sustainable Leadership Grid elements. Less complete information was available about the South African corporations but, even so, they display 12 (Alexander Forbes) and 10

(SABMiller) Rhineland criteria respectively. This represents 100 per cent conformity to Rhineland elements for which information was available among the South African firms. All these organizations show that sustainable leadership principles can be applied in successful public companies located outside Germany and Switzerland. In the next section, we look at what research shows about leadership in family businesses from different countries.

FAMILY BUSINESSES

Family businesses are found all over the world. Some scholars regard them as a viable alternative to the Anglo/US model because they are freed from an enforced emphasis on shareholder value and the short term – and some experts even consider that family businesses generally are at the cutting edge of corporate performance.[429] Perhaps this is because of predictions that the economy will shift from a focus on large corporations to smaller, entrepreneurial businesses. However, others dispute that family businesses are superior to large firms in their management and practices.[430]

Like any other form of enterprise, family businesses are not all perfect and some can be terrible places to work. Nonetheless, given that family businesses play a substantial role in many economies, it is useful to see how these businesses are typically led, and to compare their practices with the Sustainable Leadership Grid. This section looks at some of the research into family businesses, mainly in Europe and the Anglo/US world, and concludes with a more detailed look at one example, the US software company SAS.

Defining a family business is not easy. For the purposes of this book, family business includes family-owned private enterprises and family-controlled or family-influenced public companies. Non-family businesses mean all other public firms.[431] The term 'family' also includes founders. Under this definition, Dell, Marriott, Microsoft and Nordstrom are family-run public companies, even though they combine professional and family management and have multiple shareholders. These four major corporations retain the founder's strong influence at the top. Michael Dell heads Dell; Bill Marriott chairs the Marriott Group; Bill Gates and Steve Ballmer, the first business manager hired by Gates, and now CEO, are still at Microsoft; and Nordstroms run their family firm once again. The Scandinavian and South African examples provided in this chapter are all public companies. One of Atlas Copco's founding families, the Wallenbergs, still has a representative on the board. However, according to company sources, that person's association with Atlas Copco is like that of any other board member.

Among the Rhineland case study organizations covered in Part II, Allianz, Fraunhofer, Migros, Munich Re, Novartis and ZF are classified as non-family businesses; WACKER is a family and corporate owned private company; BMW, Holcim and Porsche are partially public companies still associated with the founding family (sometimes as major shareholder); leaving Aesculap, Kärcher, Loden-Frey, Rohde & Schwarz and Seele as family or founder-run businesses.

Compared with their economic significance and prevalence, family businesses have not generated a great deal of research.[432] The available evidence suggests, however, that family-run enterprises from different countries reflect many common elements of sustainable leadership, as shown in Table 6.2. For example, family businesses typically strive for independence, like Rhineland companies. They often resist entering the financial capital markets, preferring insider ownership by 'friendly' banks and companies. Research into 427 UK firms found that share ownership is closely held in family firms and owners are reluctant to sell equity to outsiders, preferring to remain independent.[433] Another study of 240 privately held companies, including family firms, concluded that these UK firms prefer to grow from their own resources first, then from debt and, finally, from external equity.[434] A majority of Italian and US family firms also prefer to avoid using outside capital and debt.[435]

Attitudes to growth are mixed in family businesses, including those based in Rhineland countries. Growth is not a high priority in some family businesses, possibly because they do not have the inclination, resources or expertise to grow.[436] Alternatively it may be strategically appropriate not to grow.[437] National background appears to make a difference. For example, growth appears more important for Italian than for US family businesses.[438]

Banks, stockholders and venture capitalists often remain skeptical about family firms, despite evidence that these firms outperform equivalent non-family firms financially.[439] Increasingly research shows that overall firms owned by founding families have higher profits and valuations than other firms. They outperform the Standard & Poor 500, for example.[440]

Ultimately whether family or non-family firms perform better financially may depend on many factors, including the context and the measures used. In Mexico, for example, about 95 per cent of businesses are wholly family-owned and run. Possibly through their greater reliance on trust, they have adapted to local conditions in a country where many institutions are considered corrupt and unreliable, and the climate for investment is poor.[441] Not having to focus on quarterly reporting, family businesses are more stable and take a long-term view, growing more slowly but more solidly than multinationals, as the Mexican research shows.[442] Radical change tends to be a considered process, given the conservatism often associated with family businesses.

Taking a long-term perspective is another feature of family businesses.[443] The average tenure for CEOs in family-run firms averages about three times that of firms with non-family member CEOs: 17.6 years, compared with 6.4 years.[444] Some researchers conclude from this that family-controlled firms are likely to be in a better position to maximize shareholder value in the long term.[445] This is generally supported by findings that family-operated firms outperform non-family-run firms, but contradicted by a study finding that, the more the family was involved in German businesses, the poorer the results.[446] Yet other research suggests that firms controlled by the founding family differ from those in non-family management or ownership by having greater market value, being operated more efficiently and carrying less debt than others.[447] These mixed outcomes possibly reflect firms' differing strategic goals: some may seek measurable financial returns while others focus on more personal goals.[448] In Italy, the family business culture does not encourage focusing on economic goals, at least in public.[449] The mixed results on financial performance may also reflect different definitions of family business.

Like Rhineland enterprises generally, family businesses apply strong ethical rules.[450] They tend to act in a more socially responsible way than non-family businesses, have clear social goals and a strong customer focus.[451] Family businesses may be more likely to adopt environmentally friendly strategies than other businesses because of their local orientation, although more research is needed here.[452] Family enterprises are also recognized as providing high quality in products and services.[453] These factors all have an effect on a firm's reputation. It may well be that, in family businesses, negative publicity tends to reflect on the owners personally. Hence there may be a greater sensitivity to questions of reputation.

Research into the complexity of the innovation process concludes that, overall, family businesses are likely to be more innovative than other firms, in that they initiate and implement more new ideas.[454] This is contrary to prevailing wisdom and older research that took fewer factors into account. Of course, smaller firms may not have the resources to invest in R&D.

Family businesses have strong cultures and values: they know what they stand for.[455] On the surface, the values may not differ greatly from those expressed by major public companies, but they are probably better implemented and practiced in a family firm where people care about the business.[456] The top values held by 100-year-old Finnish family firms are honesty, credibility, obeying the law, quality and industriousness. Interestingly values of maximizing shareholder returns, being willing to grow and desiring social recognition were rated low among these firms.[457] Spanish family entrepreneurs, like their Rhineland counterparts, tend to adopt a long-term perspective, and value seriousness, rigor, altruism, honesty and an ethical orientation.[458] In a US study, family business goals included promoting happy, proud and productive employees, financial and job security for owners and employees, quality products, personal and social growth and good corporate citizenship.[459] Family businesses in Texas highlighted valuing teamwork, which may be expressed in formal teams or simply reflect the sentiment of 'being in this together'.[460] However it is not clear whether these are self-governing or manager-led teams. Of course, just like non-family businesses, not all family firms always display the positive values they aspire to.

More research is clearly needed into family businesses, but the current evidence indicates that they conform to the Rhineland model on many criteria. In Table 6.2, research results from family-run businesses are summarized using the Sustainable Leadership Grid. Twelve elements seem common to Rhineland and family businesses: ethical behavior, independence from the financial markets, innovation, adopting a long-term perspective, developing their own managers, having a strong organizational culture, strong focus on

Table 6.2   Family businesses research findings and SAS data plotted on the Sustainable Leadership Grid

Rhineland elements on the Sustainable Leadership Grid	Family businesses	SAS
CEO concept: top team speaker	?	✓
Decision making: consensual	?	?
Ethical behavior: an explicit value	✓	✓
Financial markets: challenge them	✓	✓
Innovation: strong	✓	✓
Knowledge management: shared	?	✓
Long-term perspective: yes	✓	✓
Management development: grow their own	✓	✓
Organizational culture: strong	✓	✓
People priority: strong	✓	✓
Quality: high is a given	✓	✓
Retaining staff: strong	✓	✓
Skilled workforce: strong	?	✓
Social responsibility: strong	✓	✓
Environmental responsibility: strong	?	?
Stakeholders: broad focus	✓	✓
Teams: self-governing	?	?
Uncertainty and change: considered process	✓	✓
Union–management relations: cooperation	?	?
Total elements in conformity	12	15

Note: ✓ = conforms; ? = not known.

people, striving for high quality, retaining staff and a broad stakeholder focus; change is well considered and corporate social responsibility valued.

Given the paucity of research into family businesses, there is not enough information about some of the elements in the grid. For others it is difficult to draw conclusions because of the huge diversity among organizations classified as family businesses. Factors such as CEO as hero or team member, consensual decision making, managing knowledge, developing a skilled workforce (through training and other means), self-governing teamwork and environmental friendliness and union relations are likely to vary from enterprise to enterprise.

An innovative suggestion is that family businesses might provide an alternative to the stereotypical Anglo/US corporate model, particularly on questions of trust and integrity that arose following spectacular crashes and exposed dishonesty on Wall Street.[461] Of course, family businesses are not perfect and vary considerably. Individual firms experience their own set of problems, including succession issues and dealing with executives from outside the family.[462]

Founder-run SAS, the world's largest privately held software company, provides an example of a highly successful US organization that conforms closely to the Rhineland model (see Table 6.2).

SAS: Employees Matter to Success[463]

As the world's largest privately held software company, SAS leads the market in software for data warehousing and data mining, and offers industry-specific integrated software and support packages. Founded in 1976, SAS is headquartered in Cary, North Carolina. Founder, chairman, president and CEO James Goodnight owns about two-thirds of the company; co-founder and executive vice-president John Sall owns the remainder. In 2003, the 10 000 employees staffed 200 offices spanning 50 countries. Customers represent 96 per cent of the top 100 of the 2003 Fortune 500 and 98 per cent of the top 100 of the 2003 Forbes Super 500.

SAS's mission is to deliver superior software and services that give people the power to make the right decisions. The year 2003 marked the 27th consecutive year of growth and profitability, with global revenue totaling US$1.18 billion. SAS reinvests 25 per cent of revenues into R&D – nearly twice the average of major competitors.

SAS's success is based on the belief that treating employees as if they make a difference to the company means that they *will* make a difference to the company. In other words, satisfied employees create satisfied customers. Treating employees well provides a unique competitive advantage for the company. Table 6.3 chronicles the development of some of the many em-

Table 6.3   Employee focus and community programs at SAS, USA

Date	Growth in SAS's employee programs in the USA[464]
1976–79	Profit sharing plan and discretionary bonuses for employees; flexible work schedule, 35-hour workweek and employee perks begin, including Friday, breakfast goodies, Wednesday, chocolates, Monday, fresh fruit, complimentary drinks and snacks; parties, family events throughout the year
1980–85	Company-sponsored on-site childcare; free on-site health care center, recreation and fitness center, wellness program; subsidized café in USA
1989–96	Employees receive an additional paid week off between Christmas and New Year's Day; each year SAS appears in *Working Mother* magazine's inaugural list of the Best Companies for Working Mothers; employee assistance program; SAS named in 100 Best Companies to Work for in America and in *Companies that Care*; elder care program; child care program expanded in USA
1997–99	Paid time-off for regular part-time employees; 1998 ranked in top 10 on *Working Mother* magazine's list of the 100 Best Companies for Working Mothers (the ninth consecutive year and fifth top-10 ranking); no. 3 on *Fortune*'s list of 100 Best Companies to Work for in America; no. 4 on *Business Week*'s list of Best Companies for Work and Family; 1999 no. 3 on *Fortune*'s 100 Best Companies to Work for in America list; *CIO* magazine named SAS a Top 100 Company for operational and strategic excellence; *Triangle Business Journal*'s Platinum Rule Award for Family Friendly Practices; expansion of recreation center in USA
2000–03	2000 and 2001, second on 100 Best Companies to Work for in America list; for the 11th year, named on *Working Mother* magazine's 100 Best Companies for Working Mothers; fourth child care center opens; on 100 Best Companies to Work For list

ployee-related programs and benefits at SAS since its inception, and some of the extensive recognition it has received, while corporate performance has risen to outstanding heights.

The SAS corporate culture is legendary, according to *Business Leader Online*.[465] It was developed to stimulate creativity and prevent mistakes from overtired programmers. In addition to working out in a 35 000 square foot fitness center with company-laundered gym clothes, employees can stroll around the Cary campus, enjoying the 34 000 flowers and more than 100 acres of lawn, lunching with their children; and most leave the office by 5pm. The SAS environment fosters and encourages the integration of the company's business objectives with people's personal needs. Employee turnover, at around 4 per cent, or lower in some years, is consistently and significantly below the industry average. Other companies are now emulating this innovative workplace environment based on trust and respect.

In a 2003 press release celebrating SAS's recognition for the seventh consecutive year on *Fortune*'s Best Companies to Work For list, Jim Goodnight claimed: 'We've made a conscious effort to ensure we're hiring and keeping the right talent to improve our products and better serve our customers. To attract and retain that talent, it's essential that we maintain our high standards in regard to employee relations. Our continued presence on the *Fortune* list indicates we're doing just that.' SAS pays very competitive salaries plus good bonuses at the end of the year. An employee survey showed that 87 per cent of staff do not want SAS to go public. Being private enables the company to act in a manner contrary to the rest of the market if it considers that appropriate.

Innovation is another driver at SAS, which lives from customers renewing software licences every year. Part of the innovation system is that every user suggestion must be recorded and sent out to SAS user groups for prioritizing. From this survey, the top 10 suggestions are nearly always implemented. The company maintains close relationships with customers to gain new ideas and bring a customer-focused product to market.

Goodnight himself still enjoys programming, and the top management team understands that he prefers to spend his time that way. The team thus assumes considerable responsibility, freeing Goodnight to follow his interests.

Much of SAS's philanthropy relates to education. Cary Academy is an independent college preparatory day school that Goodnight co-founded in 1996. This model school integrates technology into all facets of education. SAS inSchool is another project centered on educational software for schools.

SAS conforms to 15 Rhineland criteria in Table 6.2, with no information available about consensual decision making, environmental responsibility, self-governing teams or union–management relations.

In this chapter we have seen that Rhineland criteria extend to public and private firms operating inside and outside the Germanic areas, the region that gave rise to the 19 criteria. Examples of public companies reflecting between 10 and 16 Rhineland elements can be found in countries as diverse as

Sweden, Finland and South Africa. Perfect correspondence with a generic model like the Sustainable Leadership Grid would be unlikely for all companies because of the highly individual circumstances they face. In some cases, obtaining information about all the criteria was not possible.

Similarly, research into family or founder-related private businesses suggests that many elements of the Rhineland model apply to them as well. SAS provides insight into the way one highly acclaimed founder-run and owned US business reflects 15 Rhineland features. It is clear that being publicly or privately owned does not prevent Rhineland principles being followed. Publicly owned German and Swiss enterprises reflect many Rhineland elements, as Chapter 5 showed. Munich Re reflects all 19 criteria.

The evidence presented here suggests that public and private organizations in different parts of the world could conform to Rhineland criteria if they wanted to. Of course, the social context in which an enterprise is embedded makes this more or less difficult to do. For example, legal constraints placed on organizations in Rhineland economies make it difficult to hire and fire as easily as in the USA. Similarly, the degree of public outrage at, or acceptance of, large-scale 'downsizing' also varies between nations.

In the next chapter, we see that some Anglo/US public companies also operate on Rhineland principles. We start with public companies that are still associated with their founders or their descendants, and conclude with examples of Anglo/US public companies that already operate on Rhineland criteria. Perhaps calls for leadership along Rhineland criteria are being heeded by Anglo/US companies after all.

7. Anglo/US public companies

The previous chapters have shown that leading European, Scandinavian and South African organizations, exhibit Rhineland practices and philosophies. Family businesses also display many Rhineland features, including the USA. But what happens in Anglo/US *public* firms? This chapter will show that some successful American, British and Australian enterprises already follow the Rhineland practices identified in the Sustainable Leadership Grid.

Certainly, outstanding Anglo/US organizations that Collins and Porras reported on in their book, *Built to Last*, display many elements of the Rhineland model. This has been corroborated in similar studies in other countries, with research into Australian 'winning' organizations,[466] and global best employer studies.[467] Box 7.1 shows that successful organizations in Australia exhibit many Rhineland elements. These include taking a long-term perspective, team-based leadership, developing leaders and promoting internally, an emphasis on training, social responsibility, staff retention, teamwork and adopting a stakeholder approach.

In what follows we consider the potential for sustainable leadership among Anglo/US public enterprises. Probably the greatest challenge for publicly listed corporations lies in resisting pressures to conform to the Anglo/US shareholder value model. This applies particularly to those companies that are professionally managed and no longer associated with their founders. This chapter highlights the good news that some outstanding Anglo/US public companies exhibit many Rhineland features. First, two US public companies that are still associated with the founding family reveal how closely they fit the Rhineland leadership elements. Then six Anglo/US public companies that are no longer associated with the founders show how it is possible for a totally public corporation to be successful when basing leadership on Rhineland criteria.

FAMILY-RUN PUBLIC COMPANIES

Acclaimed US public corporations like Marriott and Nordstrom, renowned for their people-focused philosophies and practices, still involve members of the founding family in senior management. In this section, Marriott Interna-

BOX 7.1   RHINELAND ELEMENTS IN AUSTRALIAN ORGANIZATIONS

Many Rhineland elements are common to 'winning' organizations in Australia.[468] These organizations align their people, procedures, systems and leadership in accordance with the Rhineland model. They assert that 'people are our greatest assets' and hire for cultural fit. Furthermore, while aligning the many elements involved is a challenge at times, they seek balance across them.

Although there is too little specific information to be able to apply the Sustainable Leadership Grid formally, Australian winning organizations appear to have a number of characteristics in common with the German and Swiss firms discussed in Part II:[469]

- a long-term view, even when things are not going well. This provides stability and encourages pursuit of long-term goals;
- a strong team environment;
- formal internal leadership programs and/or models for developing leadership;
- an emphasis on training and career development;
- a sense of community responsibility as opposed to just maximizing shareholder value, while usually still performing very well for shareholders;
- staff turnover that may initially be higher than the industry average shortly after appointments are made, but becomes lower than the industry average after that: it seems that those who fit the culture stay;
- promotion from within the organization;
- a balanced approach to organizational activity, using measures of financial, customer and employee stakeholder interests;
- including short-term and long-term perspectives for growth and learning measures;
- balancing the importance of the different levels: top and bottom, individual and team, small business units and large business environment;
- being conservative, managing risk;
- fostering people's commitment to the organization and pride in working for it;
- striving for distributed leadership, not just one or two powerful individual leaders.

tional and Nordstrom are compared with the elements on the Sustainable Leadership Grid.

Marriott International: 'the Spirit to Serve'[470]

Set up in 1927 by J. Willard and Alice S. Marriott, the Marriott enterprise has become the leading global company in its field, and a member of the Fortune 500. The Marriott family is heavily involved in senior management. J.W. (Bill) Marriott Jr, son of the founders, has been chairman and CEO since the 1980s. His son, John W. Marriott III, sits on the board. In 1997, J.W. co-authored *The Spirit to Serve: Marriott's Way*, from which much of the following information is taken.

Marriott International is responsible for managing over 2700 lodging properties in the USA and 68 other countries. Its expertise lies in satisfying the diverse needs of hotel customers in all parts of the globe. The focus is on the operational side of running hotels through mechanisms such as franchising. In 2003, turnover exceeded US$9 billion, an increase of almost 7 per cent over the previous year, according to Hoover's.[471] Headquartered in Washington DC, Marriott International has approximately 128 000 employees. *Fortune* consistently ranks it as the lodging industry's most admired company and one of the best places to work.

Although strongly associated with the founding family, this global public company is more than the vision of a single individual. Core values drive the organizational system, practices, culture and strategies. Integrity, taking responsibility, fairness and 'walking the talk' are central values at Marriott. A commitment to continuous improvement, overcoming adversity, hard work and fun characterizes the culture. Marriott has a relentless drive for change, improvement and renewal. It aims for the highest possible quality in service and consistency. The company is dedicated to providing exceptional service to customers, growth opportunities for employees and attractive returns to shareholders and owners. Its core purpose is to make people who are not at home feel wanted and among friends when at a Marriott hotel or other facility.

Management by walking around, called 'hands-on management', is a hallmark of the culture. Marriott is strong on systems, including its 66-step guide for cleaning a hotel room in less than half an hour, its 39-step food quality system and its 20-day process for reinforcing the Marriott values, for which each employee carries a reminder card on their person. Leadership involves providing regular opportunities for open communication and feedback, and supporting empowered employees. Management derives many ideas from associates from all over the business, listens closely to customers and is willing to experiment with new products, services and ways of doing things. Innovation is important, as is ensuring an environment where everyone can be creative. However, a balance is struck between innovating and sticking to the core business and expertise.

Marriott's philosophy is 'take care of your employees and they will take care of the customers'.[472] If employees are confident and happy, their positive attitude will be reflected in everything they do. Extensive training on technical and process topics supports this philosophy, and experienced employees mentor new employees. The company recognizes employee work–life balance needs by providing systems for helping employees cope with their complex lives. Examples include visa issues, child care, elder care, domestic abuse and housing problems. Subsidized medical care covers associates and their families. Company profit sharing helps people build retirement nest eggs, and the company adopts a strong policy of promotion from within.

Empowerment is central to human resource practices at Marriott, supported by continuing training and multiskilling. When SARS devastated the tourist industry in Hong Kong in 2003, occupancy rates fell to single-digit figures, but Marriott's restaurants boomed because people felt safe eating there. Housekeeping staff were quickly reskilled to work in the food and beverage areas, preventing any layoffs.

Recognizing employees' efforts is done daily at Marriott as well as during the company-wide annual Associate Appreciation Week. Parties, contests and special awards celebrate associates' contribution to the company's success. A strong teamwork ethic permeates the company, in which the rewards for working together outweigh those of self-interest. Even the brands work together at Marriott rather than competing, referring business to each other. The culture is basically egalitarian, with a low tolerance for individuals who seek to profile themselves highly. The company does not offer outrageous incentive packages to stop talented people leaving because its culture depends on collaboration.

Marriott International recognizes a broad range of stakeholders: associates, customers; financial stakeholders such as investors, banks and shareholders; and competitors and franchisee partnerships. Here loyalty is all-pervading. For example, the original family business went public in 1953 and, in 1997, some of the original stockholders were still Marriott owners, augmented by thousands of newer ones and associates with shareholdings.[473] Staff turnover is low by industry standards, including that among top management. At the JW Marriott hotel in Hong Kong, for example, staff turnover in 2003 was 8.9 per cent, compared with 29 per cent across the Hong Kong hotel industry. Even competitors are valued because these stakeholders provide some of the best motivation for continuing success. Marriott collaborates in teamwork with competitors via trade associations, establishing joint child care facilities or extending a helping hand to competitors in trouble, such as when their laundry service breaks down.

The company operates under a code of ethics. Ethics made the company initially resist going into gambling, given the negatives associated with gambling that do not fit the family-oriented culture at Marriott. However, Marriott eventually did acquire limited gambling interests.

Social responsibility is strong at Marriott because it wants every community in which it is located to be a better place to live and work thanks to Marriott's presence. Marriott has a tradition of supporting programs that put education, job readiness and workplace training within the reach of everyone. Helping individuals who face barriers to the workplace is accomplished through specific programs and partnerships. For example, in Hong Kong, Marriott staff work at facilities to train mentally handicapped people in housekeeping, and the JW Marriott hotel employs graduates from this program. Marriott staff support various causes, including Mothers' Choice, a program for single mothers and their children in Hong Kong. Employees volunteer their time at least once a year for this cause and the hotel holds major fund-raising events for Mothers' Choice. Volunteer activities give associates opportunities to grow, learn new skills and take pride in their contribution, both on the job and away from work.

The company believes that everybody should take action to protect the environment today and for the future. A company-wide program, Environmentally Conscious Hospitality Operations (ECHO), guides associates in five key areas: respecting and preserving wildlife, conserving water and energy, clean air initiatives, waste management and clean-up campaigns. Associates play a role by planting trees, cleaning beaches and undertaking other activities that help restore the natural resources. The company-wide policy to 'reduce/re-use/recycle' as much as possible has been augmented in various ways at the JW Marriott in Hong Kong. Energy-saving electric light bulbs are used, and cooking oil is recycled. In addition, Marriott's environmental engineering team has designed a plastics shredder to compact plastic bottles for disposal (this has now been adopted elsewhere in Hong Kong) and other advanced processes have been introduced at the Hong Kong Marriott.

J.W. Marriott's collaborator in writing *The Spirit to Serve* stresses that, from her observations, the company is not perfect but it does many things right.[474] It inspires incredible loyalty in its people, who stress the core values, but employees are open and critical when necessary. J.W. seems to form an emotional bond with many associates.

Table 7.1 compares Marriott International with the Sustainable Leadership Grid elements, showing agreement on all but three elements. No information was available for two elements: attitude to the financial markets and unions. Global companies like Marriott may relate to unions differently in different parts of the world, depending on whether the culture is cooperative or adversarial. On the remaining element, Marriott is not Rhineland: the CEO

Table 7.1   Sustainable Leadership Grid comparing Marriott and Nordstrom with Rhineland criteria

Rhineland elements on the Sustainable Leadership Grid	Marriott	Nordstrom
CEO concept: top team speaker	—	?
Decision making: consensual	✓	✓
Ethical behavior: an explicit value	✓	✓
Financial markets: challenge them	?	✓
Innovation: strong	✓	✓
Knowledge management: shared	✓	?
Long-term perspective: yes	✓	✓
Management development: grow their own	✓	✓
Organizational culture: strong	✓	✓
People priority: strong	✓	✓
Quality: high is a given	✓	✓
Retaining staff: strong	✓	✓
Skilled workforce: strong	✓	—
Social responsibility: strong	✓	✓
Environmental responsibility: strong	✓	✓
Stakeholders: broad focus	✓	✓
Teams: self-governing	✓	?
Uncertainty and change: considered process	✓	?
Union–management relations: cooperation	?	?
Total elements in conformity	16	13

Note: ✓ = conforms; — = does not conform; ? = not known.

appears to be the heroic leader who gives the final approvals, while many others initiate and execute.

Nordstrom: Obsessed with Customer Service[475]

Nordstrom's story opened this book. It grew from a single Seattle store founded in 1901 by a Swedish immigrant to the USA, John Nordstrom, into a nationwide fashion specialty chain. The chain is renowned for its service, generous size ranges and selection of fine apparel, shoes and accessories for the whole family. Nordstrom aims at providing customers with outstanding service and offering a selection of quality merchandise at fair prices. The firm seeks long-lasting relationships with its customers and other stakeholders.

Nordstrom operates about 148 stores in 27 US states, plus 31 international 'Façonnable' boutiques, primarily in Europe. It also retails online. For the fiscal year ended January 2004, sales rose to $6.49 billion, up 8.7 per cent over the previous year. Net income was $242.8 million, up from $103.6 million in the previous year. Working capital is generally financed through cash flows from operations and borrowings, and the company's focus is not on quarterly returns but on striving to be better in the long term.

The Nordstrom family retains about 30 per cent ownership in this public company and closely supervises the chain. Three members of the 2003 executive team bore the Nordstrom name. Despite the analysts' reservations, President Blake Nordstrom worked his way up from selling shoes to becoming the fourth generation of his family to run the company, at a time of crisis for the retailer, in 2000. In the course of modernizing systems and processes, his predecessor as president, an outsider, had shifted the company's traditional primary focus from customers and salespeople to shareholders. This major shift at Nordstrom was accompanied by a decline in financial performance and share price, and a marked rise in customer complaints. Other members of the Nordstrom family joined senior management. Bruce Nordstrom returned from retirement to become chairman of the board of directors. As noted at the beginning of this book, three years later, the company was once again enjoying financial success.

Everything the company does is aimed at supporting its focus on customers, starting with valuing its own people. Surprisingly Nordstrom does not provide sales training – staff just do their best to take care of the customer. Corporate heads personally visit stores to communicate with staff, being highly visible, reinforcing the concept that Nordstrom is not a faceless company.

Nordstrom's careers website refers to building relationships and loving what you do: 'Our company is our people.' That is why associates are encouraged and empowered to unlock their talent and creativity with a career they feel passionate about. In 2004, Nordstrom was again cited by *Fortune Magazine* as one of the 100 Best Companies to Work For in the USA, for the seventh consecutive year, and is listed among Fortune's 50 Best Companies for Minorities. The emphasis is on celebrating its people and their success. The company offers a generous benefits program by US standards, to enable the 52 000 Nordstrom people to stay healthy, wealthy and wise.

Analysts argue that Nordstrom's motivated workforce is a formidable competitive weapon in the service sector, and the company innovates in customer relations.[476] Success comes from working with people, not by replacing them or limiting the scope of their activities.

Nordstrom employees share in the firm's substantial financial success through commissions, but their success stems from other factors, such as encouraging people to present their own ideas, providing them with autonomy and empowering staff to use their good judgment in all situations. Promotion is from within, which helps perpetuate the culture and values, as well as ensuring that management has extensive shopfloor experience.

The Nordstrom employee handbook is legendary. It is only one page long. Rather than being a tool for organizational control, it uses ambiguous language to empower employees, who are expected to accept responsibility, be creative and operate within an ambiguous and dynamic business culture.[477] The handbook refers to 'outstanding customer service' and contains one rule: 'use your good judgment in all situations. There will be no additional rules'.

Nordstrom is committed to preserving the communities in which it does business, providing support to hundreds of community organizations through contributions, outreach programs, special events and volunteerism. In particular, it concentrates on education, human services, the arts and community development, and encourages its employees to become active in local community organizations and causes. The company monitors health and safety conditions in supplier factories.

Table 7.1 shows how Nordstrom compares with the elements on the Sustainable Leadership Grid. Based on publicly available information in 2004, this family-run company operates along 13 Rhineland elements: decision making (extensive staff empowerment) ethical behavior, independence from the financial markets (for example in appointing family members to senior positions), innovation, developing managers internally, strong organizational culture, high people priority, a long-term perspective, high quality, valuing staff retention, considering a range of stakeholders (such as customers, staff and the community) and strong social and environmental responsibility. Interestingly Nordstrom reputedly does not focus on the extensive training typical of Rhineland companies, but relies for its excellent service reputation on its associates' passion for serving customers.

Information was not available about the remaining five elements in the Sustainable Leadership Grid: how knowledge is shared, union relations, uncertainty and change management, self-governing teams (although they would be consistent with highly empowered employees) and whether the CEO is a hero or member of the top team.

Marriott and Nordstrom show that it is possible for publicly owned US corporations to correspond closely to the Sustainable Leadership Grid. Marriott fits at least 16 criteria, with no information available on two of the other elements. The relatively high profile of the CEO is the only non-Rhineland feature apparent. Nordstrom displays 13 criteria, with information not available for five other criteria. Only in not focusing on training does Nordstrom run contrary to the Rhineland model.

It is noteworthy that these two companies are still closely associated with their founders' families. What happens when there is no family bond? The next section looks at non-family enterprises based in various Anglo/US countries that conform to the Rhineland model.

ANGLO/US PUBLIC COMPANIES AND RHINELAND CRITERIA

This book has highlighted the sustainability advantages in the Rhineland model compared with shareholder value-based Anglo/US models. However, the reality is that publicly listed Anglo/US organizations, in particular, face challenges in seeking to become more sustainable. They need to blend public company requirements and existing values with long-term sustainability. The founders of Google recognized these tensions in the prospectus they issued when going public in 2004. Google intends to continue its long-term focus rather than be tempted into sacrificing long-term opportunities to meet quarterly expectations of the market. The founders warned potential investors to be prepared for decisions that benefit the long-term over short-term considerations. In this respect, the Google founders are leading the financial markets rather than simply following them.

Of course, short-term survival of the firm is essential to be able to approach the long-term, and these perspectives need to be balanced. Many firms struggle to balance the long and the short term, the needs of multiple stakeholders and shareholders, the cost and need for social responsibility, and managing costs versus retaining staff and their knowledge.[478] Finding this balance can be formidable for public corporations in particular, because pressures to focus on shareholder value can easily mortgage the future of such enterprises for short-term gains.[479]

Another challenge stems from the context and infrastructure within which Anglo/US firms operate that tend to support Anglo/US practices. Nonetheless enterprises like Honda, Nissan and a Toyota-GM joint venture provide examples of public firms that select staff for cultural fit, enter long-term commitments, have a minimum layoff policy and display similar Rhineland practices even when they operate in the Anglo/US world.[480] However, these enterprises are almost certainly influenced by the Japanese variant of the Rhineland model.

What about Anglo/US public corporations with no family ownership or Rhineland background? Finding publicly listed Anglo/US corporations that are not founder or family-influenced, but display large numbers of elements in the Sustainable Leadership Grid, has been quite a challenge. Overwhelming conformity to the Anglo/US end of the Sustainable Leadership Grid still seems to be the norm in most English-speaking countries.

In this section, six organizations from Anglo/US countries illustrate how these successful public companies display many elements of the Rhineland model: Bendigo Bank, Colgate Palmolive, Continental Airlines, HSBC, IBM and Santos. Like the Rhineland companies described in Part II, all are strong performers or leaders in their field and meet Simon's criteria for being hidden champions:[481] they strive to be the best in a defined market, deal with stakeholders directly, try to be close to the customer, continuously innovate in product and process, create clear competitive advantages in product and service, like to rely on their own strengths, value independence and invest in employees and leadership development.

The information on these companies has been derived from published documentation, particularly annual reports, sustainability indexes, industry rankings, academic case studies and websites, and often the company has provided additional information. Table 7.2 summarizes details of the companies. These companies talk about and appear to implement sustainable practices. Like the Rhineland organizations presented in Part II, these enterprises are sustainable in the sense of having existed for at least half a century, and are still performing well even if they have struck hard times from time to time. All have displayed positive growth during the last year. Table 7.3 (p. 192) summarizes how each company relates to the Rhineland criteria in the Sustainable Leadership Grid.

Table 7.2   Anglo/US public companies displaying Rhineland practices

Organization	Industry	HQ	Date	Staff	Scope	Ownership
Bendigo Bank	banking	Australia	1858	2 000	national	public
Colgate Palmolive	consumer products	US	1806	37 700	global	public
Continental Airlines	travel	US	1934	37 680	global	public
HSBC	banking	UK	1865	232 000	global	public
IBM	IT/ consulting	US	1911	255 000	global	public
Santos	energy	Australia	1954	1 700	international	public

Bendigo Bank: Community-owned Banking[482]

Bendigo Bank is based in Victoria, Australia. It started life as Bendigo Building Society in 1858 and converted to a bank in 1995. By 2003, it employed over 2000 people, had 250 branches throughout Australia, managed assets worth over A\$12 billion and serviced over 740 000 Australian customers. Profit in 2002/2003 was A\$59 million, an increase of 21 per cent on the previous year. Interestingly, even during the depressions of 1890 and 1930, the bank declared a profit.

The bank's strategy is to generate sustainable value for all stakeholders, recognizing that this requires long-term thinking. To pursue the strategy, the bank invests in people, skills, systems and structures to create a bank that looks beyond financial services to other ways of improving the prospects of its customers and communities. The intention is to position the brand in a unique niche, and one way of doing this is through franchising its Community Bank®, a concept that brings advantages to local communities.

The Community Bank® concept responded to a market need. Over 2000 bank branches belonging to various banking corporations closed across Australia between June 1993 and June 2000, reducing branch numbers by about 29 per cent in seven years and leaving many communities without banking facilities. Bendigo developed the Community Bank® to take banking back to the community and involve local people in solving their own banking needs. By January 2003, Bendigo Bank had opened branches in 86 communities, with future openings scheduled at 14-day intervals.

Communities own and operate a franchised Community Bank® through a local, publicly owned company. Locals invest A$400 000–500 000 to establish their own branch banking business, with infrastructure and support provided by Bendigo. All revenue is shared between the local branch and Bendigo Bank. The community company keeps as profit what is left over after paying its branch running costs. The idea is for the community branch to pay a reasonable return to shareholders and use the rest of the profit for local purposes, such as training, infrastructure programs and other activities that improve the quality of life for local citizens. Shareholder returns range from 4 to 10 per cent, according to the bank.

The Community Bank® illustrates how a member of the much-criticized banking sector can display corporate social responsibility, not because it is obliged to do so, but because improving its contribution in these areas will enable it to generate strong demand for its services.[483] This strategy focuses on a whole-of-community solution to help sustain its customer basis. Thus, even short-term profit is improved by looking after stakeholders.

Bendigo Bank provides employment and benefits the community directly via profits. Its innovative model is being extended to other community needs, including a telecommunications enterprise that harnesses local demand and channels it into cooperatively spirited, commercially based activities. Since it has designed new products that enhance sustainability and distinguish it from its competitors, Bendigo Bank could be placed at around stage 5 on Dunphy's sustainability taxonomy.

Bendigo separates the roles of managing director and chairman of the board, and requires directors and staff to strive for the highest standards of professional corporate ethics in conducting their operations. A set of corporate values and behaviors outlines the bank's responsibilities to its shareholders, customers, suppliers, employees and communities. The bank provides incentives for customers to reduce their impact on the environment, as well as improving its own use of energy, waste and other resources.

Promotion from within is based on managers' knowledge of Bendigo's way of banking and its strategy. In 2004, the managing director, Rob Hunt, had been with the bank for about 30 years, as had other senior executives. However, given its rapid growth, promotion from within is not always feasible, for lack of available staff. Staff turnover figures are not made public but the organization regards them as not high for an organization of its size. Relations with unions are considered harmonious and the HR department works closely with unions.

Quality and customer service are considered cornerstones to Bendigo's success. The 'Bendigo way' of banking means having someone available to speak to customers when they need it, being committed to helping customers and communities to succeed, knowing that their success will enhance the bank's own success. Staff are encouraged to express their personality when working with customers, treating people as they would want to be treated themselves, with courtesy, respect and good humor.

On the Sustainable Leadership Grid in Table 7.3, Bendigo Bank has 15 elements in common with the Rhineland model: it promotes ethical behavior, challenges the financial markets, innovates, shares knowledge, has a long-term perspective, internal management development and strong culture; people are a priority, along with high quality, retaining people and skilling staff, a broad set of stakeholders, environmental care, social responsibility and harmonious union–management relationships. No information was available for the remaining four elements: CEO concept, decision making, teams and change management.

Colgate Palmolive: 'the World of Care'[484]

In 1806, William Colgate set up a starch, soap and candle-making business in New York City, from which Colgate has grown into a US$9.3 billion consumer product company operating in over 200 countries. It is a global leader in toothpaste, dishwashing detergent, liquid hand soap, liquid cleaners and specialty pet foods, Colgate operates five businesses: oral care, personal care, household surface care, fabric care and pet nutrition. The focus is on these core businesses under a global financial strategy of increasing gross profit and reducing costs.

The company has outperformed legendary GE, according to *Fortune*.[485] Colgate has a record of strong growth and increased profitability, generated by approximately 38 000 employees. Operating profit has grown on average 14 per cent annually since 1985, translating into strong long-term returns for shareholders. The year 2003 represented the company's eighth consecutive year of double-digit earnings per share growth. In the same year, the company achieved a gross sales turnover of US$9.9 billion, yielding a net income of $1.4 billion.[486]

Chairman and CEO since 1984, Reuben Mark, favors teamwork over celebrity, and operates as a low-profile CEO.[487] He does not take the credit for a team contribution. Colgate is distinguished by the skill and depth of its leadership team, which comprises seasoned executives experienced across all geographic regions and functions. Mark has spent his entire career at Colgate, and his successor is expected to come from within.

The firm's mission is to become the best truly global consumer products company. In achieving this, Colgate people make the difference and set the company apart from the competition. Around the world, people collaborate to drive and fund growth and become the best place to work. When its people are successful, the company is successful, and so Colgate aims to provide global career opportunities for all employees, helping to increase their job satisfaction. The company continuously strives to create an even better workplace.

Colgate employees' commitment to living the company's values is regarded as a key driver of its success. The values are caring, global teamwork and continuous improvement. Living the values involves managing with respect. This means communicating effectively, valuing people's contributions, giving and seeking feedback, promoting teamwork and leading by example.

At Colgate, the core of innovation is continuous improvement, rather than the breakthrough innovation that Wall Street celebrates. In its focus on small steps, Colgate demonstrates that it does not operate just to please the financial markets. These 'small' innovations meant that, in 2002, about 38 per cent of revenues came from goods launched within the previous five years.

Colgate's strong focus on people development includes over 150 training programs, plus continuous coaching and feedback on the job. Written performance appraisals document progress towards achieving individual career goals. Rewards and recognition are an essential part of the process, as is succession planning and identifying high-potential employees for accelerated development.

Colgate's board has received prestigious awards for its corporate governance practices. The board-sponsored code of conduct and business practices guidelines promote the highest ethical standards in the company's business dealings. The company strives to communicate its commitment to ethical business practices and, in 2003 alone, 2500 managerial staff were trained in business integrity. The board continuously reviews corporate governance practices to ensure that they promote value to shareholders and other stakeholders. Since 1989, the CEO has been the only employee formally sitting on the board, but key senior managers regularly attend board meetings. This provides the board with direct access to management.

Pay is linked to company performance for employees at all levels. Remuneration is based on grade and performance and does not generate competition for remuneration among employees. About 92 per cent of a director's compensation is paid in Colgate stock. The result is that board members own significant amounts of company shares. The board is extensively involved in succession planning, people development, training and benefit programs in an effort to gain a recruitment advantage for the firm. Where staff have to be made redundant, they are compensated at the upper level of what is usual in their local environment. Colgate focuses on wellness and balancing work and life issues for employees through benefits like back-up childcare centers close to work, emergency in-home care for dependent children and adults, academic advisory services, discount shopping services, personal services (legal, financial, pet, health and wellness) and counseling services.

A range of local programs promotes well-being in the communities where Colgate operates, encouraging employees to volunteer for school mentoring programs and other enrichment activities. Protection of the environment and the health and safety of customers, staff and the communities in which they live and operate is an integral part of achieving Colgate Palmolive's mission. The company is committed to acting in a socially responsible manner and keeping its business operations environmentally sound. It is worldwide policy to manufacture and market products, and operate facilities, to comply with, or exceed, applicable local environmental rules and regulations. The company aims to produce products that have the lowest practical impact on the environment. Colgate endorses the worldwide hierarchy of solid waste management: source reduction, recycling (including re-use), incineration and land filling.

The inside view is that Colgate Palmolive practices what it preaches. In the words of one long-standing manager, the culture is 'friendly, mutually-supportive, highly collaborative, and singularly uncompetitive and apolitical'. The high degree of collaboration characteristic of the culture is attributed to the strong relationships among staff and very effective ways of sharing success 'recipes' throughout the world. Extensive knowledge management systems and practices are supported by travel, conferences and copious email communication. All this occurs within an atmosphere of easy access to managers throughout the organization.

Stefan S. Gorkin, vice president, Global Labor Relations at Colgate Palmolive Company has effectively helped Colgate management teams around the globe focus on the vital link between excellent labor–management relations and achieving business objectives. Decision making takes place within a form of 'guided democracy' that delegates most operating decisions to the shop floor teams. Key stategic decisions remain with management.

As Table 7.3 shows, Colgate Palmolive corresponds to 19 elements on the Sustainable Leadership Grid: CEO as part of a top team; consensual decision making; ethical behavior; challenging the financial markets; innovation; knowledge management; long-term perspective; management development; strong organizational culture; people priority; focus on quality; retaining staff; skilled workforce; broad stakeholder interests considered; including social and environmental responsibility; strong teamwork; incremental, considered change; and positive union–management relations.

Continental Airlines: Working Together Works[488]

With its roots dating back to 1934, US-based Continental Airlines is one of the most admired airlines, and has weathered very hard times. It bounced back from a decade of turbulence during the 1980s, when the company was nearly bankrupted, to become the third-largest airline in the USA in 1987 – only to file for bankruptcy a second time in 1990 because of rising fuel costs during the Gulf War. The company emerged from bankruptcy in 1993 after appointing a succession of 10 CEOs. It ordered 92 new aircraft to prepare for the future under a four-point Go Forward plan. The Go Forward plan's central themes, against which annual achievements are still measured, are fly to win – make prudent business decisions, fund the future – employ resources wisely, make reliability a reality – give customers what they expect and will pay for, and working together – treat each other with dignity and respect.

In 1994, Gordon Bethune became president and CEO of the company, later becoming chairman until his retirement at the end of 2004. In 1995, Continental Airlines announced the largest quarterly profit in its history, was named best stock of the year on the New York Stock Exchange and its share price skyrocketed from $6.50 in January to $47.50 in December of that year. Continental Airlines continued to prosper until 11 September 2001, posting record profits, acquiring more aircraft, expanding abroad and attaining high customer satisfaction rankings. Even in the September quarter of 2001, Continental Airlines recorded a profit, despite the terrorist attacks.

However, the 9/11 terrorist attacks in the USA created serious problems for Continental Airlines, whose planes were grounded for days afterwards, like those of other airlines. The company reacted by giving refunds to passengers stranded by the government ban on flights, and special compassion fares to assist victims' families, relief organizations and volunteers. The company was forced to suspend 12 000 employees, and the most senior executives elected to forgo all compensation for the remainder of 2001.

In 2002, Continental Airlines made a full-year loss in the aftermath of 9/11 and introduced revenue-generating and cost-saving initiatives. In 2003, sales growth was 5.6 per cent in an industry hit by difficult times, thanks to SARS, the Iraq War, high fuel prices and the advent of stiff competition from low-cost carriers. This drove some competitors towards bankruptcy but Continental Airlines survived.

Net income was US$38 million in 2003, from a US$8.87 billion turnover, bringing the company closer to its goal of breaking even in 2004. The annual report states that the company expects to fund future capital and purchase commitments through internally generated funds and financing arrangements. Shareholder value is very important at Continental Airlines, but winning for shareholders is achieved by paying and treating employees well and letting them participate in the company's winnings. Employees receive a monthly bonus for flights being on time, and the company pays about 15 per cent of pre-tax earnings to employees.

The company has continued to make long-term investments in new terminals, fleet and other facilities, which had been started in better times. Employees were urged in the 2002 annual report to remain with the company. Staff numbers at the end of 2003 were 37 680, down 14 per cent from the previous year. In the 2003 annual report, employees were asked once again to stick with the company as it implements its recovery plan, based on the Go Forward principles. About 42 per cent of employees are unionized and the company strives to reach mutual agreement with unions.

Since 1998, Continental Airlines has been named one of *Fortune*'s 100 Best Companies to Work For, and continues to receive awards for its success in many fields, including top rankings in *Fortune*'s America's Most Admired Companies. *Fortune* placed Continental Airlines among its list of 2004 Most Admired Global Companies, ranking it first in categories including innovation, employee talent, quality of management, use of corporate assets, social responsibility, long-term investment value and global reach. In 2004, it had become the world's seventh-largest airline, with over 2300 daily departures to 126 US and 101 international destinations.

Satisfied employees are essential to Continental Airlines's success and recovery. Gordon Bethune and his successor, Larry Kellner, said: 'We recognize that our future success is dependent on consistently providing an environment where employees enjoy coming to work and are fairly rewarded in both base and incentive pay for their efforts. We know that "working together" works!'[489] Under this program, people are required to function as a team and every person on that team is required to know how the airline is performing. Staff receive weekly updates and a monthly newsletter, as well as other company communications.

According to Bethune,[490] 'Running an airline is the biggest team sport there is … lots of different parts, but the whole only has value when we all work together.' The entire business can be viewed as a collection of self-managing teams that need to function as a whole. Part of Continental Airlines's challenge is getting people who are geographically dispersed and often oper-ating in different cultures to act like one airline. It does this largely through shared values, shared profits and rewards, and feedback on performance. Working together involves well-trained employees. Management operates on a collegial basis too, with members of the top team collectively agreeing on things. When asked what his greatest challenge was at Continental Airlines, Bethune replied: 'the sustainability of our winning team'.[491]

Senior management attributes Continental Airlines's recovery to staying focused on its core business: providing clean, safe and reliable air travel that includes the extra features customers want and are prepared to pay for, delivered by employees who are empowered and committed to the company's success.

Each co-worker at Continental Airlines is made familiar with the company principles of conduct, which can be summarized in one word: integrity. To Gordon Bethune, integrity means adhering to an ethical code. It also means being whole or undivided. In the introduction to the principles of conduct, Bethune emphasized various stakeholder interests when he wrote: 'When we conduct our business with integrity, the stockholders for whom we work benefit, as do our customers and our fellow co-workers. Prudent business decisions that benefit our customers and our stockholders perpetuate our business, which benefits us as employees, as well as our families and commu-nities.' In addition to the principles of conduct, a separate code of ethics has been developed for directors.

Among the principles of conduct is an environmental commitment not only to comply with environmental legislation but to minimize the potential impact of the airline's daily operations. Manuals on environmental policy and procedures are made available to all employees, and all employees have a responsibility to act in an environmentally safe manner.

Continental Airlines provides a strong fit to the Sustainable Leadership Grid in Table 7.3, matching on at least 17 criteria. While shareholder value is important to the enterprise, it balances this against a concern for other stakeholders, including its people, rather than accepting the dictates of the markets. The only element for which no explicit information is available is sharing knowledge, although this is expected to happen through the extensive teamwork at Continental Airlines.

HSBC: 'the World's Local Bank'[492]

In 1865, the HSBC Group started as the Hongkong and Shanghai Banking Corporation Limited, based in Hong Kong with a branch in Shanghai. Today, headquartered in London, the Group has about 9500 offices in 79 countries around the world, with a market capitalization of about US$100 billion. The bank is supported by 200 000 shareholders from 100 countries and serves 110 million customers. Each of these constituencies has its own set of recognized representatives whose needs must be respected: shareholders have institutional investors and shareholder groups, customers have consumer groups, and employees have unions. In addition, HSBC answers to 370 regulators around the world, the media and NGOs as part of wider society. Thus, HSBC needs to focus on a range of stakeholders in addition to its multicultural workforce where one in four of its roughly 232 000 employees is Asian, one in five Latin American, and Caucasians are in the minority. How does a global organization like HSBC lead its diverse constituents?

HSBC considers that its explicit role in society is to conduct business responsibly, serve customers expertly, provide a return to shareholders and ensure a safe and pleasant work environment for staff. Its mission is to be an admired company with its reputation derived partly by making a direct contribution to the communities it serves. Furthermore, the bank states that its success comes with a responsibility to give something back to the wider community.

For HSBC, corporate responsibility means the management of its business in a responsible, sensitive and sustainable manner. This goes beyond charitable donations, to cover everything it does every day. Sustainability involves managing the business for the long term. For example, this means winning customer trust through professional skills, integrity and transparency. Furthermore, HSBC employees recognize that their actions have an impact on society and the environment, and have set targets for improvement in the UK operations. The company contributes to educational and environmental projects. In 2003, it donated over US$47 million to charitable causes including education (especially for the less fortunate members of society) and the environment. HSBC staff devote effort, talent and time to excellent causes and are encouraged to undertake volunteer work both in and out of company time.

In terms of the environment, the bank perceives that the pursuit of economic growth and a healthy environment are linked. It strives to adopt good environmental practices in respect of its own premises, equipment and use of resources. Examples include recycling, minimizing waste and energy consumption and favoring suppliers who adopt environmental initiatives. The bank incorporates environmental considerations into credit and risk analyses and expects borrowers to comply with legal and regulatory requirements. It endorses the United Nations Environmental Program, and encourages public dialog on environmental issues. HSBC also supports specific environmental projects, including a US$50 million international eco-partnership, and is willing to send 2000 employees on conservation projects worldwide.

With this philosophy, HSBC has become one of the leading companies in the banking sector in the 2003 Dow Jones Sustainability Index and it also supports international codes of conduct. The bank's corporate social responsibility report details how it manages its social, ethical and environmental challenges. HSBC acknowledges that it has further to go, but is moving as fast as it can and faster than many others. Its espoused philosophy can be placed at around stages 5 and 6 of Dunphy's sustainability taxonomy.[493]

The financial results reflect great success. HSBC experienced a record year in 2003, when pre-tax profit was US$12.8 billion. In 2003, total income increased by 4 per cent, to US$41 billion and assets totaled US$1034 billion, up 36 per cent on 2002. The company outperformed a benchmarking group of financial industry peers and became the world's tenth largest corporation. It completed a five-year strategic plan and embarked on a new five-year plan in 2004, embedded within a 25-year planning outlook.

Activities are driven by sets of values, codes of conduct and voluntary guidelines. The bank tries to maintain ethical standards in lending. For example, it takes a careful and limited approach to financing defense equipment. The bank refuses to finance the manufacture or export of landmines: it assists landmine victims instead.

The organization likes to grow its own managers. According to Group CEO Stephen Green, it is a mistake to have too much of the top talent joining in mid-career and he prefers to recruit young graduates.[494] HSBC pays great attention to developing and retaining its senior management team, to which Green attributes the stability of the organizational culture. Staff welfare is a fundamental concern and the bank declares itself willing to work with and through recognized staff representative bodies. It is committed to equal employment opportunity and diversity. In 2003, HSBC invested the equivalent of US$750 per employee in training.

Innovation is important to the bank, as is sharing knowledge at all levels. For example, intranets provide a means of sharing information and communicating across teams, business units and geographical regions.

The overview contained in the Sustainable Leadership Grid shown in Table 7.3, suggests that HSBC has 15 elements in common with the Rhineland model: promoting ethical behavior, a long-term perspective, developing managers internally, innovation, strong organizational culture, sharing knowledge, people priority, high quality, staff retention and skilling, broad stakeholder focus, change is well considered, strong social and environmental responsibility, and willingness to cooperate with unions. Unlike typical Rhineland CEOs, top management appears to play a prominent role at HSBC. The company is dependent on the financial capital markets for its business, requiring a balanced approach to the interests of stakeholders and the capital markets. Decision making tends to vary from location to location, being sometimes consensual and sometimes manager-based, and teams tend to be predominantly manager-led.

IBM: Rethinking the Fundamentals[495]

Headquartered in New York with operations in over 160 countries, IBM strives to lead in creating, developing and manufacturing advanced information technologies. These have traditionally included computer systems, software, networking systems, storage devices and microelectronics that IBM's professional solutions and services businesses translate into value for customers. The company used to make desktop and notebook PCs, mainframes and servers, plus many peripherals, and provide software and semiconductors. Increasingly IBM focuses on its service and consulting arm, innovating to meet customer needs and incubating new high-growth businesses. It is also one of the largest global IT financiers in the world.

IBM has consistently outperformed other companies over its almost 100-year history. According to Hoovers' data, IBM is among the leaders in almost every market in which it operates, and 2003 sales revenue exceeded US$89 billion, up nearly 10 per cent on 2002. In 2003, IBM employed over 255 000 people, down by about 28 per cent from the previous year.

By many non-financial measures, IBM is a world leader. In *Forbes'* 21st annual Top Ten Most Admired Companies, IBM ranked number one in the computer industry. In 2002, it had been chosen among the top 10 list of the 100 Best Companies For Working Mothers for 15 consecutive years, was chosen number 38 among *Fortune*'s 100 Best Companies To Work For, and Hewitt and Associates' number one US company for grooming talented senior executives. A holistic approach to employee well-being, health and safety includes programs designed to assist employees in managing work–life balance. IBM is a leader in elder care, child care and regular part-time options. For the fifth consecutive year, in 2004 IBM was ranked twelfth among *Business Ethics'* 100 best corporate citizens. It was noted particularly for its relationships with minorities and women. Since 1996, IBM has raised the percentage of female executives to 18.5 per cent, with about half of its executives coming from 'minority' backgrounds.

IBM has been acclaimed by *Training Magazine* for its training investment and quality. The company invests over $750 million annually to develop the knowledge and expertise of its workforce. On average, employees spend about 55 hours each year in formal learning, about half of which is done in e-learning. Both technical and personal development programs are offered. The company shares knowledge by encouraging many communities of practice to form and interact among employees.

Compensation recognizes performance. Even during the recent downturn in the IT industry, IBM continued to perform better than its competitors and so continued to link pay to performance.

In 2004, IBM introduced a new stock options program for its 300 top executives, under which IBM's stock price has to increase by at least 10 per cent before the options can be exercised. This was an attempt to promote a longer-term management focus and overcome some of the problems with short-term options. Executives must buy the options out of their bonuses, putting their own money at risk. Furthermore, executives cannot claim their rewards until shareholders have first received a substantial increase in value. This program is intended to align the long-term interests of executives and shareholders. By having to purchase their options, executives' own real wealth is affected by the company's performance. Non-executive staff are also encouraged to hold shares in the company, and over 150 000 IBMers do so. This links employees to the firm over the long term.

The company is 'an innovator – in every dimension of that word'.[496] Investment in R&D in 2003 was over US\$5 billion, and IBM researchers earned 3288 US patents in 2002 – double that of the next closest company. However innovation goes much further than this at IBM, because the company recognizes that invention alone is no longer enough to deliver value. Innovation involves the application of invention, as it fuses new developments and approaches to solve problems. The company commits itself to innovation in delivering client success and its customers are willing to pay a premium for this. IBM abandoned relying on high-volume undifferentiated products to concentrate on playing what they call the 'high-value, innovation and integration' game. The latter route was chosen to achieve sustainable long-term success in providing quality solutions. IBM's long-term perspective is evident in some of its strategic initiatives for innovation and staff development. However, global operations are based on weekly and monthly reporting processes that provide a short-term focus for major hiring and firing decisions. If monthly targets are not being kept, staff are laid off. According to long-term employees, IBM has adopted a very short-term operational focus.

Management attributes this to a rapidly changing environment that requires IBM to adjust the skills of its workforce at times. In 2002, it hired about 12 000 new people and dismissed about 20 000 in so-called 'resource actions' to rebalance the workforce. The extent of the 2002 rebalancing (6 per cent of the workforce) was higher than the 2 per cent average over the preceding three years. Insiders report an atmosphere of fear among some employees but retrenched employees are supported by a range of programs and benefits, helping them prepare themselves for finding another job. The right to join a union is tolerated, but the company prefers to have management and workers deal directly with one another.

The company claims that it has management development embedded more deeply in its systems than any other firm. It has strong leadership depth.

Management development programs are designed to accelerate the growth of high potentials and talented IBMers still at an early career stage. Current CEO Sam Palmisano joined IBM in 1973, and came up through the ranks. He is considered a 'hands-on', prominent manager.[497]

In re-examining its traditional core values in 2003 IBM involved the entire workforce in the process. The new values are threefold: dedication to every client's success; innovation that matters, for the company and for the world; and trust and personal responsibility in all relationships. Implementing these values has an impact on the entire organization, from the performance management system, to corporate volunteering actions, relationships with investors, staff empowerment and leadership based on the values. Rather than invoking excessive controls, IBM trusts its people to make decisions and act according to the values that they themselves shaped. For IBM, relationships are the context of employees' work, including relationships within local communities.

IBM's philanthropy covers diverse and sustained programs. It supports initiatives in education, workforce development, arts, culture and the environment to benefit communities in need. Support includes grants of technology, project funding and employee time and talent through volunteerism. A policy of strategic investments has benefited communities by bringing IBM experts from all over the world to address their concerns, and has engaged IBM employees more fully in corporate citizenship. In 2002, IBM donated over $140 million (representing 1.9 per cent of operational income before taxes) in cash and kind to corporate community activities, while over 4 million hours of employee volunteer time was donated to educational and community activities.

IBM has spent nearly $1 billion over five years on environmental measures, to its clear financial benefit. Estimated savings and cost avoidance resulting from this environmental effort, after deducting costs, exceed the costs by a factor of two to one. In 2002, this meant saving over $238 million through environmental protection activities such as designing products to be environmentally friendly, disposing of waste appropriately, recycling products at the end of their life cycle, energy and water savings, pollution prevention and environmentally friendly packaging.

Even global giant IBM corresponds closely to 14 elements in Table 7.3. Deviations from the Rhineland criteria include the CEO appearing to be a driving individual rather than a low-key member representing the top team, a very short-term operational time frame, and in the staff rebalancing that periodically retrenches large numbers of staff. IBM tries to balance the competing demands of the financial capital markets with its long-term interests. The final deviation is that union activities appear to be tolerated by the employer rather than cooperative. This attitude may be influenced by the traditional adversarial relationship between unions and management in mar-

Table 7.3 *Sustainable Leadership Grid applied to Bendigo Bank, Colgate Palmolive, Continental Airlines, HSBC, IBM and Santos*

Rhineland elements on the Sustainable Leadership Grid	Bendigo Bank	Colgate Palmolive	Continental Airlines	HSBC	IBM	Santos
CEO concept: top team speaker	?	✓	✓	—	—	?
Decision making: consensual	?	✓	✓	varies	✓	?
Ethical behavior: an explicit value	✓	✓	✓	✓	✓	✓
Financial markets: challenge them	✓	✓	— balancing	— balancing	— balancing	— balancing
Innovation: strong	✓	✓	✓	✓	✓	✓ exploration
Knowledge management: shared	✓	✓	?	✓	✓	?
Long-term perspective: yes	✓	✓	✓	✓	|	✓
Management development: grow their own	✓	✓	✓	✓	✓	✓
Organizational culture: strong	✓	✓	✓	✓	✓	✓
People priority: strong	✓	✓	✓	✓	✓	✓
Quality: high is a given	✓	✓	✓	✓	✓	✓
Retaining staff: strong	✓	✓	✓	✓	|	✓
Skilled workforce: strong	✓	✓	✓	✓	✓	✓
Social responsibility: strong	✓	✓	✓	✓	✓	✓
Environmental responsibility: strong	✓	✓	✓	✓	✓	✓
Stakeholders: broad focus	✓	✓	✓	✓ |	✓	✓
Teams: self-governing	?	✓	✓	✓	✓	~✓
Uncertainty and change: considered process	?	✓		✓	—	
Union–management relations: cooperative	✓	✓		✓	tolerated	~?
Total elements in conformity	**15**	**19**	**17**	**15**	**14**	**13**

Note: ✓ = conforms; — = does not conform; ? = not known.

192

kets dominated by the Anglo/US model, such as the USA, the UK and Australia.

Santos: 'Energy that Drives us Forward'[498]

Santos, founded in 1954 in Adelaide, Australia, is in the energy sector: oil, coal, natural gas and methane constitute its core business. It has a market capitalization of over A\$4 billion, and over 84 000 shareholders. The company's activities extend outside Australia to the Asia–Pacific region and the USA. In 2002, Santos reported strong performance from its 1700 employees. Sales revenue reached near record levels at over A\$1478 million; net after tax profit was around A\$322. Strong exploration performance led to discovering three new major oil fields, and proven reserves replacement of 119 per cent. Similar financial performance was reported in 2003. Over the previous 10 years, the company's cash flow grew at an annual compounding rate of 12.6 per cent.[499] In 2001, Santos released a growth strategy based on a balanced program of exploration, commercializing its gas, acquiring other firms and optimizing its production and managing costs, which it claims is already bearing fruit.

Santos also measures itself against a broader framework of sustainability, publishing a baseline measure in its 2002 annual report. To Santos, sustainability means making economic progress, protecting the environment and being socially responsible, all on a foundation of sound corporate governance. In short, it means being ethical and 'doing the right thing'.[500] The objective is to create sustainable shareholder returns by aligning environmental and social goals with financial objectives. At Santos, these goals are complementary and, thus, sustainable practices make good business sense.

For Santos, social responsibility is multidimensional. It includes being committed to the health, safety and well-being of employees and contractors, as well as contributing to the communities to which they belong. The company is striving to improve its health and safety performance record under the slogan that 'we all go home from work without injury or illness'. Injury rates fell in 2003. Another element of social responsibility stems from the shortage of students studying petroleum engineering in Australia. This led the company to fund the School of Petroleum Engineering and Management at the University of Adelaide as a direct investment in the future workforce. The company also works with local communities, including indigenous communities, helping preserve the local cultural heritage, developing educational opportunities and supplying recreational equipment and facilities. It sponsors youth development, and various cultural activities beyond its local communities.

The company considers that employees are its greatest asset, and focuses on trying to improve its people management. Staff turnover dropped to 7.2

per cent in 2002 overall, and to 3.8 per cent among geoscientists. Employee-initiated turnover continued to fall in 2003, reaching 6 per cent. In 2002, the company spent over A\$3 million on training and development, on both technical and behavioral topics. It offers a mentoring program and conducts career path planning programs for graduates.

Santos's environmental policy is intended to 'shrink and lighten the environmental footprint of our operations'. Employees led the development of a solar-powered compressor used on gas wellheads to power safety and production control instruments. The company strives to reduce gas consumption and greenhouse gas emissions. It supports research projects to reduce the environmental impact of its operations further, and develops strategies for preventing oil spills. A company-wide Environment, Health and Safety Management System following the requirements of ISO14001 has been developed, along with a system for managing incidents and reporting near misses and hazards in its operational areas. A 2003 employee survey reported that employees recognize the company's environmental and occupational health and safety efforts. The company's first sustainability report was published in 2004.

In terms of governance, Santos has had formal guidelines in place for several years regarding board composition, attendance, compensation, external auditors, risk management and ethics. Supplementing its ethical standards, the board seeks to promote excellent corporate governance based on internal criteria that exceed prescribed legal requirements. Independent auditors praised Santos's high corporate governance standards in 2002, and again in 2003.

The company acknowledges that it is at the beginning of what its directors intend as a disciplined journey towards greater levels of sustainability, beyond consistently strong financial performance. Santos can be placed at stage 5 of Dunphy's sustainability taxonomy, with its focus on sustainability to improve the business by making it central to strategy.

From the Sustainable Leadership Grid in Table 7.3, it can be seen that Santos has 13 elements in common with the Rhineland model: promoting ethical behavior, innovation, long-term perspective, developing its own managers, strong culture, people priority, high quality, staff retention and skilling, broad range of stakeholders, change management, and strong social and environmental responsibility. Santos appears to take a balanced approach to the financial markets. Information is not available for the remaining five elements, namely how the CEO operates, how decisions are made, knowledge sharing processes, teamwork and attitudes to unions.

Clearly many elements in the Sustainable Leadership Grid derived from the original 15 Rhineland case study organizations are also evident in the eight Anglo/US public companies described in this chapter. Of the family-related public companies, Marriott fits 16 elements and Nordstrom 13. In the case of Colgate Palmolive and Continental Airlines, the correspondence covers 19 and 17, respectively, of the 19 elements in the grid. Notably, both are public companies no longer associated with their founders. The other public companies also display substantial numbers of Rhineland elements: Bendigo Bank (15), IBM (14), Santos (13) and HSBC (15). All eight companies share the following nine Rhineland elements:

- ethical behavior,
- challenging or at least balancing their approach to the financial markets,
- growing their own managers through management development processes,
- strong organizational culture, vision and values,
- making people a strong priority,
- taking high quality as a given, whether in service, product or process,
- taking account of the interests of a broad range of stakeholders,
- emphasizing social responsibility, and
- implementing environment-friendly policies.

On most other criteria, there is close agreement, with often only one company deviating from the others. For example, Nordstrom appears not to invest in formal training under its model for empowering employees, and IBM retrenches staff following a short-term process (however kindly!) to rebalance its workforce. Generally, apparant deviations arose because no information could be ascertained on some criteria for some organizations. In particular, information about whether the CEO is hero or top team representative was lacking for three enterprises. On the criterion of challenging the financial markets, all case study corporations recognize shareholders' needs for a return, but generally seek to balance them against various other stakeholders' needs. In doing so, they challenge the priority given to short-term shareholder value. Part of HSBC's core business relates to the capital markets, making it difficult for the bank to challenge the markets openly without upsetting analysts and possibly affecting its current share price. Of the eight case studies in this chapter, IBM's short-term operational perspective is most worrying, given that consistent long-term thinking is core to the Rhineland model. Although this excellent company takes a long-term view in many other areas, living under a cloud of possible dismissal can affect other Rhineland criteria, such as staff loyalty, retention and skilling, culture and sharing knowledge.

It has not been easy to identify high-performing non-family-influenced public companies in Anglo/US countries that meet substantial numbers of Rhineland elements. However the fact that there are some shows that the Rhineland model does operate in Anglo/US markets. It means that other public companies could consider following the advice of management thinkers in adopting a more sustainable model. The founders of Google clearly recognized this in their public offering documents.

Given that the Anglo/US model in particular is under pressure to adapt, and the Rhineland model provides a viable alternative, the next question is: how could Anglo/US enterprises change? Could they merge into some form of middle ground? Or are there compelling reasons for making a reasonably definitive choice between them? The final chapter looks at ways in which organizations might move towards more sustainable leadership practices.

PART IV

The future

Unfortunately, the majority of companies still see such concepts as sustainability and social responsibility as pursuits that only the rich can afford. For them, the business of business is business and should remain so. If society wants to put more constraints on the way business operates, they argue, it can pass more laws and enforce more regulations. (Charles Handy[501])

8. Towards a sustainable future

The 28 case studies presented in this book provide living examples of specific Rhineland practices and actions that leading management thinkers are calling for. The examples show how the elements in the Sustainable Leadership Grid operate in practice as part of a self-reinforcing system. They also reveal a rich variety of detail in the way sustainable development practices are implemented in successful organizations in different parts of the world. Considerable evidence suggests that the Rhineland approach, built around a philosophy of the enterprise as part of a wider community, is more sustainable over the long term than the narrower Anglo/US approach.

Political economist Will Hutton,[502] argues that the Rhineland model's success stems mainly from its innovativeness and relatively larger growth in productivity at the end of the 20th century compared with enterprises operating under the Anglo/US approach. The strong position Rhineland employees hold in their firms comes out of a much more complex view of organizational efficiency, adaptability and productivity than under the Anglo/US model. It is built on trust, loyalty and a highly skilled workforce. Rhineland workers are supported if they become unemployed.

Independently, eminent management writers, researchers and practitioners are urging leaders to adopt elements of the Rhineland model if they are not already doing so. Many experts extol the virtues of these individual leadership elements, often seemingly unaware of the Rhineland model's existence as a theoretical construct, of its proponents and of organizations that have successfully used this approach for decades. Warren Bennis, Stephen Covey, Peter Drucker, Gary Hamel, Charles Handy, Tom Peters and Margaret Wheatley are just a few well-known English-speaking academics whose work supports the Rhineland leadership philosophy and practices highlighted in this book. These and other thinkers are urging business leaders to become more people-focused, innovative, ethical and long-term in their planning and actions, and to provide for the interests of a broad range of stakeholders, including the environment and future generations. But how? What can managers do to make the appropriate shifts?

Managers endeavoring to rebuild their leadership around Rhineland philosophies and practices will need to examine many existing assumptions and behaviors closely. They will need to make decisions about where they stand now and in the near future on each grid element. To assist in this process, each element in the Sustainable Leadership Grid is discussed below, raising questions that managers seeking more sustainable leadership should ask. It is not feasible to make specific recommendations because of the huge diversity of situations and complexity that individual enterprises face. That would be like a doctor seeking to make a diagnosis without knowing anything about a patient. Nonetheless, knowing the questions to ask should provide a good start.

1. **CEO concept**: Rhineland CEOs tend not to profile themselves as heroes leading from the front, rather they act as speakers for a top team and keep a low profile. Many CEOs from the case study firms saw their role as speaker of the top team, and in some cases their profile was so low it was difficult to find public information about the CEO. For example, executives like Blake Nordstrom (Nordstrom) and Reuben Mark (Colgate Palmolive) are rarely visible in the media or other public arenas. Colgate's Mark refuses to profile himself because of his strong emphasis on teamwork, on the grounds that featuring himself takes the credit away from the team, where it belongs. At SAS, the CEO, Jim Goodnight, likes to engage in computer programming and delegates to a top team that takes some of the CEO load away from him. This is a way of developing successors in the team. Another rationale for having senior leadership operate in teams is that understanding top teams provides better predictions of organizational outcomes than just studying CEOs, even in Anglo/US firms.[503] Furthermore, research shows that the leaders of what Collins[504] calls 'great' companies, as opposed to merely 'good' companies, display 'Level 5' leadership. Level 5 leaders are humble, modest and shy rather than heroes. They shun publicity. They act with quiet determination in achieving the enterprise's goals, rather than pursuing their own ambitions. They set up the conditions for others to achieve long-term results and give others the credit for success. Although Level 5 leadership is not the only factor making these companies great, it characterized the leaders at critical times in the 11 great companies Collins identified among a sample of 1435 from the *Fortune* 500 lists since 1965. CEOs should therefore reflect on their own role, and consider empowering their top teams and others in the organization and taking themselves out of the external spotlight. Internally they may retain the roles of motivator and role model. However the power should be shared with others as much as possible, not focused just on the top person for the sake of the organization's future.

2. **Decision making**: typically based on consensus rather than a manager's decision under Rhineland leadership. Consensus is not the same as 100

per cent agreement. Consensus means that everyone can agree to go along with a particular decision even if they disagree with it. This is a strong feature of European Rhineland companies, where the workforce is highly skilled and innovation depends on harnessing employee knowledge and initiative. Not a great deal of information was available about how decisions are reached among the non-European Rhineland companies featured in this book. However, at least at three – Colgate, Continental Airlines and IBM – decision making is acknowledged as generally consensual rather than manager-based. In practice, this can be expected to vary in different countries, depending on cultural expectations about the manager's role. While it may take longer to reach agreement, getting consensus gains staff involvement and acceptance, and ensures that the knowledge in many heads has contributed to a decision. In shifting towards more sustainable leadership, managers are advised to ask whether decision-making power has been devolved to teams and individuals at the lowest relevant level. This may also require 'upskilling' of employees. The result should be fewer (expensive) managers, fewer layers of management, and better quality decisions made by those closest to the customer. How and where are decisions made in your business?

3. **Ethical behavior**: a concern with doing the right thing – is strongly evident among all the organizations covered in this book, including family businesses. Employees sign codes of conduct in many organizations, but Nordstrom trusts employees to use their best judgment instead. Ethics are a form of risk management and a way of enhancing a firm's reputation. However it has been very difficult for managers in US corporations to act ethically because the corporation's legal structure encourages managers to aim for short-term results even if this means acting irresponsibly and immorally, according to Mitchell.[505] He calls for loosening the legal and cultural constraints on US managers to enable them to act as 'natural human beings who work to increase corporate profit the way people with human moral and social values act'.[506] Instead of emphasizing trust, the US government's response has been to introduce tighter laws. Increased corporate governance standards are encouraging Anglo/US corporate boards to focus more on ethical practices, which many consider central to successful leadership. To what extent are executives in your organization really trusted, empowered and rewarded for acting as decent human beings in doing the right thing? Do you have a code of business ethics that employees adhere to? If not, *Business Ethics Magazine* pointed the way to a sample of 850 codes in its summer 2004 issue.

4. **Financial markets**: Rhineland organizations are mostly willing to challenge the capital markets in one way or another. However the reality is

that many Anglo/US companies come under enormous pressure to conform to Wall Street's demands. Even family businesses supplying goods
and services to public corporations feel the pressure to act in Anglo/US
ways, contrary to their own Rhineland values. Public companies everywhere watch their share prices, but independence of the financial markets
is a core value for many Rhineland companies and family businesses.
Even SAS employees want their company to remain private to preserve
its independence. Resisting the demands of the capital markets takes
various forms, from not producing quarterly reports (like Porsche), to
operating in the interests of the company and not the analysts (examples
include Atlas Copco, Colgate, Munich Re and Nordstrom). Others strive
to balance the needs of public listing and following the long-term
interests of various stakeholders, as Continental Airlines, HSBC, Nokia,
SABMiller and Santos do. Encouraging loyal, patient shareholders is
also in the interests of a business. Mitchell[507] argues that companies
attract the kind of investor that they deserve: enterprises with a long-
term focus are more likely to attract patient investors, whereas day-traders
are likely to be attracted to firms that maximize short-term profitability.
Managers must decide which camp they are in, and act accordingly to
attract appropriate investors. This decision will have significant implications for their other leadership behaviors. It is very difficult, if not
impossible, to be sustainable under pressure to meet quarterly targets.

5. **Innovation**: Rhineland organizations innovate continually in product,
    service and process. They invest considerably in long-term R&D, which
    is maintained even in difficult times. This is sometimes hard to do, but
    innovation and continuous improvement are central to an organizations'
    sustainability. IBM, like other Rhineland organizations, takes a much
    broader view of innovation than simply R&D investment: innovation is
    turning inventions into solutions for customers. To be able to meet
    customer needs, being close to the customer is essential. Many of the
    case studies highlight how customer feedback and needs are closely
    integrated into the innovation system. Innovation is approached in a
    systematic way, gathering ideas from the entire organization. Managers
    can usefully ask how many current products and services in their or-
    ganization were introduced over the past five years, and then benchmark
    their findings against the companies featured in this book. When was
    the last time work processes were reviewed and improved in your
    organization? Is there an easy way for people at the front line to have
    their new ideas heard and their innovations rewarded?

6. **Knowledge management**: managing knowledge is a highly valued
    element of a Rhineland organization, particularly as long-term employ-
    ees develop unique in-house skills. Holcim and other enterprises have

developed formal systems for sharing employee knowledge; Novartis and SAS have designed inspiring environments to stimulate creativity and encourage people to share their knowledge. Mentoring is strong at Marriott. Elsewhere, employees who leave are encouraged to come back as consultants or otherwise share their knowledge, and strong efforts are made to entice valued employees to stay. Retaining staff is helpful for keeping knowledge within the firm, and this knowledge can be spread through mechanisms such as promoting communities of practice, teamwork and listening to customers and suppliers. Managers should review the many ways knowledge can be retained and shared within their organization and see whether this is happening in practice.

7. **Long-term perspective**: this permeates Rhineland organizations in many ways: by developing senior managers from within and retaining them; developing long-term strategic thinking, planning, investment strategies, growth plans and renewing work processes for the future; rewarding managers via long-term stock options and other incentives that depend on the growth of stocks; and maintaining long-term stakeholder relationships. Rhineland leadership regards itself as being entrusted with the well-being of the organization for future generations. This motivation is clear in family businesses, despite practical succession issues from upcoming generations. However leaders of public corporations are also responsible for the future of their enterprises. This requires them to act in the interests of the firm and not in the short-term interests of themselves or any other single stakeholder group. Under a long-term perspective, Continental Airlines has invested in airports and ordered airplanes despite turbulent economic times for the entire industry; Marriott and Nordstrom continue to expand their hotels and stores; and Novartis is redeveloping its Basel facility into a stimulating campus. BMW, Fraunhofer Kärcher, Novartis, Porsche and WACKER have pipelines of new products that have taken years to develop. IBM espouses many long-term Rhineland leadership philosophies but is very short-term in some operations, affecting staff morale. This company will be interesting to watch, to see whether an otherwise strong Rhineland enterprise can weather a short-term operations focus. Managers focused on the long term build long-lasting relationships with employees, suppliers and other stakeholders. How long are the perspectives taken in your organization?

8. **Management development**: central to Rhineland businesses is growing their own managers rather than bringing in outsiders (except when special skills are needed). Insiders value and continue the culture; outsiders can come close to destroying it, as Nordstrom found. Most senior leadership develops through the ranks, although in a phase of rapid

expansion, as at Bendigo Bank, this is hard to maintain. Rhineland enterprises typically have extensive management and leadership development programs in place and the board and senior management take a direct interest in these programs. Innovation comes from all over the business, not just from new managers. How extensive are the management development initiatives, depth of leadership and value placed on management development where you work? Is top management involved in developing the next generation of managers?

9. **Organizational culture**: Rhineland organizations develop a strong culture, which makes them a 'special place to work'. Having a strong organizational culture characterizes the companies featured in this book, except where recent mergers have brought clashing cultures together, for example at Allianz. However, this company has put considerable effort into trying to manage the cultural differences, recognizing the importance of a strong culture. When Rhineland enterprises select outsiders, they tend to make sure the newcomers fit the culture rather than just bring technical skills. These companies place great emphasis on a shared vision and set of values, many of which revolve around innovation, quality, customers and teamwork. The exact nature of the culture varies between organizations, but, whatever kind of culture it is, employees need to fit if they are to remain for a long time. Employee surveys monitor the culture in Rhineland organizations. Does your organization have a strong culture built around positive values? Do people know what the company vision and values are? Do the formal vision and values match the values that people enact every day? Does continuing radical change or downsizing disrupt your organization's fundamental culture?

10. **People priority**: people are a core asset under the Rhineland model, with its strong focus on treating employees well. Typically, Rhineland companies provide staff benefits over and above those of competitors in their region, giving people a special reason to stay with the organization. Many of these benefits are intangible. For example, Fraunhofer caters to scientists' needs for autonomy and access to resources. Marriott celebrates staff efforts on associate appreciation days. Many Rhineland enterprises recognize the challenges employees face in balancing work and private lives, and provide counseling services, elder care and child care facilities, and flexible working hours. A culture of respect for one another and recognizing individual achievements typify many of the cases in this book. Managers seeking to enhance their people focus could consider treating employees as if they were volunteers who make a choice to come to work each day. How are people really valued in your company? Does what you say match what happens?

11. **Quality**: achieving the highest quality possible tends to be taken for granted among some Rhineland-oriented enterprises and is at the fore-front of others. This includes meeting or exceeding customer expectations and requires remaining close to the customer. IBM made a conscious strategic choice to offer quality solutions and services that customers would pay a premium for. By contrast, Colgate and SABMiller make consumer items of high quality but at low individual cost. Marriott and Nordstrom shine in quality customer service and, at Swiss retailer Migros, employees make things happen for the customer. SAS tests its quality each year when customers choose to renew their annual soft-ware licenses. Quality at BMW, Kärcher, Novartis and Porsche is known in many ordinary households. Insiders know of the legendary quality of niche players like Aesculap, Loden-Frey, Munich Re, Rohde & Schwarz, Seele, WACKER and ZF. Fraunhofer shows that quality can be achieved with a business based on research and intellectual property, even with a limited ability to pay high salaries. Nokia is renowned for its excellent IT products. Family businesses are also generally associated with pro-moting high quality. Thus, across many different industries, types of business and countries, organizations reflecting Rhineland leadership consistently strive for high-quality products and services. How is qual-ity valued and achieved in your organization? Do your processes meet the criteria of ISO9001 or similar certifications?

12. **Retaining staff**: turnover is generally very low in Rhineland organiza-tions (often around 1–2 per cent in European companies, but higher in some industries). Therefore staff development needs priority. By retain-ing and developing their staff, Rhineland companies save the heavy expenses of replacing staff, which already gives them a financial edge over competitors following the 'hire and fire' approach. The JW Marriott Hotel in Hong Kong provides some clear evidence for this with staff turnover at about one-third of the average for other hotels in Hong Kong. In order to remain competitive and innovative, long-term em-ployees require development, which is brought about in various ways, as the Rhineland organizations in this book show. Sometimes this involves mentoring, international postings, formal education and stimu-lating work challenges. When staff need to be let go, supportive programs are put in place. Others let natural attrition shave employee numbers when necessary. Rhineland organizations can become highly inventive in finding ways of retaining staff during difficult periods. The value of this extra effort is shown by US research findings that layoffs rarely increase profitability and may even achieve the opposite.[508] Managers are advised to avoid firing staff wherever possible, and to integrate human resource strategies for attracting and retaining talented people

into their overall strategy. If staff must be retrenched after all other initiatives have failed, the affected people should be supported, because it is the right thing to do and because it helps retain the loyalty of those left behind. Furthermore, the same employees or other good people may need to be (re)hired when times improve. The firm's reputation will be critical to attracting good employees in a recovering economy, particularly as competitors will also be trying to hire the most talented people. Is retaining people valued in your organization? Or are human resources considered expendable and replaceable costs? How does staff-turnover in your business compare with your industry? With Rhineland enterprises?

13. **Skilled workforce**: Rhineland firms develop employees' skills through in-house and other formal training that represents a major continuing financial investment by the employer. That this investment pays off is supported by research showing that Anglo/US firms that invest heavily in their people outperform the markets.[509] Each year, companies like BMW and IBM invest the equivalent of a medium-sized university's annual budget in developing their staff. Training is available to all employees, not just elites or managers. BMW puts every team through group training at least once every three years, in addition to other training that the teams request. At Nordstrom, formal training is not high on the agenda, rather staff mentor each other and share information and ideas. By contrast, fashion retailer Loden-Frey systematically trains its retail staff in customer service. Most of the case study organizations have extensive formal technical and managerial training programs. What is the scope and content of training provided for your employees? Is the training designed to enhance both technical and interpersonal skills? Does the training apply throughout the organization or just to some employees? Is training viewed as a cost or as an investment in the future?

14. **Corporate social responsibility**: increasingly companies are taking account of the communities within which they operate. Social responsibility underpins the corporate philosophy in Rhineland enterprises, including the philosophy in many family businesses. Larger organizations tend to invest heavily in social programs at the local, national and international level, smaller ones more modestly. Some public companies are engaging voluntarily in corporate social responsibility endeavors, while others are responding to social and governmental pressures. United by a shared commitment to sustainable development 170 international companies had joined the World Business Council for Sustainable Development (see Box 8.1). Directors of South African enterprises are encouraged to follow guidelines for corporate governance that include

---

BOX 8.1   WORLD BUSINESS COUNCIL FOR SUSTAINABLE DEVELOPMENT

Executives often find that sustainability challenges are too large for one company to handle alone. By banding together with others in their industry progress can be made towards sustainable development measured in terms of economic growth, ecological balance and social progress. One avenue is the World Business Council for Sustainable Development (WBCSD). In 2004, four of the case study companies were among the 170 members of the WBCSD: Allianz, Holcim, Nokia and Novartis. WBCSD's activities reflect the belief that the pursuit of sustainable development is good for business and business is good for sustainable development. By sharing their experiences, participants can better understand the challenges their industry will be facing, which enables them to prepare for their own firm's sustainability as well.

The WBCSD develops policies to provide a framework for business to contribute towards sustainable development. The council provides best practice examples of progress being made towards environmental and social responsibility from among its members. It also issues guidelines for helping companies raise the capital for engaging in sustainable activities. This often involves thinking creatively and seeking unconventional sources of patient capital rather than turning to conventional bank loans. For example, government development agencies and non-government organizations may have funds for specific projects in emerging economies. Funding sources like this will almost certainly have different priorities from banks, looking for the socioeconomic benefits that projects will bring to specific communities.

---

the organization's responsibility to society. The UK government is also calling for more corporate social responsibility. In complying, firms stand to enhance their reputation, attract and retain talented staff and develop future customers and workers. Social responsibility goes beyond writing checks, to providing a firm's expertise for social purposes and encouraging staff to volunteer their time during and outside working hours. Many go much further, as we have seen in the case studies in this book. One way to approach social responsibility is to make it visible by adopting a balanced scorecard to measure company outcomes. This would include economic, social and environmental indicators as a very minimum. Enterprises need to develop socially responsible initiatives that are within their means, and even small firms can do something. A first step even for small businesses could be starting with social programs that benefit the local community and involve employees applying the firm's products or services. What does your organization do in this area? How do you measure social outcomes and the impact of your enterprise on the community?

15. **Environmental responsibility**: caring for the environment is a very strong Rhineland value. Many larger enterprises typically produce environmental sustainability reports detailing their commitment, actions and outcomes. Most European companies are well advanced in environmental protection, but others, like the Australian energy company, Santos, are just beginning to acknowledge their role in environmental responsibility. Even office-based finance companies Alexander Forbes, Allianz and Munich Re focus on caring for the environment. Important in assessing a firm's genuine commitment to the environment is whether it adopts the standards of its home country in foreign places where the legal requirements are less strict, as cement producer Holcim does. Some managers are afraid that environmental protection measures will adversely affect their financial performance, but organizations like BMW, IBM, WACKER and ZF clearly show that environmental initiatives can save the firm money and provide competitive advantage. At IBM, savings outweigh the costs of environmental protection two to one, representing US$238 million in 2002. Managers need only consult these companies' environmental audit reports to gain an understanding of how comprehensive their commitment to the environment is. Why do it? Because it is the right thing to do, and also because employees are attracted to caring employers. It also reduces risk, and lenders and investors increasingly require it. And in the end it pays. What does your organization do for the environment?

16. **Stakeholder focus**: one of the distinguishing features of Rhineland approaches is that a broad range of stakeholder interests is taken into account. Stakeholders include employees, customers, suppliers, the local community, governments, the environment and society generally, as well as investors and future generations. This contrasts with the approach that favors shareholders over other stakeholders, which in some jurisdictions has been ruled to be illegal.[510] There, courts have held that shareholders have no direct interest in a company, its businesses or its assets, and their only rights are to receive dividends and vote. Since shareholders change from time to time, the courts have concluded that company directors must act in the interests of the company, separate from the interests of shareholders. This means that taking a stakeholder focus is unavoidable for companies that operate in multiple regions. As part of their philosophy, Rhineland companies take a broad stakeholder

focus. Public companies in particular struggle to balance the requirements of various stakeholder groups with those of shareholders and
financial market analysts, but a strong argument for taking a stakeholder
approach is that shareholders benefit as well.[511] Managers are advised
to identify all those groups whose interests the company should serve
and develop a plan for doing so. How extensive is the range of
stakeholders whom people genuinely consider in your firm?

17. **Teamwork**: highly developed in Rhineland enterprises, teamwork becomes self-governing in many instances and spreads throughout the
organization and between divisions. At American firms like Continental
Airlines, Colgate Palmolive, IBM and Marriott, teamwork is at the
core. Teamwork operates throughout the entire business, just as it does
at European companies like BMW. Teamwork means more than groups
being assigned to common tasks; it requires a genuine commitment to
common goals and methods of achieving those goals. The ultimate
form of teamwork is when teams are self-governing rather than manager-led. Self-governing teams not only manage their own performance
and design the work, but decide what has to be done and contribute to
strategic thinking. What is the commitment to teamwork in your organization? How widely do teams operate? Are they genuine teams working
towards to a common goal and leading themselves? Are members rewarded for teamwork or on an individual basis? Do the members receive
training in teamwork? Is the culture collaborative rather than competitive?

18. **Uncertainty and change**: Rhineland leadership values stability and
incremental change, but Rhineland enterprises are subject to pressures
for radical change, like other organizations. Radical change can affect
all or just specific parts of an enterprise. It arises from mergers and
acquisitions, through innovation, as well as from external influences,
competitor actions, changing markets and customer requirements, and
technological change. However, Rhineland enterprises do not drift with
the wind; they try to adapt to change within overall stability. They stick
to their core values and goals wherever possible when making changes.
In merging with other organizations, they consider whether or not to
intervene to meld cultures, and if so how to do it. In some cases, the
decision is to leave the culture of an acquired firm alone; at other times
deliberate change is initiated to bring the cultures together. Managers
are advised to be conservative and not to jump on every passing fad
without giving it careful consideration. If major change is to occur, it
should be appropriately supported by the organization and senior managers, and well considered before being implemented. Does your
organization embrace radical change that is planned and considered? Or

are changes implemented largely unplanned, in the hope that they will succeed?

19. **Union–management relations**: in Europe, worker codetermination mechanisms are enshrined in law, including provisions for unions and works councils, so most European organizations strive for a cooperative relationship with unions. Antagonistic relationships with unions often prevail under an Anglo/US philosophy. However, at least four of the six Anglo/US corporate case studies presented in this book foster cooperation with unions: Bendigo Bank, Colgate Palmolive, Continental Airlines and HSBC. Getting along with organized labor can lead to better relationships with the workforce, which is in the company's long-term interests. Cooperating with unions promotes industrial peace, acceptance of change and social stability. However, sometimes the industrial climate, the large number of unions in some countries, tradition and other factors make it difficult to achieve cooperation with unions, and global organizations may well cooperate with unions differently in different locations. For example, European law provides for worker representation on the boards of large firms, which may not happen elsewhere. Is the relationship between management in your organization and formal representatives of the workforce cooperative or adversarial? Do employees have a voice in your enterprise? If not, why not?

Adopting a Rhineland philosophy may sound like a daunting task for committed Anglo/US managers, particularly those who lead public companies. However, we have seen that large public companies in different parts of the world follow Rhineland principles successfully, displaying the majority of the elements if not the entire set of criteria in the Sustainable Leadership Grid. Rhineland elements occur in many global enterprises, including those identified as outstanding or winning: US visionary firms, Australian winning organizations and Best Employers worldwide.

That enterprises like German supermarket giant Aldi continue to apply Rhineland leadership abroad, including in Australia, shows that the Sustainable Leadership Grid principles can be applied in countries where Anglo/US capitalism predominates. In this context, working under the Rhineland model might disadvantage some employees who bring Anglo/US expectations. This is because long-term employees are likely to develop skills suited to one particular employer rather than acquiring more transportable skills. Here, it becomes important to manage expectations. However, if both Rhineland employer and employee accept retaining and developing staff and long-term employment as part of the employment 'contract', there should be little reason for employees to leave or lose their jobs under foreseeable circumstances. These expectations enable both parties to engage in long-term planning and investment, including employees' developing employer-specific skills. The employer can commit himself or herself to training and developing staff knowing they are likely to remain with the firm; employees undertake those developmental opportunities expecting to continue with that employer for the long term.

We have seen that Rhineland principles apply in diverse industries as well, from Alexander Forbes, Allianz, Bendigo Bank, HSBC and Munich Re in finance; Marriott in hospitality; Loden-Frey, Migros and Nordstrom in retailing; IBM in IT; and Santos in the energy sector to many manufacturing and other knowledge-based enterprises.

One often-mentioned reservation is that Rhineland capitalism and leadership are not suited to modern high-tech industries. First, Nokia's success in the telecommunications industry belies this belief because Nokia effects strong Rhineland leadership. Another disconfirming example comes from a comparison of the biotechnology industries in Germany and the UK. Casper and Kettler puzzled about the reason for the German biotechnology industry suddenly taking off, given its supposedly inhospitable climate for entrepreneurs.[512] At the same time, biotechnology in the UK was stagnating, despite seeming to have institutional frameworks very similar to those in the USA, where biotechnology thrives. The authors concluded that German firms are succeeding because of, and not in spite of, a mix of new and established corporate practices. The firms combine relatively stable elements of German institutional frameworks with elements of more entrepreneurial business models. The traditional preference in the German economy for incremental innovation in established technologies has been combined in the biotechnology sector with government policy and private sector reforms. These changes encourage financial institutions to support entrepreneurial technology firms via means such as venture capital.[513] Interestingly, no changes occurred to German labor or corporation laws in order to stimulate the new technologies. It appears that Rhineland firms are not daunted by the institutional context they operate within, but can adapt this context to deal with changing markets.

Thus, industry, form of incorporation and country of operation do not seem to act as barriers to implementing Rhineland leadership. Nonetheless some potential barriers need to be addressed.

POTENTIAL BARRIERS

We have seen that enduring organizations practice leadership consistent with the Rhineland model in both European and Anglo/US contexts. If the Rhineland approach to leadership is recognizably more sustainable than the Anglo/US model, what stops Anglo/US firms from changing? There are probably many reasons. One reason could be lack of awareness of an alternative and how it could work. One purpose of this book is to increase awareness of sustainable leadership practices by providing concrete examples of ways in which these practices can be implemented.

Second, it might seem as if legislation, regulations or the financial markets would prevent Rhineland leadership occurring in the Anglo/US world. We have seen that this is not true. Some highly successful organizations reflect Rhineland principles in different parts of the world and are directly involved with the financial capital markets. Rhineland philosophies in essence provide a strong social backbone for an organization, and this can be achieved in Anglo/US contexts too.

A third potential barrier is that the Sustainable Leadership Grid comprises a series of elements that tend to be aligned, forming self-reinforcing systems, at least at the two extremes. The proper performance of individual elements in the models depends on the other parts. Breaking out of one paradigm and creating another can be a daunting task because so many elements need to be changed at once – but then, going out of business can also be a daunting experience. We have also seen that even Rhineland firms do not necessarily conform to all Rhineland criteria in the Sustainable Leadership Grid, only to the majority of them. This suggests that some elements could be chosen to lead the way towards Rhineland leadership, as discussed below.

A fourth reason why Anglo/US leadership may be slow to change is that tension can arise within and between the various elements in the grid. For example, a focus on the short term often distracts from long-term goals, innovation and investing in people, which many business leaders recognize as essential for sustainability. Survival in the short term is essential as well, but easy staff dismissal, implemented to serve the short run, can destroy employee long-term loyalty. This means that, when times are hard, employees do not support the firm, do not acquire skill according to the firm's needs, and become cynical about the organizational culture and vision. Public firms concerned about their store prices often seek to balance elements in the Sustainable Leadership Grid, such as their attitudes towards the capital markets. Another example of tension occurs when radical change is needed. Rhineland leadership strives to maintain the overall organizational culture and preserve the core values while accommodating the changes. How a firm responds to tensions between and within the elements is very much a question of leadership values and philosophy.

A fifth barrier might be that changing costs money, particularly in fostering corporate social responsibility. As Box 8.1 shows, there are numerous nonconventional funding sources that could support sustainable development.

Finally, the context in which a firm operates may dampen change. For example, it may be hard to introduce Rhineland concepts of worker participation to Anglo/US firms, given that systems of industrial relations are specific to each country and reflect the customs, attitudes and traditions of that society.[514] In Germany, worker participation in the organizations that employ them is viewed as an expansion of democracy. This motivation is absent in the US labor movement, which tends to be more adversarial and focuses on more basic issues of pay, benefits and working conditions rather than on participation and workplace democracy. Denying German workers participation would be as 'challenging' to German workers as requiring it in the Anglo/US system would be to US workers. In global enterprises this is likely to lead to different degrees and kinds of worker involvement to suit local conditions rather than implementing a one-size-fits-all approach. However, the overall approach to labor–management relations can still be cooperative even though it is influenced by local circumstances. Similarly, other elements may need adjusting to local circumstances in the way they are implemented. What is important is that as many elements as feasible reflect Rhineland principles if sustainability is the goal.

MAKING A START

Where should management begin in breaking the self-perpetuating cycle? A sensible approach would be to start with an audit of the firm's current sustainability status, using the Sustainability Leadership Grid as a framework. This would reveal internal or external elements that need adjusting. For some enterprises, only a few elements will need to be brought into line; for others a major overhaul might be necessary.

Managers of large enterprises might find it appropriate to start with particular business units or divisions as a first step. Success in small areas can then lead to more widespread change. Entrepreneurs have more scope for creating a Rhineland culture in new businesses. They can even 'go public' if they specify their intention to follow the Rhineland model in the prospectus and concentrate on long-term investors.

Major financial institutions are paving the way for change by demanding that the companies and properties that they invest in meet sustainability criteria. Allianz, HSBC and Munich Re, for example, have integrated sustainability into their core businesses. The finance industry as a whole has been strongly criticized for driving the shareholder value model and its associated short-term focus. Interestingly, this same industry may well drive the change for sustainable leadership through its emerging focus on socially responsible and ethical investing, environmental risk assessments, and other sustainable practices, according to the UK-based Forum for the Future.[515]

In some contexts, the way to start by establishing harmonious union relationships. In this way, working conditions and enhanced staff retention provide the stable environment for employees to develop their skills on behalf of the firm. This would raise the quality of the firm's products or services, increase innovation within the firm and provide time for a strong organizational culture to emerge, uninterrupted by unexpected loss of staff. Colgate Palmolive provides an example of this through its efforts to use labor–management relationships to further its business objectives.

Alternatively, one could begin with a focus on a broad range of stakeholders, enhancing relationships with staff, customers, suppliers and the local community as well as thinking about future generations. This encourages a long-term perspective, corporate social responsibility, environmental initiatives and ethical practices. These in turn contribute to attracting and retaining a talented workforce willing to innovate and develop with the firm, which in turn characterizes Rhineland leadership. Bendigo Bank illustrates this approach with its Community Bank® concept.

An important step is to make the worker central, treating employees as assets rather than as costs or liabilities. This can be rationally justified in terms of the enhanced performance found in those firms that do invest heavily in their people.[516] It reflects the starting point of the Rhineland model: that enterprises comprise people who are there to serve society rather than just to maximize profits. This would lead to a focus on a broader range of stakeholders, including society and the environment, retaining staff, teaching skills developing people and promoting from within. In turn, this generates a long-term perspective and encourages ethical behavior. It may also mean standing up to some financial analysts, and possibly changing the financial and ownership models underpinning the firm. Thus a sustainable cycle begins.

WHAT ELSE CAN BE DONE?

Changing how business is done requires leadership courage. It needs top management's long-term commitment to the organization and its future. It requires patience on the part of investors and boards. Mitchell[517] proposes that many of the problems with the shareholder value model could be fixed without destroying the essence of the model, merely by modifying it around the edges. He suggests changes such as appointing boards for five-year terms, breaking the nexus between managers and stock options and making boards independent of shareholders. Financial measures need to be supplemented by social and environmental criteria so that all three criteria come to managers' attention. Some of this is starting to happen. Mitchell further suggests lengthening the interval at which financial reporting is done, from quarterly to several years if appropriate to the firm, but essentially letting the firm decide when to report. Making these basic structural and legal requirements is relatively straightforward.

Mitchell calls for replacing the vulnerability that stems from the hire-and-fire and control mentality in the Anglo/US system with trust, which is another form of vulnerability. Managers should be freed from the heavy legal constraints and monitoring they are currently under, and trust put in their place. This would allow the common decency that we tend to observe in family-run businesses to rise again in public organizations.[518]

Trust reduces the need for monitoring staff and managers, makes the workplace a happier place to be and, most likely, enhances performance.[519] Nordstrom and WACKER provide explicit examples of using trust. Family firms generally enjoy greater trust than other businesses from customers, suppliers and most other stakeholders. Trust is mentioned frequently among the exceptional Anglo/US case study companies that display Rhineland leadership, and underpins European Rhineland organizations.

Government also has a role. For example, policy makers need to encourage firms to coordinate more with one another to improve both their own performance and more general economic performance.[520] This includes promoting greater cooperation among unions and employers, and increased sharing of information among private sector actors. Doing so will alter the various actors' uncertainty about what other parties will do, and so contribute to raising the level of trust. In turn, this enables leaders to reach decisions based more broadly on consensus rather than on an individual basis.

However, it is difficult to establish cooperation and trust in the absence of a supporting framework, such as Rhineland capitalism provides.[521] Firms like Alexander Forbes, Atlas Copco, Colgate Palmolive, Continental Airlines, HSBC, IBM, Marriott, Nokia and Nordstrom may be large enough to provide the necessary support for themselves, but smaller firms would benefit from institutionalized support. This could be done through a framework that mimics the function of an employers' association where it does not exist.[522] The association would provide member firms with information about the business sector. Culpepper[523] suggests that an employers' association alone is insufficient. Reforms need to be conducted *in association with* government, which shoulders some of the risk and costs involved. According to Culpepper, the state would then be building up the power of private associations that it would not be able to control, but the government would reap other benefits from increased employment and taxes. Clearly, existing infrastructure can act as a barrier to change. Providing appropriate supporting frameworks such as through employer associations or other initiatives would help remove these obstacles.

For many companies, a major challenge lies in confronting some basic assumptions. Assumptions include that the pressures of the financial capital markets are inevitable, and that a firm cannot pull back from them to gain control over its own future; that quarterly growth and quarterly reporting really are essential and value-adding rather than resource-consuming and distracting from the long-term goals of the organization; that 'downsizing' is the optimal way to save money in the short term rather than focusing on the long-term consequences of such decisions.

Other questions to consider include how much of a future an enterprise has without consistent and substantial investment in R&D and its people. What is the future of an organization that is alienated from the society around it? How much longer can the environment be exploited rather than protected?

Additional assumptions commonly held by Anglo/US managers that should be questioned include the following:

- the importance of retaining heroic leadership and manager-driven decisions;
- that innovation comes from staff turnover rather than from systems embedded in an enterprise full of highly skilled and trained people;
- that it does not matter if people leave and take corporate knowledge with them;
- that stakeholders' views are not particularly relevant to an enterprise's future;
- that engaging in social and environmental responsibility is a luxury for wealthy organizations.

This book is not alone in calling for a fundamental requestioning of the basic model on which most business in the Anglo/US world is based. As the quotations at the beginning of each section in Chapters 3, 4 and 5 show, such calls are coming from many directions. The problem is that practitioners may not have seriously considered alternatives to what they currently do. The case studies presented in this book are about organizations displaying Rhineland leadership that have weathered hard times. Most of them have experienced major disruptions: Continental Airlines following 9/11 springs immediately to mind as an example, as does 'Big Blue' IBM that had to reinvent itself after it missed the PC market and mistakenly focused on mainframes. Rhineland principles do not prevent bad things happening to a company. However, Rhineland leadership may well ensure survival by providing a strong social core.

Not only has this book identified key elements in Rhineland leadership, but it has shown how sustainable organizations implement this kind of leadership. Some outstanding organizations in the English-speaking world are on this journey, and are becoming well known for their sustainable approaches. If they can make the shift to more sustainable leadership, surely others can too? Corporations based in emerging economies have a choice between Rhineland or Anglo/US leadership. Hopefully, they will opt for sustainable leadership in a form that suits their local conditions.

One important question remains unanswered: which criteria in the Rhineland model are crucial? Which ones are really needed to promote sustainability? If we listen to management writers and thinkers, the answer is 'all of them'. The key differentiators between the two models are the long-term, stakeholder and contextual focus of the Rhineland model versus the short-term, shareholder-oriented and self-centered approach of the Anglo/US approach. The evidence indicates that the Rhineland model is more sustainable in that it enriches not only the enterprise but also those who come into contact with it. The Anglo/US model typically enriches certain individuals, mainly shareholders and senior managers, but impoverishes others. This undermines, not only its own sustainability, but the sustainability of the broader community.

To make this book more palatable to those who untiringly and against all the available evidence promote the Anglo/US model, it might have been tactically astute to recommend a blending of the models. The research does not support such an approach and it would have been unethical for me to promote it. I unashamedly suggest, therefore, that the Rhineland approach represents a more sustainable and better way of doing business – for all stakeholders. Shareholders should take note and demand satisfaction.

Notes

1. Dunphy (2003, p. 10).
2. Mintzberg (2004).
3. Mintzberg *et al.* (2002).
4. For example, Bruyn (1991), Epstein (1999), Handy (2002a), Hutton (2002).
5. For example, Globescan (2004).
6. Hutton (2002).
7. Albert (1992, p. 22).
8. Hall and Soskice (2001).
9. Ibid.
10. Yergin and Stanislaw (1998).
11. Epstein (1999).
12. Albert (1993, p. 3).
13. Stiglitz (2002).
14. Sardar and Davies (2002).
15. Hutton (2002).
16. Albert (1993).
17. Lehrer (2001).
18. Ozaki (1991).
19. Stiglitz (2002).
20. Thanks are due to Dr S. Kantabutra, Mahidol University, Bangkok for this information.
21. National Economic and Social Development Board (2004).
22. For example, Bass (1985), Collins and Porras (1994), Kotter (1990).
23. Albert (1993).
24. Hall and Soskice (2001).
25. Hutton (2002).
26. Shearer (2002).
27. Mintzberg *et al.* (2002).
28. For example, Hutton (2002), Kennedy (2000), Mitchell (2001), Schuler (2003), Stiglitz (2002), Westwood (1997).
29. Ketz (2002).
30. Hutton (2002), Vitols (2001).
31. For example, Albert (1993), Hutton (2002).

32.   Albert (1993, p. 15).
33.   Glunk *et al.* (2001).
34.   Kennedy (2000, p. ix).
35.   Mitchell (1993, p. 112).
36.   Martin (2002, p. 70).
37.   Economist Intelligence Unit (2003c).
38.   Economist Intelligence Unit (2003c).
39.   Mintzberg *et al.* (2002).
40.   Clarkson (1998).
41.   Shearer (2002).
42.   Ibid.
43.   Albert (1992), Vitols (2002).
44.   Albert (1992).
45.   Kennedy (2000).
46.   Albert (1992).
47.   Bruyn (1991), Regini (2003).
48.   Epstein (1999), Hutton (2002), Mitchell (1993).
49.   For example, Albert (1992), Hutton (2002), Kennedy (2000), Mitchell (2001).
50.   Malik (2002a).
51.   Champlin and Knoedler (2003), Mitchell (2001), Zalewski (2003).
52.   Vitols (2002).
53.   Malik (2002a).
54.   Ibid.
55.   Bond (2002).
56.   Albert (1992, p. 15).
57.   Mitchell (2001).
58.   Kennedy (2000).
59.   Vogel (2001).
60.   For example, Gelb and Strawer (2001), Willmott and Flatters (1999).
61.   For example, Mitchell (2001).
62.   Albert (1993).
63.   Ibid.
64.   Ibid.
65.   Karsten (1985).
66.   Neumann and Egan (1999).
67.   Economist Intelligence Unit (2003a, 2003b).
68.   Economist Intelligence Unit (2003a).
69.   Ibid.
70.   Müller-Armack (1989).
71.   Hodges and Woolcock (1993).
72.   Betts (2002b), Vogel (2001).

73. Druckrey (1998).
74. Walter (1995).
75. Hodges and Woolcock (1993).
76. Albert (1992).
77. Ibid.
78. Flecker and Schulten (1999).
79. Ibid.
80. Vogel (2001).
81. Wever and Allen (1992).
82. Ibid.
83. Lane (2000).
84. Ibid.
85. Casper and Kettler (2001).
86. Mitchell (2001).
87. Mintzberg *et al.* (2002).
88. Freeman (1998, p. 126).
89. For example, Albert (1993), Hutton (2002).
90. Rodenstock (2002).
91. Caldwell (2001), Stiglitz (2002).
92. Groenewegen (1997).
93. Betts (2002b).
94. Albert (1992).
95. Bruyn (1991).
96. Lang (2002).
97. Ibid.; Mintzberg *et al.* (2002).
98. Mitchell (2001).
99. OECD (1996), Dahlin (2001).
100. Flecker and Schulten (1999).
101. Dahlin (2001).
102. Bischof and Campbell (2000).
103. Vogel (2001).
104. Groenewegen (1997).
105. For example, Parnell (1999), Tetlock and Goldgeier (2000).
106. Grant (2000), Hutton (2002).
107. Hutton (2002).
108. OECD (2003).
109. Shlaes (1994).
110. Hutton (2002).
111. Albert (1992), Betts (2002a).
112. Albert (1992), Epstein (1999), Hutton (2002), Schuler (2003).
113. Epstein (1999).
114. Hall and Soskice (2001).

115. *Economist* (2003).
116. Reichel (2002).
117. *Economist* (2002).
118. Weihrich (1999).
119. Langguth (1999).
120. Ibid.
121. Ibid.
122. Yergin and Stanislaw (1998).
123. Hutton (2002).
124. Vogel (2001).
125. Statistisches Bundesamt (2002).
126. Weihrich (1999).
127. Albert (1993).
128. Walter (1995).
129. Elliott (2002).
130. Rodenstock (2002).
131. Weihrich (1999).
132. Rodenstock (2002).
133. Lauder *et al.* (1994).
134. Rodenstock (2002).
135. Parnell (1999).
136. Hutton (2002), OECD (2003).
137. Hutton (2002).
138. Benson (2003).
139. Mitchell (1993).
140. Albert (1993).
141. Oxley *et al.* (1997).
142. OECD (2004).
143. Mintzberg *et al.* (2002, p. 72).
144. For example, Mitchell and Scott (1990).
145. Akula (2000).
146. For example, Bellah *et al.* (1985).
147. Ibid.
148. Albert (1992, 1993), Hall and Soskice (2001), Hutton (2002), Mitchell (2001).
149. PriceWaterhouseCoopers (2003).
150. Laughlin (1995).
151. Glaser and Strauss (1967).
152. *Manager Magazin* (2004).
153. Simon (1996).
154. B. Braun, *News File*, 05.07.2002/website.
155. Source: Hoovers' on-line at URL (www.hoovers.com).

156. Sold off in June, 2004.
157. *Manager Magazin* (2002).
158. Dr Harald Bergsteiner (2004), personal communication.
159. Bennis (2003, p. 5).
160. Avery (2004).
161. Kakabadse *et al.* (1995).
162. Gemmill and Oakley (1992), Kouzes and Posner (1995).
163. Hubbard *et al.* (2002).
164. Kotter (1982).
165. Mintzberg *et al.* (2002).
166. Avery (2004).
167. Pfeffer (1981).
168. Judge (1999).
169. Lucier *et al.* (2002, p. 2).
170. Nadler and Tushman (1990).
171. Finkelstein and Hambrick (1996).
172. Hambrick (1995).
173. For example, Finkelstein and Hambrick (1996).
174. For example, Kuchinke (1999).
175. Schnebel (2000).
176. Vaill (1989).
177. Howell *et al.* (1990).
178. Hofstede (2003).
179. Glunk *et al.* (2001).
180. Hastings (2003).
181. Kakabadse *et al.* (1990).
182. Covey (2003, p. 8).
183. Miller and Monge (1988).
184. Collins (1997).
185. Bennis (2003, p. 5).
186. Zadek *et al.* (1997).
187. Ciulla (1995).
188. Singer (1994).
189. Recardo (2000).
190. Seidman (2004), Verschoor (2001).
191. *Management Services* (2002).
192. Preuss (1999).
193. Holcim (2001).
194. Bennis (2003, p. 5).
195. Kennedy (2000).
196. For example, Mitchell (2001).
197. Coggan (2003).

198. Neff and Ogden (2001).
199. Booz Allen Hamilton (2003).
200. Neff and Ogden (2001).
201. Finkelstein and Hambrick (1996).
202. Booz Allen Hamilton (2002).
203. Lucier *et al.* (2002).
204. Wiersema (2002).
205. Neff and Ogden (2001).
206. Sahlman (2002).
207. Hewitt (2004).
208. Cashman (2003, p. 6).
209. Mitchell (2001).
210. For example, Estes (1996), Hutton (2002).
211. Estes (1996).
212. Estes (1996), Handy (2002b).
213. Carroll (1998).
214. Collins and Porras (1994).
215. Donaldson and Preston (1995), Jones (1995), Scott and Lane (2000).
216. Hillman and Hitt (1999).
217. Henriques and Sadorsky (1999).
218. Donaldson (1999).
219. Ogden and Watson (1999).
220. Anderson *et al.* (1994).
221. For example, Berman *et al.* (1999); Jones (1995).
222. Preston and Donaldson (1999).
223. Dyer and Singh (1998).
224. Leana and Rousseau (2000).
225. Singer (1994).
226. Kennedy (2000).
227. Zadek *et al.* (1997).
228. Malik (2002b).
229. Covey (2003, p. 8).
230. Avolio (1996).
231. Lawler (1986).
232. For example, Avery (2004), Hackman (1986), Manz (1986, 1990, 1992), Manz and Sims (1980).
233. Manz (1990).
234. Hackman (1986).
235. Manz (1990).
236. Drath (1998).
237. Ibid.
238. For example, Katzenbach and Smith (1993).

239.   Leede *et al.* (2000).
240.   Warnecke (1993).
241.   Wiener (2003).
242.   Wiener (2003, p. 35).
243.   Byham (2003, p. 9).
244.   Collins and Porras (1994).
245.   Ibid.
246.   Booz Allen Hamilton (2003).
247.   Conger and Benjamin (1999).
248.   Holcim (2001).
249.   Holcim (2001, p. 3).
250.   Covey (2003, p. 7).
251.   Lewis (1992, p. 48).
252.   Schnebel (2000).
253.   For example, Ott (1989), Schein (1985).
254.   Schein (1985).
255.   For example, Deal and Kennedy (1982).
256.   Collins and Porras (1994).
257.   Wheatley (1999).
258.   Handy (2002a, p. 51).
259.   For example, Hamel and Prahalad (1989), Kantabutra and Avery (2002), Oswald *et al.* (1997).
260.   Larwood *et al.* (1995).
261.   Hewitt and Associates (2002).
262.   For example, Collins and Porras (1994), Kouzes and Posner (1995).
263.   Collins and Porras (1994).
264.   Collins and Porras (1994, p. 9).
265.   Collins (1999).
266.   Schnebel (2000).
267.   Ibid.
268.   Warnecke (1999, p. II).
269.   Müller (1995).
270.   Wheatley (2003, p. 11).
271.   Handy (2002a, p. 52).
272.   Hewitt and Associates (2002).
273.   Pfeffer *et al.* (1995).
274.   Ibid.
275.   Ibid.
276.   Mitchell (2001).
277.   Ibid.
278.   Muller (1999).
279.   For example, Fairholm (1998).

280. Kennedy (2000).
281. Handy (2002a).
282. BMW 2001/2002 Sustainability Report.
283. Peters (2003, p. 16).
284. Mintzberg *et al.* (2002).
285. Hall and Soskice (2001).
286. Hodges and Woolcock (1993).
287. Cascio (2002), Glebbeek and Bax (2004).
288. Jacobs (2002).
289. Cascio (2002).
290. Roth (2002).
291. Dess and Shaw (2001).
292. Böhmer and Reuss (2003).
293. Wiener (2003).
294. Sung (2003, p. 15).
295. OECD (2001).
296. Gibson (2002).
297. For example, Devins and Johnson (2003).
298. Hall and Soskice (2001).
299. Bassi and McMurrer (2004).
300. OECD (2001).
301. Dowling and Albrecht (1991).
302. Vereinigung der Bayerischen Wirtschaft (2002).
303. Levitan and Werneke (1984).
304. Bechtold (2000), Crossan *et al.* (1999).
305. Sugarman (2000).
306. Albert (1993).
307. Weihrich (1999).
308. Manz (1996).
309. Argyris (1982a, 1982b), Mills (1983).
310. Drucker (2003, p. 3).
311. Drucker (2003).
312. Coulson-Thomas (1992).
313. Jakobs (2003).
314. Munich Re 2001 Annual Report.
315. Drucker (2003, p. 3).
316. Upchurch (2000).
317. Weihrich (1999).
318. Lane (2000).
319. Ibid.
320. Dahlin (2001).
321. Albert (1992).

322. Albert (1993, p. 123).
323. Dore (2002).
324. Ibid.
325. Hall and Soskice (2001).
326. Lawler *et al.* (1995).
327. Levitan and Werneke (1984).
328. Vitols (2001).
329. Betts (2002a), Levitan and Werneke (1984).
330. Dore (2002).
331. Lane (2000).
332. Vogel (2001).
333. Drucker (2003, p. 3).
334. World Economic Forum (2004).
335. Hutton (2002).
336. Barca and Becht (2001).
337. Becht and Mayer (2001).
338. Ibid.
339. Ibid., p. 7.
340. Hodges and Woolcock (1993, p. 4).
341. Slywotzky and Wise (2002).
342. Ibid.
343. Simon (1992).
344. Handy (2002b).
345. *Der Spiegel* (2002).
346. CFO.com (2001).
347. Malik (2002b).
348. Porsche Annual Report 2000/2001, p. 5.
349. Porsche AG (2002).
350. Porsche Annual Report, 2000/2001.
351. *BBC News* (2003).
352. Hamel (2003, p. 11).
353. OECD (2002).
354. Hall and Soskice (2001).
355. Ibid.
356. Lawler *et al.* (1995).
357. For example, Hubbard *et al.* (2002).
358. Hall and Soskice (2001).
359. Mitchell (2001).
360. Meyer (2002).
361. Mitchell (2001).
362. Lane (2000).
363. Wheatley (2003, p. 11).

364. Janz and Prasarnphanich (2003).
365. Sveiby (2000).
366. Herbert (2000), Janz and Prasarnphanich (2003).
367. Casper and Kettler (2001).
368. Block (2003, p. 17).
369. World Economic Forum (2004).
370. Albert (1992).
371. For example, Anderson *et al.* (1994), Lawler *et al.* (1995).
372. Lawler *et al.* (1995).
373. WACKER (1997).
374. Bennis (2003, p. 5).
375. Kennedy (2000).
376. Marinetto (1998).
377. Zalewski (2003).
378. *Management Services* (2002).
379. Gelb and Strawer (2001), Schueth (2003), Watt (2003), Willmott and Flatters (1999).
380. Hillman and Keim (2001), Morgan Stanley and Oekom (2004).
381. Mays (2003), Morgan Stanley and Oekom (2004).
382. Dunphy (2004).
383. Maitland (2003).
384. *World Economic Forum* (2004).
385. Zalewski (2003).
386. Kaplan and Norton (1992).
387. BMW Sustainable Value Report, 2001/2002.
388. Hoffman (2000).
389. Ladd (1970).
390. Rockefeller (2003, p. 136).
391. Handy (2002a).
392. Bansal (2002).
393. Ibid.
394. Harrison and Freeman (1999), Martin (2002).
395. Philpott (2003).
396. Hoffman (2000).
397. Seis (2001).
398. Chandrashekar *et al.* (1999).
399. Seis (2001).
400. Hoffman (2000).
401. Seis (2001).
402. Hoffman (2000).
403. Martin (2002).
404. Dunphy (2003).

405. URL: http://www.allianz.com, accessed 27.05.2004.
406. BMW 2002 Annual Report.
407. Hutton (2002, pp. 242–3).
408. *Economist* (2003).
409. *Forbes Magazine* (2003).
410. *Economist* (2003).
411. Ibid.
412. Ibid.
413. Thanks are due to Ms Heidi Giævér Oram, Vice President Public Affairs, Atlas Copco, Sweden and Mr Gerry McDonald, former Group Human Resources Manager, Australia for their generous assistance with this case study.
414. Source: Hoover's on-line at http://www.hoovers.com.
415. 2003 Atlas Copco, *Facts in Brief.*
416. This case is based on publicly available information.
417. Source: Hoover's on-line at http://www.hoovers.com.
418. Hutton (2002).
419. URL: http://www.nokia.com, accessed March 2004.
420. Ibid.
421. This case is based on publicly available information.
422. Alexander Forbes 2003 annual report.
423. Ibid.
424. http://www.alexanderforbes.com.
425. This case is based on publicly available information.
426. Source: Hoover's on-line at http://www.hoovers.com.
427. http://www.sabmiller.com/CAR2003_assurancestate, accessed 17 March 2004.
428. Ibid.
429. For example, Adams *et al.* (2002), Kleiman *et al.* (1995).
430. For example, Parker (2001).
431. Adams *et al.* (2002).
432. Bird *et al.* (2002), McConaughy *et al.* (2001), Moores and Mula (2000), Sharma *et al.* (1997).
433. Westhead *et al.* (2001).
434. Poutziouris (2001).
435. Corbetta and Montemerlo (1999).
436. Bhagwat (2002).
437. Groenewegen (1997).
438. Corbetta and Montemerlo (1999).
439. McConaughy *et al.* (2001).
440. Anderson and Reeb (2003).
441. *Economist* (2004).

442. Ibid.
443. Adams *et al.* (2002), McConaughy *et al.* (2001).
444. McConaughy (2000).
445. For example, Adams *et al.* (2002).
446. Klein (2000).
447. McConaughy *et al.* (2001).
448. Poza *et al.* (1997).
449. Corbetta and Montemerlo (1999).
450. Adams *et al.* (2002).
451. Adams *et al.* (2002), Gallo (2004), Wittmeyer (2003).
452. Post (1993).
453. Adams *et al.* (2002), Poza *et al.* (1997).
454. Gudmundson *et al.* (2003).
455. Dyer (1986), Poza *et al.* (1997).
456. Poza *et al.* (1997).
457. Koiranen (2002).
458. García-Álvarez and López-Sintas (2001).
459. Tagiuri and Davis (1992).
460. Sorenson (2000, p. 198).
461. Adams *et al.* (2002).
462. Corbetta and Montemerlo (1999), Poza *et al.* (1997).
463. Thanks are due to Dev Mookerjee, from SAS Australia, for his generous assistance with this project.
464. SAS website, accessed 13/02/2004.
465. *Business Leader Online* (November 1999, http://www.businessleader.com/bl/nov99/cover.html).
466. Hubbard *et al.* (2002).
467. Hewitt and Associates (2002).
468. Hubbard *et al.* (2002).
469. Ibid.
470. Thanks for their generous assistance with this case study are due to June M. Farrell, vice president, International Public Relations Marriott International, Inc.; Barbara Powell, director, International Community Relations, Marriott Hotels International Ltd, London; Therese Necio-Ortega, director of communications, JW Marriott Hotel, Hong Kong; and Alice Cheng, account manager, JW Marriott Hotel, Hong Kong.
471. Source: Hoover's on-line at http://www.hoovers.com.
472. Marriott and Brown (1997, p. 34).
473. Ibid.
474. Brown (1997).
475. This case is based on publicly available information.
476. Anonymous (1994), Pfeffer *et al.* (1995).

477. Goodall (1992).

478. Simon (1996).

479. Albert (1992, 1993), Hutton (2002), Kennedy (2000).

480. Groenewegen (1997).

481. Simon (1996).

482. Thanks are due to Emma McKenzie, Public Relations, Bendigo Bank, Australia for her generous assistance with this case study.

483. Bendigo Bank, 2001/2002 annual report.

484. Consistent with its policy of avoiding publicity, Colgate Palmolive was unable to comment officially on this case study, which is based largely on publicly available information.

485. Schwartz (2001).

486. Source: Hoover's on-line at http://www.hoovers.com.

487. Lardner (2002).

488. This case is based on publicly available information.

489. Continental Air, 2003 annual report, p. 12.

490. Puffer (1999, p. 1).

491. Ibid., p. 34.

492. Thanks are due to Andrew Donohoe, senior corporate communications manager, HSBC, Sydney, Australia, for generous assistance with this case study.

493. Dunphy (2003).

494. Green (2003).

495. This case is based largely on publicly available information.

496. IBM, 2003 annual report.

497. O'Heir (2004).

498. This case is based on publicly available information, particularly the 2002 annual report.

499. Santos, 2003 annual report.

500. Ibid.

501. Handy (2002a, p. 53).

502. Hutton (2002).

503. Finkelstein and Hambrick (1996).

504. Collins (2001).

505. Mitchell (2001).

506. Ibid., p. 3.

507. Mitchell (2001).

508. Cascio (2002).

509. Bassi and McMurrer (2004).

510. King Report (2002).

511. Kennedy (2000), Preston and Donaldson (1999).

512. Casper and Kettler (2001).

513. Ibid.
514. Levitan and Werneke (1984).
515. http://www.forumforthefuture.org.uk.
516. Bassi and McMurrer (2004).
517. Mitchell (2001).
518. Ibid.
519. Ibid.
520. Hall and Soskice (2001).
521. Culpepper (2001).
522. Ibid.
523. Ibid.

References

Adams, F.A., True, S.L. and Winsor, R.D. (2002), 'Corporate America's search for the "right" direction: Outlook and opportunities for family firms', *Family Business Review*, **15**(4), 269–76.

Akula, J.L. (2000), 'Business crime: What to do when the law pursues you', *Sloan Management Review*, **41**(3), 29–41.

Albert, M. (1992), 'The Rhine model of capitalism: an investigation', *European Business Journal*, **4**(3), 8–22.

Albert, M. (1993), *Capitalism vs Capitalism: How America's Obsession With Individual Achievement and Short-term Profit Has Led it to the Brink of Collapse*, New York: Four Walls Eight Windows.

Anderson, E.W., Fornell, C. and Lehmann, D.R. (1994), 'Customer satisfaction, market share and profitability: Findings from Sweden', *Journal of Marketing*, **58**, July, 53–66.

Anderson, R.C. and Reeb, D.M. (2003), 'Founding-family ownership and firm performance: Evidence from the S&P 500', *Journal of Finance*, **58**(3), 1301–27.

Anonymous (1994), 'Nordstrom: respond to unreasonable customer requests!', *Planning Review*, **22**(3), 17–19.

Argyris, C. (1982a), *Reasoning, Learning and Action: Individual and Organizational*, San Francisco: Jossey-Bass.

Argyris, C. (1982b), 'The executive mind and double-loop learning', *Organizational Dynamics*, **11**, 5–22.

Avery, G.C. (2004), *Understanding Leadership: Paradigms and Cases*, London: Sage.

Avolio, B.J. (1996), 'What's all the Karping about Down Under? Transforming Australia's leadership systems for the twenty-first century', in K.W. Parry (ed.), *Leadership Research and Practice: Emerging Themes and New Challenges*, Melbourne: Pitman.

Bansal, P. (2002), 'The corporate challenges of sustainable development', *Academy of Management Executive*, **16**(2), 122–31.

Barca, F. and Becht, M. (eds) (2001), *The Control of Corporate Europe*, Oxford: Oxford University Press.

Bass, B. (1985), *Leadership and Performance Beyond Expectations*, New York: Free Press.

Bassi, L. and McMurrer, D. (2004), 'How's your return on people?', *Harvard Business Review*, **82**(3), 18.

BBC News (2003), 'Porsche sues Frankfurt exchange'; accessed on line on 13.04.03 at http://newsvote.bbc.co.uk/go/pr/fr/-/2/hi/business/2926603.stm.

Becht, M. and Mayer, C. (2001), 'Introduction', in F. Barca and M. Becht (eds), *The Control of Corporate Europe*, Oxford: Oxford University Press. pp. 1–45.

Bechtold, B.L. (2000), 'Evolving to organizational learning', *Hospital Material Management Quarterly*, **21**(30), 11–25.

Bellah, R.N., Madsen, R., Sullivan, W.M., Swidler, A. and Tipton, S.M. (1985), *Habits of the Heart: Individualism and Commitment in American Life*, Berkeley, CA: University of California Press.

Bennis, W. (2003), 'Flight of the phoenix: authentic leaders find a way to fly', *Executive Excellence*, Australian edn, **20**(5), 2–5.

Benson, E. (2003), 'Rehabilitate or punish?', *Monitor on Psychology*, **34**(7), 46–7.

Berman, S.L., Wicks, A.C., Kotha, S. and Jones, T.M. (1999), 'Does stakeholder orientation matter? The relationship between stakeholder management models and firm financial performance', *Academy of Management Journal*, **42**, 488–506.

Betts, P. (2002a), 'Slump intervenes in capitalist culture-clash', *Financial Times*, 6 November, p. 13.

Betts, P. (2002b), 'Germany's evangelist for cautious reform: interview with Gerard Cromme', *Financial Times*, 13 March, p. 13.

Bhagwat, Y. (2002), 'The role of going public in family businesses' long-lasting growth: a study of Italian IPOs by Pietro Mazzola, Gaia Marchisio', *Family Business Review*, **15**(2), 149–51.

Bird, B., Welsch, H., Astrachan, J.H. and Pistrui, D. (2002), 'Family business research: the evolution of an academic field', *Family Business Review*, **15**(4), 337–50.

Bischof, B. and Campbell, A. (2000), 'Views from different angles', *Financial Times*, 13 April, p. 15.

Block, P. (2003), 'Expect more of yourself: stop looking up to bosses for answers', *Executive Excellence*, Australian edn, **20**(5), 17.

Böhmer, R. and Reuss, A. (2003), 'Wettlauf gegen die Zeit', *Wirtschaftswoche*, **23**, 88–91.

Bond, J. (2002), 'Managing in a complex world – Can business satisfy shareholders, customers and society at the same time?', First Roberts Lecture, 24 October, University of Sheffield, UK.

Booz Allen Hamilton (2003), 'Results of global CEO survey published in *strategy + business in 2002*'.

Brown, K.A. (1997), 'Afterword', in J.W. Marriott Jr and K.A. Brown, *The Spirit to Serve: Marriott's Way*, New York: Harper, pp. 165–73.

Bruyn, S.T. (1991), *A Future for the American Economy: The Social Market*, Stanford, CA: Stanford University Press.

Byham, W.C. (2003), 'Identifying potential: achieve gold-medal results', *Executive Excellence*, Australian edn, **20**(5), 9.

Caldwell, C. (2001), 'Europe's "social market"', *Policy Review*, **109**, 29–45.

Carroll, A.B. (1998), 'Understanding stakeholder thinking: themes from a Finnish conference', in M.B.E. Clarkson (ed.), *The Corporation and Its Stakeholders: Classic and Contemporary Readings*, Toronto: University of Toronto Press, pp. 71–80.

Cascio, W. (2002), *Responsible Restructuring: Creative and Profitable Alternatives to Layoffs*, San Francisco, CA: Berrett-Koehler.

Cashman, K. (2003), 'Awakening authenticity', *Executive Excellence*, Australian edn, **20**(5), 5.

Casper, S. and Kettler, H. (2001), 'National institutional frameworks and the hybridization of entrepreneurial business models: the German and UK biotechnology sectors', *Industry and Innovation*, **8**(1), 5–31.

CFO.com (2001), 'Porsche faces delisting from index as Deutsche Boerse readies decision'; accessed on line on 13.05.03 at http://www.cfo.com/printarticle/1,5317,4480l,00.html.

Champlin, D.P. and Knoedler, J.T. (2003), 'Corporations, workers, and the public interest', *Journal of Economic Issues*, **37**(2), 305ff.

Chandrashekar, A., Dougless, T. and Avery, G.C. (1999), 'The environment is free: the quality analogy', *Journal of Quality Management*, **4**(1), 123–43.

Ciulla, J.B. (1995), 'Leadership ethics: mapping the territory', *Business Ethics Quarterly*, **5**, 5–28.

Clarkson, M.B.E. (1998), 'Introduction', in M.B.E. Clarkson (ed.), *The Corporation and Its Stakeholders: Classic and Contemporary Readings*, Toronto: University of Toronto Press. pp. 1–9.

Coggan, P. (2003), 'Listing loses its allure', *Financial Times*, 5 September.

Collins, J. (1997), 'And the walls came tumbling down', in F. Hesselbein, M. Goldsmith and R. Beckhard (eds), *The Organization of the Future*, The Drucker Foundation, San Francisco, CA: Jossey-Bass, pp. 19–28.

Collins, J. (2001), 'Level 5 leadership: the triumph of humility and fierce resolve', *Harvard Business Review*, **79**(1), 67–76.

Collins, J. and Porras, J. (1994), *Built to Last*, New York: HarperCollins.

Collison, D. and Kozuma, Y. (2002), 'After Enron, is "Japan Inc" a better business model?', *Accounting & Business*, September, 4–35.

Conger, J.A. and Benjamin, B. (1999), *Building Leaders: How Successful Companies Build the Next Generation*, San Francisco, CA: Jossey-Bass.

Corbetta, G. and Montemerlo, D. (1999), 'Ownership, governance, and management issues in small and medium-size family businesses: a comparison of Italy and the United States', *Family Business Review*, **12**(4), 361–74.

Coulson-Thomas, C. (1992), 'Strategic vision or strategic con? Rhetoric or reality?', *Long Range Planning*, **25**(1), 81–9.

Covey, S. (2003), 'Seven habits revisited', *Executive Excellence*, Australian edn, **20**(5), 7–8.

Crossan, M.M., Lane, H.W. and White, R.E. (1999), 'An organizational learning framework: from intuition to institution', *Academy of Management Review*, **24**, 522–37.

Culpepper, P.D. (2001), 'Employers, public policy and the politics of decentralized cooperation in Germany and France', in P.A. Hall and D. Soskice (eds), *Varieties of Capitalism: The Institutional Foundations of Comparative Advantage*, Oxford: Oxford University Press, pp. 275–306.

Dahlin, B. (2001), 'Unemployment and labor market rigidities within the OECD: 1989–2000', *OECD Employment Outlook*; accessed at http://www.duke.edu/~bgd3/bgd0201.pdf on 23 April 2004.

Deal, T.E. and Kennedy, A.A. (1982), *Corporate Cultures: The Rites and Rituals of Corporate Life*, Reading, MA: Addison-Wesley.

Der Spiegel (2002), 'Morgan Stanley auf 1000 Millionen Euro Schadenersatz verklagt'; accessed on 27.11.02 at http://www.spiegel.de/wirtschaft/0,1518,224522,00.html.

Dess, G.G. and Shaw, J.D. (2001), 'Voluntary turnover, social capital, and organizational performance', *Academy of Management Review*, **26**, 446–56.

Devins, D. and Johnson, S. (2003), 'Training and development activities in SMEs', *International Small Business Journal*, **21**(2), 213ff.

Donaldson, T. (1999), 'Making stakeholder theory whole', *Academy of Management Review*, **24**, 237–41.

Donaldson, T. and Preston, L.E. (1995), 'The stakeholder theory of the corporation: concepts, evidence and implications', *Academy of Management Review*, **20**, 65–91.

Dore, R. (2002), 'Will global capitalism be Anglo-Saxon capitalism?', *Asian Business & Management*, **1**(1), 9ff.

Dowling, M.J. and Albrecht, K.-O. (1991), 'Technical workers and competitive advantage: what can we learn from the Germans?', *Business Horizons*, **34**(6), 68–73.

Drath, W.H. (1998), 'Approaching the future of leadership development', in C.D. McCauley, R.S. Moxley and E. van Velsor (eds), *The Center for Creative Leadership Handbook of Leadership Development*, San Francisco, CA: Jossey-Bass, pp. 403–39.

Drucker, P.F. (2003), 'Future of Management', *Executive Excellence*, Australian edn, **20**(5), 3.

Druckrey, F. (1998), 'How to make business ethics operational: responsible care – an example of successful self-regulation?', *Journal of Business Ethics*, **17**(9/10), 979–85.

Dunphy, D. (2003), 'Corporate sustainability: challenge to managerial orthodoxies', *Journal of the Australian and New Zealand Academy of Management*, **9**(1), 2–11.

Dunphy, D. (2004), 'Sustainability: seize the strategic opportunity', *Executive Excellence*, **21**(1), 19.

Dyer, J.H. and Singh, H. (1998), 'The relational view: cooperative strategy and sources of interorganizational competitive advantage', *Academy of Management Review*, **23**, 660–97.

Dyer, W.G. (1986), *Cultural Change in Family Firms: Anticipating and Managing Business and Family Transitions*, San Francisco: Jossey-Bass.

Economist (2002), 'An uncertain giant: a survey of Germany', *The Economist*, 7 December.

Economist (2003), 'A midsummer night's dream: survey – the Nordic Region', *The Economist*, 12 June.

Economist (2004), 'Still keeping it in the family: the family business model not only survives in Mexico, it prospers', *The Economist*, 20 March.

Economist Intelligence Unit (2003a), 'Viewswire Germany'; accessed 28 November 2003 at http://www.viewswire.com/index.asp?/layout=oneclick&pubcode=VW&country_id=DE.

Economist Intelligence Unit (2003b), 'Viewswire Switzerland'; accessed 28 November 2003 at http://www.viewswire.com/index.asp?/layout=oneclick&pubcode=VW&country_id=CH.

Economist Intelligence Unit (2003c), 'Viewswire United States of America'; accessed 28 November 2003 at http://www.viewswire.com/index.asp?/layout=oneclick&pubcode=VW&country_id=US.

Elliott, L. (2002), 'Germany should regard Brown as a flexible friend', *The Guardian*, 15 July, p. 21.

Epstein, E.M. (1999), 'The continuing quest for accountable, ethical and humane corporate capitalism: an enduring challenge for social issues in management in the new millennium', *Business & Society*, **38**(3), 253–67.

Estes, R. (1996), *The Tyranny of the Bottom Line: Why Corporations Make Good People Do Bad Things*, San Francisco, CA: Berrett-Koehler.

Fairholm, G.W. (1998), *Values Leadership: Toward a New Philosophy of Leadership*, New York: Praeger.

Finkelstein, S. and Hambrick, D. (1996), *Strategic Leadership: Top Executives and Their Effects on Organizations*, St Paul, MN: West.

Flecker, J. and Schulten, T. (1999), 'The end of institutional stability: what future for the "German model"?', *Economic and Industrial Democracy*, **20**(1), 81–115.

Forbes Magazine (2003), 'Proud little Finland tops world rankings', 10 October 2003; accessed 6 May 2004 at http://www.forbes.com/topnews.html.

Freeman, R.E. (1998), 'A stakeholder theory of the modern corporation', in M.B.E. Clarkson (ed.), *The Corporation and Its Stakeholders: Classic and Contemporary Readings*, Toronto: University of Toronto Press, pp. 125–38.

Gallo, M.A. (2004), 'The family business and its social responsibilities', *Family Business Review*, **17**(2), 135–49.

García-Álvarez, E. and López-Sintas, J. (2001), 'A taxonomy of founders based on values: the root of family business heterogeneity', *Family Business Review*, **14**(3), 209–30.

Gelb, D.S. and Strawer, J.A. (2001), 'Corporate social responsibility and financial disclosures: an alternative explanation for increased disclosure', *Journal of Business Ethics*, **33**(1), 1–13.

Gemmill, G. and Oakley, J. (1992), 'Leadership: An alienating social myth?', *Human Relations*, **45**(2), 113–29.

Gibson, I. (2002), 'Report of automotive innovation and growth team (AIGT)', Executive Summary, URL: http://www.autoindustry.co.uk/companies/aigt/index.html, accessed 27 July 2003.

Glaser, B.G. and Strauss, A.L. (1967), *The Discovery of Grounded Theory*, Chicago: Aldine Publishing.

Glebbeck, A.C. and Bax, E.H. (2004), 'Is high employee turnover really harmful? An empirical test using company records', *Academy of Management Journal*, **47**(2), 277–86.

Globescan (2004), '2004 corporate social responsibility monitor: global public opinion on the changing role of companies', URL: http://www.globescan.com, accessed 19 April 2004.

Glunk, U., Heijltjes, M.G. and Olie, R. (2001), 'Design characteristics and functioning of top management teams in Europe', *European Management Journal*, **19**(3), 291–300.

Goodall, H.L. Jr (1992), 'Empowerment, culture and postmodern organizing: deconstructing the Nordstrom employee handbook', *Journal of Organizational Change Management*, **5**(2), 25–30.

Grant, J. (2000), 'America's hedonism leaves Germany cold: US methods of price indexing, particularly for computer-related products, exaggerate output compared with European rivals', *Financial Times*, 4 September, p. 15.

Green, S. (2003), 'Perspectives: in search of global leaders', *Harvard Business Review*, **81**(8), 40.

Groenewegen, J. (1997), 'Institutions of capitalisms: American, European and Japanese systems compared', *Journal of Economic Issues*, **31**(2), 333–46.

Gudmundson, D., Tower, C.B. and Hartman, E.A. (2003), 'Innovation in small businesses: culture and ownership structure do matter', *Journal of Developmental Entrepreneurship*, **8**(1), 1–18.

Hackman, J.R. (1986), 'The psychology of self-management in organizations', in M.S. Pollack and R.O. Perloff (eds), *Psychology and Work: Productivity Change and Employment*, Washington, DC: American Psychological Association, pp. 85–136.

Hall, P.A. and Soskice, D. (2001), 'An introduction to varieties of capitalism', in P.A. Hall and D. Soskice (eds), *Varieties of Capitalism: The Institutional Foundations of Comparative Advantage*, Oxford: Oxford University Press, pp. 1–68.

Hambrick, D.C. (1995), 'Fragmentation and other problems CEOs have with their top management teams', *California Management Review*, **37**, 110–27.

Hamel, G. (2003), 'Radical innovation', *Executive Excellence*, Australian edn, **20**(5), 11.

Hamel, G. and Prahalad, C.K. (1989), 'Strategic intent', *Harvard Business Review*, May–June, 63–76.

Handy, C. (2002a), 'What's a business for?', *Harvard Business Review*, **80**(12), 48–55.

Handy, C. (2002b), *The Elephant and the Flea: New Thinking for a New World*, London: Arrow.

Harrison, J.S. and Freeman, R.E. (1999), 'Stakeholders, social responsibility and performance: empirical evidence and theoretical perspectives', *Academy of Management Journal*, **42**(5), 479–85.

Hastings, M. (2003), 'Living by Uncle Sam's rules: many Europeans and Asians want to know why they have to suffer for the sins of Enron and Worldcom', *Newsweek (International Edition)*, 17 February, p. 42.

Henriques, I. and Sadorsky, P. (1999), 'The relationship between environmental commitment and managerial perceptions of stakeholder importance', *Academy of Management Journal*, **42**, 87–99.

Herbert, I. (2000), 'Knowledge is a noun, learning is a verb', *Management Accounting*, **78**, 68–9.

Hewitt and Associates (2002), *Best employers to work for in Australia study 2000 – Summary of findings*, Sydney: Hewitt and Associates.

Hewitt and Associates (2004), 'Hewitt study shows companies revamping executive long-term incentive programs', Press release, 8 April.

Hillman, A.J. and Hitt, M.A. (1999), 'Corporate political strategy formulation: a model of approach, participation and strategy decisions', *Academy of Management Review*, **24**(4), 825–42.

Hillman, A.J. and Keim, G.D. (2001), 'Shareholder value, stakeholder management and social issues: what's the bottom line?', *Strategic Management Journal*, **22**, 125–39.

Hodges, M. and Woolcock, S. (1993), 'Atlantic capitalism versus Rhine capitalism in the European Community', *West European Politics*, **16**(3), 329–44.

Hoffman, A.J. (2000), 'Integrating environmental and social issues into corporate practice', *Environment*, **42**(5), 22–33.

Hofstede, G. (2003), 'Cultural constraints in management theories', reprinted in L.W. Porter, G.A. Bigley and R.M. Steers (eds), *Motivation and Work Behavior*, New York: McGraw-Hill, pp. 344–57.

Holcim (2001), 'Selecting and developing the leaders for tomorrow: management development concept and guidelines for Group companies', report 9/2001.

Howell, J.P., Bowen, D.E., Dorfman, P.W., Kerr, S. and Podsakoff, P.M. (1990), 'Substitutes for leadership: effective alternatives to ineffective leadership', *Organizational Dynamics*, Summer, 21–38.

Hubbard, G., Samuel, D., Heap, S. and Cocks, G. (2002), *The First XI: Winning Organisations in Australia*, Milton, Queensland: Wiley.

Hutton, W. (2002), *The World We're In*, London: Little Brown.

Jacobs, H. (2002), 'Vision impaired', *Sydney Morning Herald*, 9–10 November, pp. 1–7.

Jakobs, G. (2003), 'Nachfolger gesucht', *Manager Magazin*; accessed on line 14.03.03 at http://www.managermagazin.de/artikel/0,2828,druck-237775,00.html.

Janz, B.D. and Prasarnphanich, P. (2003), 'Understanding the antecedents of effective knowledge management: the importance of a knowledge-centered culture', *Decision Sciences*, **34**(2), 351–84.

Jones, T.M. (1995), 'Instrumental stakeholder theory: a synthesis of ethics and economics', *Academy of Management Review*, **20**, 404–37.

Judge, W.Q. (1999), *The Leader's Shadow: Exploring and Developing Executive Character*, Thousand Oaks, CA: Sage.

Kakabadse, A., Alderson, S., Myers, A. and Bryce, M. (1990), *Boardroom Skills; The Top Executive Survey*, Cranfield, UK: Cranfield School of Management.

Kakabadse, A., Myers, A., McMahon, T. and Spony, G. (1995), 'Top management styles in Europe: implications for business and cross-national teams', *European Business Journal*, **7**(1), 17–27.

Kantabutra, S. and Avery, G.C. (2002), 'Effective visions: components and realization factors', *SASIN Journal of Management*, **8**(1), 33–49.

Kaplan, R. and Norton, D. (1992), 'The balanced scorecard – measures that drive performance', *Harvard Business Review*, **70**, 71–9.

Karsten, S.G. (1985), 'Eucken's "social market economy" and its test in postwar West Germany: the economist as social philosopher developed ideas that paralleled progressive thought in America', *The American Journal of Economics and Sociology*, **44**, 169ff.

Katzenbach, J.R. and Smith, D.K. (1993), *The Wisdom of Teams: Creating the High-performance Organization*, Boston, MA: Harvard Business School Press.

Kennedy, A.A. (2000), *The End of Shareholder Value: The Real Effects of the Shareholder Value Phenomenon and the Crisis it is Bringing to Business*, London: Orion Business Books.

Ketz, J.E. (2002), 'A variety of CEOs on the defensive and all wet', *Accounting Today*, **16**(19), 8–9.

King, M.E. (2002), *Report on Corporate Governance for South Africa*, Parktown, South Africa: Institute of Directors in Southern Africa.

Kleiman, R., Petty, W. and Martin, J. (1995), 'Family controlled firms: an assessment of performance', *Family Business Annual*, **1**, 1–13.

Klein, S.B. (2000), 'Family business in Germany: significance and structure', *Family Business Review*, **13**(3), 157–80.

Koiranen, M. (2002), 'Over 100 years of age but still entrepreneurially active in business: exploring the values and family characteristics of old Finnish family firms', *Family Business Review*, **15**(3), 175–88.

Kotter, J.P. (1982), *The General Managers*, New York: Free Press.

Kotter, J.P. (1990), *A Force for Change: How Leadership Differs from Management*, New York: Free Press.

Kouzes, J.M. and Posner, B.Z. (1995), *The Leadership Challenge*, San Francisco, CA: Jossey-Bass.

Kuchinke, K.P. (1999), 'Leadership and culture: work-related values and leadership styles among one company's U.S. and German telecommunication employees', *Human Resource Development Quarterly*, **10**, 135–54.

Ladd, J. (1970), 'Morality and the ideal of rationality in formal organizations', *The Monist*, **54**, 488–516.

Lane, C. (2000), 'Globalization and the German model of capitalism – erosion or survival?', *British Journal of Sociology*, **51**(2), 207–34.

Lang, K. (2002), 'Unglücksfälle oder Systemkrise?', *Mitbestimmung online*, November; accessed on line 27.11.02 at http://www.boeckler.de/mitbestimmung/.

Langguth, G. (1999), 'Germany in the age of globalization', *The Washington Quarterly*, **22**(3), 91–108.

Lardner, J. (2002), 'In praise of the anonymous CEO', *Business 2.0*, **3**(9); accessed on line, 14/4/2004.

Larwood, L., Falbe, C.M., Kriger, M.R. and Miesling, P. (1995), 'Structure and meaning of organizational vision', *Academy of Management Journal*, **85**, 740–69.

Lauder, D., Boocock, G. and Presley, J. (1994), 'The system of support for SMEs in the UK and Germany', *European Business Review*, **94**(1), 9ff.

Laughlin, R.C. (1995), 'Empirical research in accounting: alternative approaches and a case for "middle-range thinking"', *Accounting, Auditing and Accountability Journal*, **8**(1), 63–87.

Lawler, E.E. (1986), *High Involvement Management*, San Francisco, CA: Jossey-Bass.

Lawler, E.E., Mohrman, S.A. and Ledford, G.E. Jr (1995), *Creating High Performance Organizations: Practices and Results of Employee Involvement and Total Quality Management in Fortune 1000 Companies*, San Francisco, CA: Jossey-Bass.

Leana, C.R. and Rousseau, D.M. (eds) (2000), *Relational Wealth*, Oxford: Oxford University Press.

Leede, J. de, Nijhof, A.H.J. and Fisscher, O.A.M. (2000), 'The myth of self-managing teams: a reflection on the allocation of responsibilities between individuals, teams and the organization', *Journal of Business Ethics*, **21**(2/3), 203–15.

Lehrer, M. (2001), 'Macro-varieties of capitalism and micro-varieties of strategic management in European airlines', in P.A. Hall and D. Soskice (eds), *Varieties of Capitalism: The Institutional Foundations of Comparative Advantage*, Oxford: Oxford University Press, pp. 361–86.

Levitan, S.A. and Werneke, D. (1984), 'Worker participation and productivity change', *Monthly Labor Review*, **107**(9), 28–33.

Lewis, D. (1992), 'Communicating organizational culture', *Australian Journal of Communication*, **19**(2), 47–57.

Lucier, C., Spiegel, E. and Schuyt, R. (2002), *Why CEOs fall: The Causes and Consequences of Turnover at the Top*, report published by Booz Allen Hamilton, Sydney.

Maitland, A. (2003), 'Half top companies report on environmental conduct', *Financial Times*, 9 September , p. 6.

Malik, F. (2002a), 'Perpetuierung falscher Corporate Governance', *Manager Magazin*; accessed on line on 27.11.02 at http://www.manager-magazin.de/koepfe/mzsg/0,2828,217433,00.html.

Malik, F. (2002b), *Die Neue Corporate Governance: Richtiges Top-Management, Wirksame Unternehmensaufsicht*, 3rd edn, Frankfurt am Main: Frankfurter Allgemeine.

Management Services (2002), 'Ethical issues score badly in poll of small businesses', **46**(5), 7.

Manager Magazin (2002), 'Ranking on shareholder-value-performance (Germany)'; accessed on line 27.11.02 at http://www.manager-magazin.de/geld/euro500/0,2828,218049,00.html.

Manager Magazin (2004), 'Ranking on image profile (Germany)'; accessed on line 28.04.04 at http://www.manager-magazin.de/unternehmen/imageprofile.html.

Manz, C.C. (1986), 'Self-leadership: toward an expanded theory of self-influence in organizations', *Academy of Management Review*, **11**, 585–600.

Manz, C.C. (1990), 'Beyond self-managing work teams: toward self-leading teams in the workplace', in R. Woodman and W. Pasmore (eds), *Research in Organizational Change and Development*, Greenwich, CT: JAI Press.

Manz, C.C. (1992), 'Self-leadership ... the heart of empowerment', *The Journal for Quality and Participation*, **15**, 80–89.

Manz, C.C. (1996), 'Self-leading work teams: moving beyond self-management myths', in R.M. Steers, L.W. Porter and G.A. Bigley (eds), *Motivation and Leadership at Work*, 6th edn, New York: McGraw-Hill, pp. 581–99.

Manz, C.C. and Sims, H.P. (1980), 'Self-management as a substitute for leadership: a social learning theory perspective', *Academy of Management Review*, **5**, 361–7.

Marinetto, M. (1998), *Corporate Social Involvement: Social, Political and Environmental Issues in Britain and Italy*, Aldershot, UK: Ashgate Publishing.

Marriott, J.W. Jr and Brown, K.A. (1997), *The Spirit to Serve: Marriott's Way*, New York: Harper.

Martin, R.L. (2002), 'The virtue matrix: calculating the return on corporate responsibility', *Harvard Business Review*, **80**(3), 68–75.

Mays, S. (2003), *Corporate Sustainability – an Investor Perspective*, Canberra: Department of Environmental Heritage.

McConaughy, D.L. (2000), 'Family CEOs vs nonfamily CEOs in the family-controlled firm: an examination of the level and sensitivity of pay to performance', *Family Business Review*, **13**(2), 121–31.

McConaughy, D.L., Matthews, C.H. and Fialko, A.S. (2001), 'Founding family controlled firms: performance, risk and value', *Journal of Small Business Management*, **39**(1), 31–49.

Meyer, C. (2002), 'Survival under stress', *MIT Sloan Management Review*, Fall, 96.

Miller, K.I. and Monge, P.R. (1988), 'Participation, satisfaction and productivity: a meta-analytic review', *Academy of Management Journal*, **29**, 727–53.

Mills, P.K. (1983), 'Self-management: its control and relationship to other organizational properties', *Academy of Management Review*, **8**, 445–53.

Mintzberg, H. (2004), *Managers not MBAs: A Hard Look at the Soft Practice of Managing and Management Development*, San Francisco, CA: Berrett-Koehler.

Mintzberg, H., Simons, R. and Basu, K. (2002), 'Beyond selfishness', *MIT Sloan Management Review*, Fall, 67–74.

Mitchell, L.E. (2001), *Corporate Irresponsibility: America's Newest Export*, New Haven, CT: Yale University Press.

Mitchell, T.R. (1993), 'Leadership, values and accountability', in M.M. Chemers and R. Ayman (eds), *Leadership Theory and Research: Perspectives and Directions*, San Diego, CA: Academic Press.

Mitchell, T.R. and Scott, W.G. (1990), 'America's problems and needed reforms: confronting the ethic of personal advantage', *Academy of Management Executive*, **4**, 23–35.

Moores, K. and Mula, J. (2000), 'The salience of market, bureaucratic, and clan controls in the management of family firm transitions: some tentative Australian evidence', *Family Business Review*, **13**(2), 91–106.

Morgan Stanley and Oekom Research (2004), *Sustainability as a Style of Investment Offering Double Dividends*, Munich: Oekom Research.

Muller, M. (1999), 'Enthusiastic embrace or critical reception? The German HRM debate', *Journal of Management Studies*, **36**, 465–82.

Müller, W.R. (1995), 'Der Mythos der Machbarkeit in der Führungsausbildung', *Organisationsentwicklung*, **14**(4), 20–28.

Müller-Armack, A. (1989), 'The meaning of the social market economy', in A. Peacock and H. Willgerodt (eds), *Germany's Social Market Economy: Origins and Evolution*, New York: St Martins, pp. 82–6.

Nadler, D. and Tushman, M. (1990), 'Beyond the charismatic leader: leadership and organizational change', *California Management Review*, **32**, 77–97.

National Economic and Social Development Board (2004), *What is the Sufficiency Economy?*, Thailand: National Economic and Social Development Board.

Neff, T. and Ogden, D. (2001), 'Anatomy of a CEO', *Chief Executive – Sixth Annual Route to the Top*, vol. 164; accessed 4 September, 2003 at http://www.chiefexec.net/depts/routetop/anatomyofaceo.html.

Neumann, S. and Egan, M. (1999), 'Between German and Anglo-Saxon capitalism: the Czech financial markets in transition', *New Political Economy*, **4**(2), 173–95.

OECD (1996), *Employment Outlook*, OECD, no. 65.

OECD (2001), *Economic Outlook*, OECD, no. 70.

OECD (2002), *Economic Outlook*, OECD, no. 71.

OECD (2003), 'Main Economic Indicators', August 2003; downloaded 2.09.02 from http://www.oecd.org.

OECD (2004), 'Economic Survey – United States 2004'; accessed 19.04.2004 from http://www.oecd.org/home/.

Ogden, S. and Watson, R. (1999), 'Corporate performance and stakeholder management: balancing shareholder and customer interests in the UK privatized water industry', *Academy of Management Journal*, **42**, 526–38.

O'Heir, J. (2004), 'Sam I am: getting down to business at IBM', *CRN*, 13 April; accessed online, 14/4/2004.

Oswald, S., Stanwick, P. and LaTour, M. (1997), 'The effect of vision, strategic planning, and cultural relationships on organizational performance: a structural approach', *International Journal of Management*, **14**, 521–9.

Ott, J.S. (1989), *The Organizational Culture Perspective*, Pacific Grove, CA: Brooks/Cole.

Oxley, H., Burniaux, J-M., Dang, T-T. and d'Ercole, M.M. (1997), 'Income distribution and poverty in 13 OECD countries', *OECD Economic Studies*, no. 29, 1997/II.

Ozaki, R. (1991), *Human Capitalism: The Japanese Model of Market Economies*, New York: Kodansha.

Parker, R. (2001), 'The myth of the entrepreneurial economy: employment innovation and small firms', *Work, Employment and Society*, **15**(2), 373–84.

Parnell, M.F. (1999), 'Globalization, Eastern Germany and the "Mittelstand"', *European Business Review*, **99**(1), 32–41.

Peters, T. (2003), 'Brand inside: meter your energy, spirit and spunk', *Executive Excellence*, Australian edn, **20**(5), 16.

Philpott, J. (2003), 'The great stakeholder debate', *People Management*, **9**(16), 20.

Pfeffer, J. (1981), *Power in Organizations*. Boston, MA: Pitman.

Pfeffer, J., Hatano, T. and Santalainen, T. (1995), 'Producing sustainable competitive advantage through the effective management of people', *Academy of Management Executive*, **9**(1), 55–72.

Porsche AG (2002), 'Porsche verzichtet auf Listing in New York', Press release dated 16.10.2002; accessed on line 13.05.03 at http://www3.porsche.de/german/deu/company/investorrelations/news/pressreleases/021016.

Post, J.E. (1993), 'The greening of the Boston Park Plaza Hotel', *Family Business Review*, **6**(2), 131–48.

Poutziouris, P. (2001), 'The views of family companies on venture capital: empirical evidence from the UK small to medium-size enterprising economy', *Family Business Review*, **14**(3), 277–91.

Poza, E.J., Alfred, T. and Maheshwari, A. (1997), 'Stakeholder perceptions of culture and management practices in family and family firms: a preliminary report', *Family Business Review*, **10**(2), 135ff.

Preston, L.E. and Donaldson, T. (1999), 'Stakeholder management and organizational wealth', *Academy of Management Review*, **24**(4), 619–20.

Preuss, L. (1999), 'Ethical theory in German business ethics research', *Journal of Business Ethics*, **18**(4), 407–19.

PricewaterhouseCoopers (2003), *A Comparison of the King Report 2002 and the Sarbanes–Oxley Act of 2002*, South Africa: Institute of Directors.

Puffer, S.M. (1999), 'Continental Airlines' CEO Gordon Bethune on teams and new product development', *Academy of Management Executive*, **13**(3), 28–35.

Recardo, R.J. (2000), 'Best practices in organizations experiencing extensive and rapid change', *National Productivity Review*, Summer, 79–85.

Regini, M. (2003), 'Tripartite concentration and varieties of capitalism', *European Journal of Industrial Relations*, **9**(3), 251–64.

Reichel, R. (2002), 'Germany's postwar growth: economic miracle or reconstruction boom?', *Cato Journal*, **21**(3), 427–42.

Rockefeller, R.C. (2003), 'Turn public problems to private account', *Harvard Business Review*, **81**(8), 129–36 (reprinted from 1971).

Rodenstock, R. (2002), 'Der Mittelstand in der Vereinigung der Bayerischen Wirtschaft', paper given to the Wirtschaftsbeirat der Union Bezirksgruppe Kulmbach, 4 February 2002, 10am, Kulmbach.

Roth, D. (2002), 'How to cut pay, lay off 8,000 people, and still have workers who love you', *Fortune*, **145**(3), 62–8.

Roy, A. (2002), untitled article, *The Guardian*; accessed on 22 January 2002, at http://www.guardian.co.uk.

Sahlman, W.A. (2002), 'Expensing options solves nothing', *Harvard Business Review*, **80**(12), 90–96.

Sardar, Z. and Davies, M.W. (2002), *Why Do People Hate America?*, Cambridge: Icon Books.

Schein, E.H. (1985), *Organizational Culture and Leadership*, San Francisco, CA: Jossey-Bass.

Schnebel, E. (2000), 'Values in decision-making processes: systemic structures of J. Habermas and N. Luhmann for the appreciation of responsibility in leadership', *Journal of Business Ethics*, **27**, 79–88.

Schueth, S. (2003), 'Socially responsible investing in the United States', *Journal of Business Ethics*, **43**(3), 189–94.

Schuler, T. (2003), *Immer im Recht: wie America sich und Seine Ideale Verrät*, Munich: Riemann.

Schwartz, N.D. (2001), 'Colgate cleans up', *Fortune*, **143**(8); accessed online, 14/4/2004.

Scott, S.G. and Lane, V.R. (2000), 'A stakeholder approach to organizational identity', *Academy of Management Review*, **25**, 43–62.

Seidman, D. (2004), 'The case for ethical leadership', *Academy of Management Executive*, **18**(2), 134–8.

Seis, M. (2001), 'Confronting the contradiction: global capitalism and environmental health', *International Journal of Comparative Sociology*, **42**(1–2), 123–44.

Sharma, P., Chrisman, J.J. and Chua, J.H. (1997), 'Strategic management of the family business: past research and future, *Family Business Review*, **10**(1), 1–35.

Shearer, T. (2002), 'Ethics and accountability: from the for-itself to the for-the-other', *Accounting, Organizations and Society*, **27**, 541–73.

Shlaes, A. (1994), 'Germany's chained economy', *Foreign Affairs*, **73950**, 109ff.

Simon, H. (1992), 'Lessons from Germany's midsize giants', *Harvard Business Review*, **70**(2), 115–23.

Simon, H. (1996), 'You don't have to be German to be a "hidden champion"', *Business Strategy Review*, **7**(2), 1–13.

Singer, A.E. (1994), 'Strategy as moral philosophy', *Strategic Management Journal*, **15**, 191–213.

Slywotzky, A.J. and Wise, R. (2002), 'The growth crisis – and how to escape it', *Harvard Business Review*, **80**(7), 72–83.

Sorenson, R.L. (2000), 'The contribution of leadership style and practices to family and business success', *Family Business Review*, **13**(3), 183–200.

Statistisches Bundesamt (2002), *Die Europäische Union: Zahlen und Fakten*, May, Wiesbaden: Statistisches Bundesamt.

Stiglitz, J. (2002), *Globalization and its Discontents*, London: Penguin.

Sugarman, B. (2000), 'The learning organization and organizational learning', at URL http://www.leskey.edu/faculty/sugarman/loandtd.htm, accessed September.

Sung, T. (2003), 'People power: link training to goals', *Executive Excellence*, Australian edn, **20**(5), 15.

Sveiby, K. (2000), 'The knowledge-focussed manager'; accessed October from URL: http://www.sveiby.com.au/KnowledgeManagement.html.

Tagiuri, R. and Davis, J.A. (1992), 'On the goals of successful family companies', *Family Business Review*, **5**(1), 43–62.

Tetlock, P.E. and Goldgeier, J.M. (2000), 'Human nature and world politics: cognition, identity and influence', *International Journal of Psychology*, **35**, 87–96.

Upchurch, M. (2000), 'The crisis of labour relations in Germany', *Capital and Class*, **70**, spring, 65–93.

Vaill, P.B. (1989), *Managing as a Performing Art*, San Francisco, CA: Jossey-Bass.

Vereinigung der Bayerischen Wirtschaft (2002), *Weiterbildung*; accessed 28.11.02 at http://www.bayerischewirtschaft.de/demo/bildung/bildung.html#bach.

Verschoor, C.C. (2001), 'Are companies paying more attention to ethics?', *Strategic Finance*, **82**(8), 22–4.

Vitols, S. (2001), 'Varieties of corporate governance: comparing Germany and the UK', in P.A. Hall and D. Soskice (eds), *Varieties of Capitalism: The Institutional Foundations of Comparative Advantage*, Oxford: Oxford University Press, pp. 337–60.

Vitols, S. (2002), 'Risse in der Glitzerfassade', *Mitbestimmung online*, November; accessed 27.11.02 at http://www.boeckler.de/mitbestimmung.

Vogel, S.K. (2001), 'The crisis of German and Japanese capitalism: stalled on the road to the liberal market model?', *Comparative Political Studies*, **34**, 1103–33.

Wacker, D. (1997), *Preserving a Heritage*, Munich: WACKER-Chemie.

Walter, N. (1995), 'The evolving German economy: unification, the social market, European and global integration', *SAIS Review*, **15**, Special Issue, 55–81.

Warnecke, H.-J. (1993), *Revolution der Unternehmenskultur – das Fraktale Unternehmen*, Berlin: Springer.

Warnecke, H.-J. (1999), 'Growing old but staying young', *Fraunhofer-Gesellschaft: The 50th anniversary*, Munich: Fraunhofer-Gessellschaft.

Watt, D. (2003), 'Is SRI sustainable?', *Benefits Canada*, **27**(8), 62–5.

Weihrich, H. (1999), 'Analyzing the competitive advantages and disadvantages of Germany with the TOWS matrix – an alternative to Porter's model', *European Business Review*, **99**(1), 9–22.

Westhead, P., Cowling, M. and Howorth, C. (2001), 'The development of companies: management and ownership imperatives', *Family Business Review*, **14**(4), 39–85.

Westwood, R. (1997), 'Harmony and patriarchy: the cultural basis for "paternalistic headship" among the overseas Chinese', *Organizational Studies*, **18**(3), 445–80.

Wever, K.S. and Allen, C.S. (1992), 'Is Germany a model for managers?', *Harvard Business Review*, **70**(5), 36–43.

Wheatley, M.J. (1999), *Leadership and the New Science: Discovering Order in a Chaotic World*, 2nd edn, San Francisco, CA: Berrett-Koehler.

Wheatley, M.J. (2003), 'Prepare for the future: engage people in meaningful work', *Executive Excellence*, Australian edn, **20**(5), 10–11.

Wiener, D. (2003), 'The art of productivity: creating high-performance workplaces', *Pathways: The Novartis Journal*, July/September, 30–35.

Wiersema, M. (2002), 'Holes at the top: why CEO firings backfire', *Harvard Business Review*, **80**(12), 70–77.

Willmott, M. and Flatters, P. (1999), 'Corporate citizenship: the new challenge for business?', *Consumer Policy Review*, **9**(6), 230–37.

Wittmeyer, C. (2003), 'The *Practice of Management*: Timeless views and principles', *Academy of Management Executive*, **17**(3), 13–14.

World Economic Forum (2004), 'Voice of the leaders survey', available February 2004 at http://www.weforum.org./security/survey.

Yergin, D. and Stanislaw, J. (1998), *The Commanding Heights: The Battle Between Government and the Marketplace that is Remaking the Modern World*, New York: Simon & Schuster.

Zadek, S., Pruzan, P. and Evans, R. (1997), *Building Corporate Accountabil-*

ity: Emerging Practices in Social and Ethical Accounting, Auditing and Reporting, London: Earthscan.

Zalewski, D.A. (2003), 'Corporate objectives – maximizing social versus private equity', *Journal of Economic Issues*, **37**(2), 503ff.

Index